123 14 16

19 20 26

27 30 34

55

15 — 50

THE ORGANIZATIONAL SOCIETY

AN ANALYSIS AND A THEORY

BY

Robert Presthus

A Caravelle Edition

VINTAGE BOOKS

A DIVISION OF RANDOM HOUSE
New York

VINTAGE BOOKS

are published by ALFRED A. KNOPF, INC.

and RANDOM HOUSE, INC.

Reprinted by arrangement with Alfred A. Knopf, Inc.

MANUFACTURED IN THE UNITED STATES OF AMERICA

FOR

Anita, Lesley, Toni,

and Jeffrey

PREFACE

THIS BOOK *is an interdisciplinary analysis of big organizations and their influence upon the individuals who work in them. Conceptually, the analysis operates at three distinct but interrelated levels: society as a whole; the big, rational organization; and the individual. Organizations are defined as "miniature societies" in which the dominant values of society are inculcated and sought in a more structured, spatially restricted context. A major object is to show how individuals work out an accommodation in this milieu, and to develop a theory of organizational behavior that posits three ideal types of accommodation to big organizations: "upward-mobiles," "indifferents," and "ambivalents." It must be said that I am under no illusion that the mass of evidence cited throughout the book validates this theory. Such evidence can only be illustrative. The difficult task of testing the theory by empirical research remains.*

The analysis and the theory draw upon several social sciences. My own discipline, political science, contributes the grounding in the democratic-humanistic values that provide the normative framework of the book. Political science also contributes a conception of power in its various forms, as well as considerable data about the structure and processes of political organizations. Economic theory and research provide the major source of information about the changing structure of our economy, including the rise of large-scale organizations; the separation of ownership from management; the decline of the traditional competitive economy; and its replacement by a system of "administered" prices, production, and relationships between capital and labor. Sociological constructs and data are used to illuminate the structural aspects of big organizations, including specialization, hierarchy, oligarchy, rationality, centralized authority, status anxiety, role conflict, the displacement of values, and the emergence of "informal" centers of power, prestige, and communication.

Sullivan's interpersonal theory of psychiatry is turned to the analysis of individual behavior in big organizations. The compelling impact of society and culture upon individual personality is similarly put in an organizational context. The resulting "socialization process" suggests how personality is largely determined by the authoritative values of society. Specifically, I attempt to show how the big organization enlists such attitudes as anxiety and deference toward authority in the service of its major goals. Psychological formulations are also used to isolate individual needs of security, recognition, self-realization, and autonomy; these needs in turn are set against the structural characteristics of the "bureaucratic situation" with its demands for loyalty, predictability, and conformity. While such a multifaceted analysis necessarily sacrifices some rigor, I hope the attempt is warranted by a clearer picture of organizational behavior and the meaning of work in contemporary society.

ROBERT PRESTHUS

Ithaca, New York

ACKNOWLEDGMENTS

LIKE EVERY BOOK, *this one is the product of many minds and of many sources of inspiration. My main intellectual debt is to Thorstein Veblen, Max Weber, C. Wright Mills, Robert K. Merton, and Harry Stack Sullivan. Although I have known none of these men personally, their work has had great influence on my own thinking about our society, its values and organizations, and the most useful ways of analyzing them. I am grateful to colleagues in political science, sociology, and social psychology who have saved me from many errors: to William Delany, Herbert Kaufman, and Victor Thompson who read the entire manuscript; to Donald L. Garrity and James M. Holt who criticized the chapter on culture and personality; and to Andrew Hacker and Leif Braaten who read respectively the chapters on the "upward-mobile" and the "ambivalent" types. None of them of course is responsible for any errors of fact or interpretation which may occur. These are my own responsibility.*

I am also indebted to the Ford Foundation for a grant during 1959-60, which enabled me to study the social sciences, and to complete the first draft of the manuscript.

Finally, I want to thank my wife, Anita, for her help and understanding during the time the book was taking shape.

CONTENTS

THE ORGANIZATIONAL SOCIETY

CHAPTER I

BIG ORGANIZATIONS: DEFINITIONS AND DYSFUNCTIONS

THIS BOOK concerns the influence of social values and bureaucratic structure upon members of the big organizations that pervade our society. More specifically, it attempts to define the patterns of individual accommodation that occur in the bureaucratic milieu. Contemporary organizations have a pervasive influence upon individual and group behavior, expressed through a web of rewards, sanctions, and other inducements that range from patent coercion to the most subtle of group appeals to conformity. Indeed, bureaucratic organizations often seem less concerned with the self-realization of their members than with the relevance of such individuals for organizational goals of size, power, and survival. Ironically, members often accept this instrumental bargain; and why they do so is a matter of central interest here. We shall also be concerned with the larger social consequences of big organizations. Does organizational logic enhance the survival chances of our society, or does it limit our ability to meet the demands of change in a swiftly changing world?

The organizations with which we are concerned may be

defined as large, fairly permanent social systems designed to achieve limited objectives through the co-ordinated activities of their members. We are concerned with organizations in which people spend their working lives. The boundaries of such organizations are relatively distinct. Membership and responsibility can be assigned and "organizational" activities, values, and expectations can be differentiated from those that are extraorganizational. Such organizations have both manifest and latent goals. The manifest goal of private corporations is to produce and sell certain products at a profit. Their latent or "unofficial" goals, however, include all the aspirations of their members for security, recognition, and self-realization. Such latent goals and the methods used to gain them are often regarded as aberrations. They seem to subvert organizational ends. However, a major assumption here is not only that such aspirations and methods are legitimate, but that they often help the organization achieve its manifest goals.

The bureaucratic model used throughout this study has various structural characteristics, including specialization, hierarchy, oligarchy, i.e., a tendency toward control by the few, and interpersonal relations that are explicitly differentiated by authority. As C. Wright Mills says, "An organization is a system of roles graded by authority." Such characteristics appear most clearly in *big organizations*, which are defined for the moment as those in which the sheer number of participants and the scale of operations prohibit face-to-face relationships among most of their members. Size by itself introduces a pathological element in organizations that eases the problem of analysis by dramatizing their other characteristics. Although hierarchy appears in both the small group and the army, its intensity and effects are more sharply evident in the larger system.

In our analysis the terms "big organizations" and "bureaucratic structures" are synonymous. The total environment provided by such institutions will be called the *bureaucratic situation.* The classical analysis of bureaucratic organization is by

Max Weber, who attached no invidious connotation to the term but indeed believed that bureaucracy was absolutely essential for both the modern state and the corporation. "The decisive reason for the advance of bureaucratic organization has always been its purely technical superiority over any other form of organization."[1] "Precision, speed, unambiguity, knowledge of files, continuity, discretion, strict subordination, reduction of friction and of material and personal costs—these are raised to the optimum point in the strictly bureaucratic administration." [2] Ideally, this system eliminates "from official business love, hatred, and all purely personal, irrational, and emotional elements which escape calculation." [3]

According to Weber, bureaucracy has the following characteristics:

1. Fixed and official jurisdictional areas, which are regularly ordered by rules, that is, by laws or administrative regulations.
2. Principles of hierarchy and levels of graded authority that ensure a firmly ordered system of super- and subordination in which higher offices supervise lower ones.
3. Administration based upon written documents; the body of officials engaged in handling these documents and files, along with other material apparatus, make up a "bureau" or "office."
4. Administration by full-time officials who are thoroughly and expertly trained.
5. Administration by general rules which are quite stable and comprehensive.[4]

[1] Max Weber: "Bureaucracy," in Hans Gerth and C. Wright Mills: *From Max Weber* (New York: Oxford University Press, Inc.; 1946), p. 214.

[2] Ibid., p. 214.

[3] Ibid., p. 216.

[4] Max Weber: *Theory of Social and Economic Organization,* trans. by A.M. Henderson and T. Parsons (New York: Oxford University Press; 1947), pp. 333-6.

The position of the bureaucratic official has the following characteristics.[5] His job is a permanent vocation, a career for which he has been specifically trained. In most societies its conditions include a certain social esteem. Ideally, the official is *appointed* to his job by some superior authority. Bureaucratic demands for subordination and discipline would be fractured by election which would deflect responsibility to those outside the organization. Normally, the individual has life tenure which insures "a strictly objective discharge of specific official duties." Finally, the official receives a regular, money salary, determined by his rank and length of service.

Weber's analysis provides a good beginning, but it has serious limitations for the kind of study proposed here. Not only are the psychological consequences of the model for individuals ignored, but their latent goals are regarded as errant deviations that necessarily subvert the organization's rational means and ends. The critical distinction and the inevitable tension between the authority of position (hierarchy) and the authority of skill are unexamined. The influence of informal groups and the organization's part in socialization are similarly neglected. In sum, Weber deals almost exclusively with the formal, manifest functions of bureaucracy and gives little attention to their unanticipated consequences, both functional and dysfunctional. This orientation is explained in part (Weber's own values were democratic and humanistic) by the social context in which he lived and wrote, namely, Germany at the turn of the century, with its patent class stratification, its patriarchal family system, its extreme respect for authority, and its highly disciplined military and governmental bureaucracy. In the next chapter we shall outline a bureaucratic model that rests upon Weber yet includes the latent, "informal" aspects characteristic of organizations in contemporary American society.

When they occur together, as they usually do in large bureaucratic systems, hierarchy, specialization, and authority

[5] Ibid., p. 203.

produce a distinctive psychological climate. Members are expected to be loyal to the organization, to behave consistently and rationally according to technical and professional criteria, and to defer to the authority of the organization's leaders. The social and psychological basis of this accommodation is the major concern of this book.

A basic assumption throughout our analysis is that social values and institutions mold individual personality and behavior. This occurs through a process called socialization. Society, in effect, provides a web of values and expectations that determines the individual's character, his ethical beliefs, and his ideas about progress, success, and failure. "Those drives which make for the differences in men's characters, like love and hatred, the lust for power and the yearning for submission—are all products of the social process." [6] Men may, for example, be born with an impulse to dominate others, but social values such as the democratic ideal of equality determine the manner and extent to which this impulse can be gratified. When men choose, they choose within this context of socially determined values. While our society provides a broad scope for individual choices, organizational influences traced here have significantly changed the conditions under which they are made.

Big organizations impose socialization through their patent authority systems, their rational procedures, and their limited objectives. In this context organizations will be defined as miniature social systems in which the mechanics and the consequences of socialization are sharply defined. The big organization resembles a school or a church in that it inculcates approved ideals, attitudes, and behavior, all calculated to enhance the organization's competitive chances. This educational function is apparent in the organization's authority system which encourages members to accept uncritically its legitimacy and rationality. The tensions arising from such

[6] Erich Fromm: *Man for Himself* (New York: Rinehart & Co., Inc.; 1947), p. 241.

organizational conditions are sharper than those existing in the larger society where differences in status and income are more fluid, transitory, and generally less invidious.[7]

The organization's socializing influence and the individual's accommodations to its claims are, however, always worked out through interaction with other people. This condition is analyzed by using an *interpersonal theory of behavior*. Interpersonal theory insists that personality and indeed most forms of individual behavior are the result of one's perceptions of himself in relation to others. Personality is mainly the result of social interaction rather than of biological impulse. In big organizations such interactions occur in a highly structured context in which authority, rank, power, and status are clearly differentiated. This accounts for the consistency of behavior in the typical big organization.

The specialization and discipline of big organizations have both functional and dysfunctional consequences. Their gains in material rewards, industrial efficiency, and military power are clear enough. Their dysfunctions are more subtle and pervasive, raising problems of individual autonomy, integrity, and self-realization. Prominent among them today is a *displacement of value* from the intrinsic quality of work to its by-products of income, security, prestige, and leisure.[8] This displacement stems from the impersonality, the specialization, and the group character of work in the typical big organization. Its larger significance may appear in an alienation from

[7] Robin M. Williams: *American Society: A Sociological Interpretation* (New York: Alfred A. Knopf; 1951), pp. 128-35. For a discussion of the feasibility and the difficulty of moving from the family level of analysis to the organizational and occupational level, see Talcott Parsons: "The Relation Between the Small Group and the Larger Social System," in Roy R. Grinker: *Toward a Unified Theory of Human Behavior* (New York: Basic Books, Inc.; 1956), pp. 190-200; and T. Parsons and Robert F. Bales, *et al.*: *Family, Socialization, and Interaction Process* (Glencoe, Illinois: The Free Press; 1955).

[8] Robert K. Merton: *Social Theory and Social Structure* (Glencoe, Illinois: The Free Press; 1957), pp. 197-202; and "The Unanticipated Consequences of Purposive Social Action," *American Sociological Review*, Vol. 1, pp. 894-904.

work, resulting from such factors as the economy's frequent concern with essentially trivial products. The organization's capacity to meet the demands of change may suffer, since criticism and innovation tend to be muffled by its demands for conformity.

Such organizational conditions and expectations have fostered the growth of certain personality types whose skill and behavior meet the demands of the organizational society. We shall define three such types as the *upward-mobiles*, the *indifferents*, and the *ambivalents*.[9] The upward-mobiles now tend increasingly to gain control of the efforts and rewards of professionals, scientists, and other highly trained men. Veblen's separation of the engineers and financiers, with its attending dysfunctions, is being repeated in many organizations, economic, educational, artistic, religious, and military. The unexpected consequences include the alienation of the professional, the aggrandizement of administration, a tendency toward oligarchy, and as the concluding chapter argues, impaired survival power of both organizations and society as the quality of decisions suffers from lack of participation by those who are best qualified to make them.

[9] While lending themselves to oversimplification and misinterpretation, such types have a long and distinguished intellectual history, beginning in the Western world with Plato's "philosopher-kings," "guardians," and "workers," and Aristotle's "democratic" and "oligarchic" types of political states. More recent examples (cited throughout the analysis) include Pareto's "lions" and "foxes," Mosca's "ruling class," Tönnies's "Gemeinschaft" and "Gesellschaft," Weber's "charismatic" and "bureaucratic" leaders, Veblen's "financiers" and "engineers," Lasswell's "political administrators," and "political agitators," Riesman's "inner-and-other-directed" men, Merton's "locals" and "cosmopolitans," and Mills' "abstracted empiricists" and "grand theorists." Psychology of course is replete with typologies, including Jung's "introverts" and "extroverts," James' "tender-minded" and "tough-minded," Adorno's "authoritarian" personality, as well as the gamut of psychopathological categories of mental illness. Used judiciously, such types have the great virtue of helping one order the infinite complexity of the real world. Indeed, it is hard to see how conceptualization in any field can proceed without such generalizations.

It is important to discuss further the kinds of organizations with which this book is concerned. By "big organizations" we mean systems that have a large number of employees and operate in large-scale terms. A good example would be the 500 largest industrial corporations in the United States, which in 1961 had a net worth of over 100 billion dollars, employed over nine million people, and ranged in total assets from 10 billion (Standard Oil of New Jersey) to a mere 48 million (Maremont Corporation).[1] Such organizations are a common instrument of modern society, featuring scientific procedures, standardization, objective recruitment, impersonality, machine operations, an exquisite division of labor, a hierarchy of authority and status, and a tendency to demand complete loyalty from their members. They dominate basic industry and have made deep inroads into educational and artistic areas. The indexes of size include number of employees, capitalization, proportion of total production, and the amount of capital required for entry into a given field. But an enterprise need not have all these characteristics to be classified as "big." Financial enterprises, for example, may control vast concentrations of capital, yet their total number of employees is relatively small. Similarly with self-conscious public agencies like the Foreign Service and the Marine Corps. Although it is difficult to get agreement on definition, in this book the organizations we regard as "big" include the twenty largest of our 1,850 universities and colleges, which have almost twenty percent of 3,610,000 students (1960). They include enterprises like General Motors with 500,000 employees, U. S. Steel with 269,400, General Electric with 227,000, Standard Oil with 241,000, Dupont with 92,000, the big insurance companies, and the big banks like the Bank of America and Chase-Manhattan.

The Small Business Administration, whose clientele is determined by size, defines an organization as "big" if it has over 1,000 employees. However, this figure varies with employ-

[1] "The Fortune Directory," *Fortune,* Vol. 64 (July, 1961), pp. 167-86.

ment size and with dollar-volume standards, which change from industry to industry. Independent ownership and competitiveness in their field are the Administration's main qualitative standards for small businesses. In the end one must probably rely on certain general attitudes about bigness in our society. Certainly there is a consensus that General Motors and U.S. Steel are big industrial organizations; that our seventy-odd billion-dollar corporations are big; that New York University and the University of California are huge academic organizations; that the AFL-CIO is a giant labor organization; and that the Farm Bureau Federation and the Farmer's Union are giants in agriculture.

As one descends the scale from these obvious examples, disagreement will increase. However, the importance of size for our purposes is that large numbers of employees and large-scale operations result in a bureaucratic situation whose structural characteristics and psychological climate evoke certain patterns of individual accommodation. If this is true, it is not necessary to set down a precise index of size. We can define "big organizations" as all bureaucratic systems large enough to prevent face-to-face interpersonal relations among most of their members. Regardless of their product, such organizations tend to operate similarly. They all arrange individual skills and relationships in order to secure continuity and stability. They all develop standardized methods to handle their major activities. They all exhibit a built-in conflict between authority based upon position and authority based upon skill. They are consciously designed to achieve a major purpose, i.e., to produce steel, automobiles, public service, news, educated men, entertainment, etc.

A common problem in organizational analysis is where to draw the boundaries of one's inquiry. In the present study big organizations are conceptualized as satellites of a larger social system; the behavior of their members is shaped by the values of the larger society. Indeed, such organizations now provide the major arena in which individual claims for success, income, and security are resolved. But one cannot understand organizational behavior unless he brings to bear upon it the insights of several disciplines. Cultural psychology shows us how social values mold personality; sociology deals with the structure and consequences of social institutions; political science deals with power and with the resulting allocation of scarce values. Each treats of individual and group behavior. Together, they provide the theoretical basis for this book.

If social structure is critical in molding individual behavior and personality, the big organization can usefully be conceived as a small society whose characteristics of specialization, hierarchy, and authority have a similar influence upon its members. The mechanisms that society employs to inculcate its values may also be seen at work within the organization. The organization, in a word, socializes its members in a way similar to that of society. It co-opts the learned deference to authority inculcated by institutions such as the family and the church. We may assume that the patent authority and prestige structure of the typical big organization enhances the effectiveness of the authority-deference mechanism.

Such a mode of analysis clearly requires the insights and conceptual tools of several disciplines. But the existing structure and values of the intellectual market place inhibit such an approach. Each discipline tends to define organizations in terms of its own image, with the result that organizational phenomena are divided into political, economic, sociological, and psychological compartments. Professional commitments and power struggles among university departments discourage the integration of social-science theory and methods. The reasons for this situation are found in the conditions of participation set down by academia today. They provide ironic evidence of our major theme by illustrating the extent to which organizational expectations and rewards influence individual behavior.

Unless one has experienced graduate training and apprenticeship in American higher learning, the stress involved in broadening one's approach beyond a single discipline is hard to imagine. Academic training instills a compelling inhibition against venturing beyond a given segment of knowledge. The underlying reason is the passionate specialization of university organization. All the dynamics of training, of values, and of professional recognition push one toward restricted fields of analysis. As a result, trained incapacity, technical introversion, and bureaucratic infighting are characteristic of most university departments. Each discipline carves out for itself a narrow segment of human behavior, concentrates mightily on developing it through research, theory, and immaculate terminology, and in the process accumulates such a bewildering array of facts and fables that the apprentice is submerged by what is called the "basic knowledge in the field." To presume to challenge or to go beyond this revealed wisdom is to risk the most crushing label in the academic lexicon: *dilettante.*

The dilemmas of specialization are aggravated by competing "schools" within each discipline. There exists within each discipline opposing conceptions of the field, its scope, and the proper ways of doing research. And, of course, each "school" has its priests, acolytes, and true believers. C. Wright Mills has shown that American sociology is sharply divided between at least two schools, the "grand theorists" and the "abstracted empiricists," representing broadly a division between rationalists and positivists.[2] The implications of academic organization and its claims for appropriate professional behavior are suggested by the fact that several reviewers of Mills' work concluded: "Here is a man who will never be president of the American Sociological Society." Political science is similarly divided among those who regard the field as an aspect of political and moral philosophy and those who define it as a "science" resting upon empirical analyses of electoral behavior, political attitudes, leadership, etc. Conflicts such as these give academia a rather humorless quality, and a competitive impulse that does credit to an Oriental bazaar.

In studying organizational behavior one can thus be eclectic not only about the disciplines to which he turns but also

[2] *The Sociological Imagination* (New York: Oxford University Press, Inc.; 1959), Chs. 2-3.

with regard to method. Certainly the kinds of questions raised in this book require both the "traditional" and "scientific" conceptions of inquiry. Also, one cannot ignore the pressing normative questions that are engaged here. The autonomy of the individual in an organizational society is too important an issue to be stifled by methodological inhibitions. The present analysis will therefore draw upon all sources that seem helpful in understanding bureaucratic structure and individual accommodations to it.[3] We can now consider some of the tools that help us order the bureaucratic situation. There is an analytical fiction known as the "ideal-type" concept that recognizes the diversity of big organizations yet enables one to study them with the hope of building generalizations. Max Weber called this tool a "generalized rubric within which an indefinite number of particular cases may be classified." By this conception, it is not essential to work out an iron-clad definition of "big organizations." As the term suggests, an "ideal type" is actually an illusion, a sort of Platonic ideal or composite of all cases in a given class. The assumptions of classical economics provide an example. To analyze behavior in the market place, economists posited a ficitious setting in which men were always rational, saved their money, and enjoyed the luxury of free choice in a competitive, self-regulating system. Most theorists knew, although their apostles sometimes forget, that such conditions existed only in their own minds. But the ideal made the real more understandable by providing a model which helped them analyze the existing system.

Our "ideal type" is a "big organization," a generalized model of all large-scale institutions. Such a tool gives us a bench mark against which we can measure "an indefinite number of particular cases." This model, the main elements of

[3] I am encouraged in attempting this broad-gauged approach by the comments of Alex Inkeles urging a synthesis of sociological and psychological method in analyzing social affairs, "Personality and Social Structure," in Robert K. Merton, *et al.*: *Sociology Today* (New York: Basic Books, Inc.; 1959), pp. 249-76.

which will be set down in the next chapter, provides the framework for our analysis in Chapters 6, 7, and 8, where we characterize the three bureaucratic types already mentioned: the *upward-mobile,* the *indifferents,* and the *ambivalents.* The *upward-mobiles* are those who react positively to the bureaucratic situation and succeed in it. The *indifferents* are the uncommitted majority who see their jobs as mere instruments to obtain off-work satisfactions. The *ambivalents* are a small, perpetually disturbed minority who can neither renounce their claims for status and power nor play the disciplined role that would enable them to cash in such claims.

Like the economist's classical model, these types are oversimplified and idealized, but they have a similar value as conceptual tools. Most research begins with similar premises that permit one to study particular institutions or events. In a word, the student of organizational behavior does not reason in a vacuum, but instead he develops frameworks that help in the selection and classification of information. In addition to bureaucratic structure and types, our guides include a number of democratic-humanistic values against which the consequences of big organizations can be set. The values include equality of opportunity, freedom of thought and expression, and self-realization. The consequences include the remarkable concentration of social and economic power characteristic of American society today. This concentration, which is documented in Chapter 3, is evidenced by the size and proportion of markets, by the number of employees, by the percentage of total capital investment, and by the social power that big organizations now exert in many areas.

But such organizations are more than mere devices for producing goods and services. They have critical normative consequences. They provide the environment in which most of us spend most of our lives. In their efforts to rationalize human energy they become sensitive and versatile agencies for the control of man's behavior, employing subtle psychological sanctions that evoke desired responses and inculcate consistent patterns of action. In this sense, big organizations are a major disciplinary force in our society. Their influence spills over the boundaries of economic interest or activity into spiritual and intellectual sectors; the accepted values of the organization shape the individual's personality and influence his behavior in extravocational affairs.

Because such values are supported by organized power, they become reinforced not only for those immediately concerned but for society generally. They provide the criteria of personal worth, success, and power. Increasingly such values can be achieved only in big organizations. Meanwhile, the latters' drive for efficiency and control, their long-run goals, and their precious self-images compel them to demand wider and deeper loyalty from their members. Such demands are usually justified by honorific abstractions such as "the good of the organization." Many individuals accept such demands, and some become as disciplined as the organization itself. Most of their interpersonal relations and their social life are bent toward career ends. Big organizations therefore become instruments of socialization, providing physical and moral sustenance for their members and shaping their thought and behavior in countless ways.

These human consequences are the result of the growth of science, technology, and specialization in our society during the past seventy-five years. Structural changes in the economy during that period and the growing size and power of organizations had striking implications for the traditional ideals of individual autonomy that had characterized a simpler social system. While new conditions brought many new opportunities based mainly upon the expanding specialization of labor, such opportunities existed in a different context which demanded new personal skills and discipline. Ironically, instead of bringing contentment, new opportunities often encouraged insecurity. A vague dissatisfaction persisted as men became afraid that the job they had was not as good as the one available. With one eye focussed on the main chance, the individual tended to lose the intrinsic satisfaction of work as work tended to become a mere means to other ends. The specialization and impersonality of bureaucratic tasks were further causes in the alienation of men from their work, which increasingly became a means of buying escape in the form of organized recreation and entertainment.

Big organizations have brought impressive gains in American living standards and national power, and have become models for economic development in poorer countries.[4] Our society is deeply committed both to the gains and to the instruments that have helped make them possible. This analysis implies in no way, therefore, a preference for anarchy or a longing for a rural utopia. It seeks instead to raise questions about the social and psychological impact of big organizations and, by implication, to suggest greater discrimination in their use. It maintains that their impersonal, long-range objectives, patent control mechanisms, size, and tendency toward absolutism may have dysfunctional, anxiety-producing results for their members. Such by-products, the unanticipated consequences of the bureaucratic situation, become most clear when organizational claims are set against democratic ideals of free expression, individual worth, and spontaneity.

For example, the bureaucratic situation tends to foster an adaptive personality type who develops the ability to play "tough-minded" roles, that is, those that give the organization's claims priority over any conflicting demands such as loyalty to friends or to personal ideals. The "good of the organization" becomes the highest value. As Erich Fromm and others have shown, such behavior is often unhealthy, encouraging self-alienation and anxiety, primarily because of its exploitative and manipulative character.

The size and impersonality of organizations may also encourage anxiety. Feelings of helplessness and of frustration occur as organizational power and demands checkmate the individual's claims for autonomy. Personal freedom and

[4] Robert Presthus: "The Social Bases of Bureaucratic Organization," *Social Forces*, Vol. 38, pp. 103-9; "Weberian v. Welfare Bureaucracy in Traditional Society," *Administrative Science Quarterly*, Vol. 6, pp. 1-24.

growth, in terms of effective choices and real participation in decisions that affect one directly, tend to be submerged by the centralized power and decision making that characterize big organizations. Because success and psychic ease often require an uncritical acceptance of such conditions, security is often purchased with conformity. But the attending decline of personal responsibility in favor of collective irresponsibility may result in a subtle corrosion of integrity.

Such results may be the price for technical efficiency and material progress; but one must ask, what are the consequences for individual freedom and development? Writing in the 1830's, Tocqueville could say, "I know of no country in which there is so little independence of mind and real freedom of discussion as in America." [5] One must again ask, how has the organizational society affected this condition? Although we admire bigness and productivity, the organizations that symbolize these tend to weaken the humanistic ideal that men must be treated as ends rather than as means. The effects of big organizations in such terms are only vaguely felt, and understandably so, because they are subtle and cummulative.

Where the trend toward bigness has been analyzed, mainly in government and economics, conclusions have differed widely. Some view the rise of big government, big labor, and big agriculture as "bad," on the grounds that it stifles competition and prevents equal access to raw materials and capital. On the other hand, economic concentration is sometimes regarded as a healthy by-product of the liberal theory of competition, providing a countervailing force that prevents exploitation by any single Leviathan.[6] However, there is no doubt that the consumer can be hurt by collusion among the giants, as seen in such practices as price fixing and built-in obsolescence; and smaller firms competing against the big organiza-

[5] Alexis de Tocqueville: *Democracy in America* (New York: Alfred A. Knopf, Inc.; 1954), Vol. 1, p. 263.

[6] John K. Galbraith: *American Capitalism* (Boston: Houghton Mifflin Co.; 1956).

tions in any given field are greatly disadvantaged by relative lack of capital and by their attending inability to influence major decisions concerning the industry.[7] This latter eventuality can pertain even where smaller firms still outnumber the big ones.

Studies of concentration and size have usually been restricted to structural and competitive change, often attempting to show that the competitive market remains viable. There has been little concern with the normative implications of such trends. The effects of organizational tools such as authority and status anxiety upon individual self-realization have not been carefully traced. Such problems tend to be repressed, one suspects, because they underscore the disparity between organizational power and democratic ideals. Our liberal ethic avoids the problem of power because it happily assumes that self-interest necessarily ends in community advantage. Yet, unequally distributed power insures the unequal distribution of social rewards and opportunity. The resulting decline of personal autonomy often proves inadmissible in a society bred on individualism. The conception that the power of big organizations must be matched by an equal measure of social responsibility is resisted.

We tend moreover to restrict our thinking about individual freedom to government, concluding that freedom is assured when public power is controlled. But somehow the logic of freedom which is so compelling in this public context is often neglected where private power is concerned. There, despite the intimate relationship between conditions of work and of self-realization, the implications of the concentrated power now characteristic of our society have usually been ignored. The extension of material equality has been uncritically accepted as insuring the freedom necessary to make good our democratic ideals. Despite the tragic example of Russia, we have often regarded individual freedom as an inevitable by-product of economic advance.

[7] In agriculture, for example, see Grant McConnell: *The Decline of Agrarian Democracy* (Berkeley: University of California Press; 1953).

Meanwhile, big organizations threaten the social equilibrium that makes democracy possible by encouraging both conflict and compromise. As Chapter 3 will show, such organizations have invaded areas far removed from the industrial world where they first appeared. For this invasion, our idolatry of size and our faith in technical solutions for human problems seem mainly responsible. As a result, artistic, educational, and spiritual activities have embraced bureaucratic organization, seeking efficiency, and confusing size with grandeur as fully as their industrial counterparts. In adopting the techniques of commerce, they have inevitably adopted some of its values, and their character has changed accordingly. In terms of quality and of human values, the effect of big organizations on art, liberal education, and mass communications is, therefore, a disturbing question.

Moreover, as will be suggested in Chapter 9, the expansion of organizational values has serious implications for national security. Insofar as weapons and space superiority now depend upon pure research, the balance-sheet mentality of big organizations and the practical objectives of their research have weakened our competitive position. Although "pure" science has become eminently practical, research cannot be administered according to organizational logic, particularly the demand that it have practical short-run consequences. It is significant that a refugee physicist, asked to explain European superiority in atomic theory, replied simply, "Leisure." Research suffers in a bureaucratic context where utilitarian values and hierarchical control dominate.

Such changes in the character of the work place tend to change the character of work. Here, the altered role and status of the professional man is of particular interest. Professional standing becomes precarious in big organizations where power, loyalty, and status rather than skill are the source of influence. It seems clear that the professional's traditional independence and his style of work are being undercut. Increasingly he has become an employee in a huge organization which alone can provide the capital plant, the laboratory, and the instruments necessary for the use of his skill. He becomes part of an intensely pragmatic bureaucratic structure. Since he no longer works for himself, it becomes increasingly difficult for him to set his own pace, to decide how his energy will be spent, and to work in terms of knowledge rather than of time.

The decline of the independent professional is matched by the rise of the administrator. Often possessing little technical knowledge beyond a somewhat intangible ability to organize others, he now controls the distribution of the organization's resources. Since his role involves co-ordinating and arbitrating the conflicting demands of specialists, he tends to regard them in terms of power and strategy. Specialists are themselves not entirely innocent of the tactics of survival. But the administrator's own constant power orientation reinforces his perception of the specialist as an introverted "fact grubber." (This alienation may be subtly reinforced if he has abandoned his own technical or research aspirations.) Where administrative posts are a reward for professional achievement (as in a few eminent universities, for example), this schism is eased. However, loyalty and seniority, qualities hardly calculated to inspire professional enthusiasm, have become the main bases for succession to administrative posts in big organizations. Combined with the higher status and income of administrators, this condition disenchants some professionals and intrigues others, with unfortunate results in either case.

In business and industry, the administrator's role was shaped mainly by the change in ownership structure that began early in this century. The risk-taking entrepreneur, who dominated American industry from 1875 to 1910, was replaced by a salaried, professional executive. His was a "management" job in which "human relations" was among the critical skills. The rise of specialists in market analysis, tax policy, advertising, design, finance, and engineering brought diffused decision making. The ability to work effectively in committees and small groups took on a new significance. While the executive's main job was one of co-ordinating specialists, he also became an "industrial statesman." Aware that economics and politics were inextricably joined and that most people knew it, he kept in touch with publics who influenced the political framework in which his organization operated. Since he personally initiated less policy, while group decision making enabled him to share responsibility, taking risks became less appealing. Science, planning, market research, human inertia, and the creative wonders of advertising provided some insurance against fluctuations in demand. In sum, the counsel of his scientific entourage and his company's financial resources reduced both the need and the appeal of individual responsibility and risk taking.

Although such innovations brought new opportunities, they were often accompanied by a new dependence. Increasingly the organization set the conditions for individual work. The technician required a big organization to accommodate his talent. Without its physical plant, its administrative and capital resources, his skill was useless. His prestige was a function of the organization's prestige. Undefined by such tangible indexes, he tended to count for little. This left him exceptionally vulnerable. The relatively small number of power centers in the economy made possible a swift and far-reaching control. Like the radio actors and the screen writers blacklisted for political indiscretion, offenders could be disciplined on a national scale.[8] Their trained incapacity meant that they could turn to alternative work only at considerable financial sacrifice. And here again, diffused responsibility was clearly apparent. Those who expelled them were remote and evasive, unknown clients who worked through advertising agencies and interest groups unknown to the public.

The substitution of political and personal criteria for objective judgments of work changed individual orientations toward work. The self-realization assured by the creation of a finished product had been impaired by specialization. Now the loss of intrinsic joy in work encouraged a preoccupation with

[8] John Cogley: *Report on Blacklisting* (New York: Fund for the Republic, Inc.; 1956), 2 Vols.

means. Conviviality, "personality," and dependency became important career skills. As C. Wright Mills says, "Our society has become a great showroom in which the individual must merchandize his personal wares if he is to compete successfully."[9] Like other commodities, the individual found that standardization had its sales value. One refrain runs throughout the well-known *Fortune* interviews with executives and their wives: the fear of being thought different. One must be "common," nonintellectual, and above all, "able to put others at ease." He must realize the importance of "constructive friendships," i.e., friendships that have career utility. This ethic reflects in part existing group theory and the "adjustment" theme of mass education. The group decides and the individual conforms. To be "well-adjusted" is the object. But the relationship is also clear between such sanctions and the standardization attending machine production and mass markets. As Veblen found, this economic value permeates every aspect of social life.

Even the employee's wife is caught in the bureaucratic net. As one executive put it, "Management has a challenge and an obligation to plan deliberately and to create a favorable, constructive attitude on the part of the wife that will liberate her husband's total energies for the job."[1] Corporations knew the kind of wife they wanted: highly gregarious, adaptable, one who realized that "her husband belongs to the corporation." The junior executive, inspired by such values, might well wonder if his wife had become a handicap in the competitive race. "Most corporations keep tabs on the wife's growth as an index to the executive's availability for certain positions."[2]

[9] This process of "adult socialization" is treated in C. Wright Mills: *White Collar* (New York: Oxford University Press, Inc.; 1951), pp. 182-8; and H.S. Becker and A. Strauss: "Careers, Personality, and Adult Socialization," *American Journal of Sociology,* Vol. 62, pp. 253-63.

[1] William H. Whyte, Jr.: "The Wives of Management," *Fortune,* Vol. 44 (October, 1951), p. 86.

[2] Ibid.

Similar demands are made by most big organizations, often, one thinks, without realizing their larger implications. A report on standards of conduct for international civil servants prepared for the United Nations provides an example.[3] "The international civil servant must accept special restraints in his public and private life . . ."[4] "Integrity, international loyalty, independence and impartiality, and the subordination of private interests to the interests of the organization, are daily requirements."[5] Moreover, "integrity" is defined as the individual's capacity to regulate "his conduct with the interests of the international organization *only* in view."[6]

The private life of the staff member is also covered:

> "*In principle,* the private life of the international staff member is his concern and should not be intruded upon by his organization. At the same time, in order that his private life will not bring his organization into disfavor, he must set himself a high standard of personal conduct —one that is more complex in some respects than that demanded of national civil servants. He must bear in mind that his conduct, whether connected or unconnected with official duties, must be such that it will not infringe upon any demonstrable interests of the organization he serves, bring it into discredit, or offend the community in which he lives. Such restraint must be exercised even in the use of rights recognized by existing legislation if this use is likely to reflect unfavorably upon the organization. Not only must the international civil servant be careful and discreet himself, but *he should impress upon members of his household the necessity of*

[3] International Civil Service Advisory Board: *Report on Standards of Conduct in the International Civil Service* (New York: United Nations; 1954).

[4] Ibid., p. 15.

[5] Ibid., p. 14.

[6] Ibid., p. 4.

maintaining a similar high standard of conduct."[7]

Such prescriptions emphasize the tension between organizational and individual claims.

Although the present analysis obviously favors individual self-realization over other claims, the writer does not accept the Freudian view that man is inevitably in conflict with society. Social organizations, on the contrary, often enhance his freedom and opportunity. In this respect every social organization, the family, the church, the university, the union, and the corporation, has a Janus-like character. On the one hand, it encourages individual autonomy by inculcating the skills and values necessary for self-realization. On the other, it demands conformity with its ends and the means used to achieve them. Striking a balance between these claims has always been difficult. But today it seems that organizational demands have distorted the organizational-individual equation.

While affirming one's belief in individual autonomy is something like coming out in favor of an early spring, the fact remains that a vital measure of a democratic society is the respect and freedom it provides the individual. Today, however, big organizations tend to view man instrumentally. Their acquisitive demands restrict his discretion; they subordinate his values and aspirations to the major purposes of the organization. They dispense great rewards, but these are always distributed in terms of *collective* values which the individual must accept if he is to compete for them. Administrators often try to reconcile the organization's interests with those of the individual, but they tend nevertheless to view human beings as instruments designed to achieve ends considered by the organization to be more important than those of any individual person. As a result, organizational values become the bench mark for evaluating and rewarding the individual. Man, in effect, is made for the organization. *He may succeed and prosper within it, but the organization al-*

[7] Ibid., p. 15, italics added.

ways defines the terms of success. Yet, given his dignity as a human being and his capacity for reason, man ought not to be viewed as an instrument. As Dostoevsky insisted: "The whole purpose of man surely consists in proving to himself that he is a man and not a cog in a machine."

CHAPTER 2

THE BUREAUCRATIC MODEL

WE NOW TURN to an analysis of the structural characteristics of the typical big organization. While such organizations obviously differ in size, product, age, and tradition, they are quite similar in form, procedure, and the claims they make upon their members for loyalty and consistency. Most of them have the following characteristics: large size, specialization, hierarchy, status anxiety, oligarchy (rule by the few), co-optation (selection of their successors by the organization's elite), "efficiency," and rationality. The bureaucratic model to be described here is an ideal type. It has no exact counterpart in the real world. However, although every big organization may not exhibit all these characteristics, we can safely assume that most of them will. While all big organizations may not be bureaucratic, most bureaucratic organizations will be big. Such organizations provide a distinctive psychological climate in which authority and status are nicely differentiated. As a result, behavioral expectations are clearly prescribed; interpersonal relations occur in a structured context. Ideally, there is very little ambiguity in bureaucratic organizations.

Although all the characteristics of the bureaucratic model are mutually reinforcing, size is among its most significant features. "Size," of course, has many dimensions, including the organization's scale of operations, volume of work, extent of capital resources, number of clients or customers, and the geographical scope of its activities. However, since our interest is precisely in the influence of the organization upon its own members, "size" refers here to organizations in which the number of members is large enough to prohibit face-to-face relations among most participants.

Durkheim has shown that as societies increase in size, density, and urbanization, the division of labor increases rapidly.[1] Like suicide, *specialization* is a function of increasing civilization. This is because the members of the undifferentiated society find themselves in too intense competition. They therefore turn to a division of labor which will permit each segment to pursue its own goals with a minimum of conflict. "The division of labor . . . is a result of the struggle for existence."[2] Showing that organisms "prosper more when they differ more," Darwin found 200 species of insects living upon one tree, some feeding upon its leaves, some upon its fruit, and others upon its bark and roots. "Men submit to the same law. In the same city different occupations can co-exist without being obliged to destroy each other, for they pursue different objects."[3]

Big organizations reveal similar motives and degrees of specialization. Specialization was one of the main weapons of the scientific management movement in its drive for greater productivity in industrial organizations. To some extent man undoubtedly becomes more proficient as he confines himself to a given field or activity. The organization of university departments along disciplinary lines and the impetus this gives to specialization is an example. Perhaps as recently as

[1] Emile Durkheim: *Division of Labor in Society* (Glencoe, Illinois: The Free Press; 1952).

[2] Ibid., p. 270.

[3] Ibid., p. 267.

100 years ago, a scholar was often competent in two or three fields. Francis Bacon's major role was that of lawyer, but his reputation rests in philosophy. Today, the sheer volume of knowledge and the complexity of civilization mean that the intellectual is almost always limited to a single discipline, and perhaps to only one of its major segments.

As organizations grow larger, we may say with Durkheim that they *necessitate* a greater division of labor. This differentiation attracts and accommodates the different interests and abilities of individuals, enabling each to find his place. In economic systems it permits those displaced by mergers to continue as parts of the new combination. "The small employer becomes a foreman; the small merchant becomes an employee." [4] And, we may add, the farmer-owner becomes a skilled worker in a nearby city. As the highly developed role of specialists and middlemen in our economy attests, specialization permits the survival of a great number of individuals who in simpler societies "would be condemned to extinction."

Some qualification of Durkheim's assumption that specialization is generally beneficial seems required. There is an inherent tension in organizations between those in hierarchical positions of authority and those who play specialized roles. Each feels that his role is more essential to the organization. The specialist deplores the fact that those in hierarchical roles have appropriated to themselves the definitions of success in our society.[5] In the university, for example, the

[4] Ibid., p. 269. Organizational size is treated as a critical variable in Mason Haire, ed.: *Modern Organization Theory* (New York: John Wiley & Sons, Inc.; 1959). For studies that stress the relationship between large size and bureaucratization and survival power, see O. Grusky: "Corporate Size, Bureaucratization, and Managerial Succession," *American Journal of Sociology*, Vol. 47 (November, 1961), pp. 261-9; T. Caplow: "Organizational Size," *Administrative Science Quarterly*, Vol. 1 (March, 1957), pp. 484-505.

[5] Victor A. Thompson: "Hierarchy, Specialization and Organizational Conflict," *Administrative Science Quarterly*, Vol. 5, pp. 508-11; also, *Modern Organization* (New York: Alfred A. Knopf; 1961), Ch. 4.

major rewards in prestige and income go to those in administrative (hierarchical) positions. The most eminent faculty member must become an administrator if he is to secure larger shares of these values. In industrial and academic research organizations the specialist resents the fact that he must go to the nonspecialist administrator to secure the resources necessary to carry out his technical work. This is especially frustrating because it means that in allocating such resources authority based upon hierarchy takes precedence over that based upon knowledge.

On the other hand, those in hierarchical positions often find the specialist difficult. Rarely can he be persuaded that his own department does not deserve the lion's share of the organization's resources. His "trained incapacity" makes it difficult for him to see that the administrator's role is inevitably one of achieving compromise among competing units within the organization. The conflict is often one between the organization-wide view of the administrator and the restricted, introverted perspective of the specialist. Moreover, specialists disturb the equilibrium of the organization by fighting among themselves about resources and recognition. In large organizations such conflicts are less amenable to accommodation based upon personal association and friendship. Each department or division tends to become a world in itself. Indeed, there are political and professional sanctions against collaborating with the enemy, because the internal discipline and unity of each subunit becomes so important in its competitive success. In this sense, size and attending specialization can become pathological.

Size has other dysfunctions. We know that as size increases morale decreases.[6] While the relationship is less consistent, lower productivity and absenteeism are also associated with

[6] James C. Worthy: "Organizational Structure and Employee Morale," *American Sociological Review*, Vol. 15, p. 173; R. Marriott: "Size of Working Group and Output," *Occupational Psychology*, Vol. 23, pp. 44-57; D. Hewitt and J. Parfit: "A Note on Working Morale and Size of Group," *Occupational Psychology*, Vol. 27, pp. 38-42.

organizational size. This is apparently because men find it difficult to identify with the large number of people found in the typical big organization. While small-group membership eases this problem, it does not necessarily improve the individual's rapport with the organization qua organization. Individuals tend to feel unimportant and somewhat alienated by its size, anonymity, and power. They do not seem to count. The pecuniary nexus between the organization and the individual may contribute to this self-perception. In mass-production industry, the highly rationalized work process encourages alienation by reducing the skill demands of the job. Such attitudes toward the organization, which are characteristic of the "indifferent" type, will be fully developed in Chapter 7. There is also considerable evidence that size contributes to hierarchy, to which we now turn.

Hierarchy may be defined as a system for ranking positions along a descending scale from the top to the bottom of the organization. Ordinarily hierarchy refers to "line" relationships rather than to those among "staff" specialists who presumably do not give orders. Although this distinction has become tenuous because of the growing influence of specialists, certainly the main decisions in big organizations are made by line officials. Hierarchy, which is as old as history, is of religious origin where it referred to the ranking of the officialdom set up to administer religious values.[7] As Weber shows, the change from charismatic authority, based upon revelation or magic, to *bureaucratic authority,* occurred in both religion and politics. This "routinization of charisma" brought *rules and officials* to administer them. The discretion of each official was necessarily limited, however, and the power

[7] M. Weber: "Bureaucracy," in Gerth and Mills: *From Max Weber* (New York: Oxford University Press, Inc.; 1946), p. 282. Both Weber's conception of ideal types and the historical evolution of organizations from "charismatic" to "bureaucratic" bases of operation may have been influenced by F. Tönnies, whose earlier (1887) work contained both concepts, *Community and Association,* trans. by C.P. Loomis (London: Routledge, Kegan Paul, Ltd.; 1955).

he exercised was not personal but legal. Therefore, "a hierarchy of superiors, to which officials may appeal and complain in an order of rank, stands opposite the citizen or member of the association . . . This situation also holds for the hierocratic association that is the church." [8] Hierarchy, then, is the result of the separation of personal, charismatic authority from official authority.

Nevertheless, as Victor Thompson shows, charismatic authority remains strong in modern organizations.[9] This is because hierarchy and the prestige attaching to it are more easily maintained when a person's roles are not clearly defined. This ambiguity is one of the essential differences between hierarchical and specialist roles. It is well known that the farther away one is from those in high organizational posts the greater the tendency to hold them in awe, to attribute to them charismatic or magical powers. Hierarchical differences in status, power, and income reinforce this perception. The higher one goes in the hierarchy the more his activities become differentiated and unamenable to precise evaluation. Contrast this situation with the role of the specialist who is assigned responsibility for a given functional task. Communication barriers between elite and rank and file aggravate this condition. In sum, the deference accorded organizational leaders is highly charged with charismatic implications. Such deference validates the individual's need to impute superiority to those above him. It also honors the American creed which holds that there are significant personal differences in ability between those who succeed and those who do not.

Hierarchy is nicely illustrated by military organization. Ranks and authority are graded from the top to the bottom of the organization. Ideally, this apparatus provides a chain of command extending throughout the entire system, in which each person from commanding general to buck private is under the control of the man immediately above him. At the

[8] Weber: op. cit., p. 295.

[9] Thompson: *Modern Organization*, pp. 493-7.

same time he is himself the supervisor of the person directly below him in the hierarchy. It is not only *positions* that are ranked in terms of authority, but relative amounts of authority, status, deference, income, and other perquisites of office are ascribed to each position. Such perquisites are allocated disproportionately. They tend to cluster near the top and to decrease rapidly as one descends the hierarchy. This inequitable distribution of scarce values is characteristic of all big organizations; it provides a built-in condition of inequality and invidious differentiation. Hierarchical monopoly of the distribution system augments the power of those at the top since rewards can be allocated to reinforce elite definitions of "loyalty," "competence," and so on. A related objective of this inequality is to reinforce the organization's status system, which in turn reinforces the authority and legitimacy of its leaders. Such consequences of the bureaucratic situation will be considered in Chapter 5.

Hierarchy gives those at the top control of the formal communication system whose channels follow hierarchical lines. Since information is obviously a prerequisite for participation, this control enables the elite to manipulate both the issues and those who help resolve them. Hierarchy permits elites to determine what kind of issues will be raised for organizational consideration. Potential solutions can be delimited by hierarchical control of meetings. By proposing only one or two alternatives and by indicating his preference among them, the formal leader can exercise disproportionate influence. The conditions of individual participation, that is to say, are always affected by hierarchy. Often, the places that individuals take around a conference table are an accurate index of their rank and status in the organization. The ensuing discussion tends to follow such rankings, with senior members dominating. As in other contexts, the weight attached to propositions is often a function of the status of their originator. The informal groups that appear in organizations are similarly structured by the relative influence, skill, seniority, and conviviality of their members.

Perhaps the main function of hierarchy is to assign and to validate authority along a descending scale throughout the organization. The resulting allocations surely constitute the basic authority structure of the organization. However, any discussion of authority in organizations must recognize that there are several bases for legitimating it. The whole burden of this book is upon the generalized deference to authority of many kinds that characterizes most individuals. We have seen that hierarchical authority has charismatic elements. But the greatest deviation from the hierarchical system of authority is the authority that specialists enjoy by virtue of their technical skill and training. The steady accumulation of knowledge which characterizes modern Western society underlies this development. New skill groups arise and demand recognition of their expertise; a self-consciousness born of knowledge, introversion, and the desire to control the market for their skills brings professionalization. Soon specialists attempt to redefine the conditions of organizational participation. While hierarchical elites insist that the question of "what should be done" remains their prerogative, specialists insist that they are entitled to a larger role in substantive policy. Knowledge, in a word, challenges hierarchical definitions of authority and role.

The resulting competition often leads to considerable legerdemain whereby mock recognition is given to line authority when in fact a decision has been made by specialists. Such fictions permit the traditional image of hierarchical supremacy to remain unchallenged by the relentless advance of scientific knowledge. Perhaps the best current example (see Chapter 9) is the management of federal atomic weapons and missile research by high ranking military officers whose experience has been restricted to the command of an army division or a ship.

The legitimation of authority by rapport or personal empathy has also become critical in big organizations. This development has come about in part as a result of human relations techniques, which rest upon deep-seated individual needs for friendship and recognition. Moreover, as bureaucratic conditions of work become more common and more standardized, the primary distinctions among white collar jobs often include such subjective factors as sympathetic work relations. In this way the interpersonal skill and the work climate provided by organizational leaders and supervisors become a basis for individual acceptance of their authority. Research shows that both the amount of influence that a leader exerts and the amount he *attempts* to exert increase with group acceptance of him as a person.[1] There is some evidence, moreover, that executives rarely fail because of lack of substantive knowledge; inadequate personal relations are more often the cause.

Despite the challenges of expertise and emotion, hierarchy remains a critical basis of organizational authority. From the human side, hierarchy is a graded system of interpersonal relationships, a society of unequals in which scarce values become even scarcer as one descends the hierarchy. Some tension inevitably results since freedom, rewards, and influence are unequally shared by those in the organization. This condition is aggravated because the career chances of any given individual rest in the hand of his immediate superior. This provides serious obstacles for those at lower ranks in the form of innumerable veto barriers which requests for rewards or promotion must penetrate. Not only can the request be denied at any level, but if such requests are negated some distance up the hierarchy, those concerned may never learn the reasons for the veto nor at what point it occurred. This condition tends to increase the common feelings of remoteness and powerlessness among members of big organizations.

Hierarchy has other functions. By delegating authority to the point where the skill necessary to carry out tasks resides, hierarchy links authority with skill. By monopolizing the dis-

[1] R.P. French and R. Snyder: "Leadership and Interpersonal Power," in Dorwin Cartwright, ed.: *Studies in Social Power* (Ann Arbor: University of Michigan Institute for Social Research; 1959), pp. 118-49.

tribution system, elites increase their control of those in the organization. Big organizations therefore tend to exhibit an "upward looking" posture and a certain anxiety. When this atmosphere is set against democratic values of individual autonomy and self-realization, considerable tension may result. A serious operational dysfunction may occur as individuals, forced to choose between initiative and risk on the one hand and clearance and safety on the other, tend to choose the latter. They resist delegation. Those in higher positions are also reluctant to delegate because this makes them responsible for the potential error of others. Such resistance is explained by the organization's drive to increase control, but since control is achieved only by limiting delegation, the organization tends to slow down. This unanticipated consequence refutes the claim that power must be centralized if big organizations are to act expeditiously: there still remains the gap between those who make decisions and those who carry them out.

Closely articulated with hierarchy in big organizations is the *status* system. Status refers to the allocation of different amounts of authority, income, deference, rights, and privileges to the various positions in the hierarchy. Prestige is the deference attached to each position, and generally it follows hierarchy. The largest amounts of deference are assigned to those at the top of the hierarchy, and the relative amounts decrease at a disproportionate rate as one descends. Ideally, both status and prestige are accurate indexes of a person's contributions to the organization. As we have seen, however, the existing system of distribution insures that those in hierarchical "line" positions receive disproportionate rewards in comparison with those in specialist roles. The status system's functional consequences include concrete recognition of individual worth and achievement. Its dysfunctions include invidious comparisons of individual contributions, comparisons which are not always objectively based. Perhaps its main operational consequence is to reinforce the authority of those at each hierarchical level in the organization. Those in the upper levels of the organization are more highly reinforced because status indexes are skewed toward the top.

We can now consider the social and psychological bases of status. It seems clear that the current emphasis upon status symbols reflects a change from an economy of scarcity to one which Veblen called "conspicuous consumption." But conspicuous consumption is difficult today for the reason that mass production has made the symbols of material success available on so large a scale. The resulting disenchantment of elites is seen in the Middle East where the periphery of material benefits is being slowly extended through industrialization and inflation. There the elite feels deprived as a result of the loss of indexes that once differentiated it from the masses. In the U.S. the decline of this psychic income means that status aspirations will be shifted to other areas, and that subtle, nonmaterial distinctions will become more highly valued since they are more difficult to establish. The importance of power and personal influence in our society seems in fact to nourish a neurotic drive for any symbol that will enhance one's status.

The social framework of status also suggests that its symbols become a substitute for values no longer attainable. The difficulty of achieving independence through owning one's business, a difficulty which reflects the trend toward bigness and concentration; the employment of the "independent" professions on a bureaucratic, salaried basis; the devaluation of the term "professional"—all seem conducive to increased status anxiety and striving. In a larger context, the whole trend toward big organization is involved, in the sense that size and anonymity result in sustained attempts by the individual to preserve status in compensation for the loss of autonomy. C. Wright Mills speaks of the "status panic" that characterizes life in the white-collar world.

Also related is the mock "professionalization" of ordinary jobs through increased educational requirements. Ludicrous efforts to borrow prestige by substituting status-laden titles for socially devalued jobs: "news analyst" for reporter; "mortician" for undertaker; the crisp term "executive," e.g., "sales executive" for salesman; the title "engineer" for all sorts of routine jobs; the co-optation of the honored symbol, "professional"—all suggest the effort to achieve status by word magic. In a deeper sense this trend may reflect decreased occupational mobility. If one cannot ascend the ladder as easily as before, why not enhance the status of that which is obtainable?

The American assumption of upward-mobility generation by generation is thus related to status idealization. A comparison with class-bound European and Middle Eastern societies suggests that sheer age, the maturing of the economy, and declining personal autonomy in the U.S. will increase status consciousness, and that a greater emphasis will come to be placed upon artificial, bureaucratic distinctions as the more objective means to status become more difficult to achieve. A free and easy democracy requires a unique social and economic situation with relatively equal access to abundant natural resources. The organizational society checkmates this situation as the lessons of power are learned by many groups and as their countervailing power results in a rough equilibrium between major social interests. In this milieu, big organizations naturally turn to subtle status rewards as compensation for economic and personal dependence and limited mobility. The honoring of seniority is an obvious example. The small gap between initial and upper-level incomes in the bureaucratized professions further encourages the use of psychic rewards such as graduated ranks, titles, name plates, and "atmosphere."

Members are clearly differentiated according to their role and status. Types of sanction, forms of communication, dress, and conduct in off-work activities are determined by one's position in the organizational hierarchy. As a rule those who deal with the public enjoy exceptional status reinforcements, including large, well-appointed offices, expense accounts (and hence greater social mobility), more staff and secretarial assistance, and those mechanical and human props that formalize access, create an impression of preoccupation with important matters, and encourage attitudes of deference. Such behavioral consequences of the status system will be considered in detail in Chapter 5 under the psychological aspects of big organizations.

The assignment of authority and status along hierarchical lines means that the conditions of participation in big formal organizations are determined by a minority. This characteristic of the bureaucratic model may be called *oligarchy,* which means "rule by the few." Although oligarchy has usually meant rule by the wealthy, modern oligarchs are often salaried employees whose status and power are based upon their *control,* not their ownership of great organizational resources. Although the power of such elites is limited in their external relations by the power of similar minorities elsewhere, our concern is with the *internal* aspects of organizations where oligarchy seems relatively unrestrained. This is not to say oligarchy is inevitable, but merely that it is a highly probable feature of big organizations.

One must qualify the oligarchic generalization in other ways. Constraints against oligarchy vary from one kind of organization to another. From casual observation we may assume that the tendency toward oligarchy is probably greater in industrial organizations than in political ones. The constituencies (the potential opposition) in the industrial context are relatively limited in number and interest, in contrast to political organizations which usually include members representing a variety of interests. Such members moreover have at their disposal critical sanctions such as the failure to vote for the party in question or to provide the funds or volunteer efforts necessary to keep the association solvent. Again, in a broad social context, the extent of oligarchy will vary with the degree of literacy and participation existing among members of the community. The skills and interests required for true bargaining between leaders and led exist in different measure in different societies. Oligarchy, as a result, will be more probable in underdeveloped societies where political and organizational skills are the monopoly of relatively limited groups. There, in Pareto's phrase, the "circulation of elites" occurs within a small group. In Western society, on the other hand, relatively high literacy rates and greater participation in a greater number of associations mean that the skills which make oligarchy possible are more widely distributed. As a result, its effects are somewhat modulated.

It is always necessary to add that while "oligarchy" means the power of the few over the many, this does not mean that the majority is powerless. Even Machiavelli's Prince was admonished to have due regard for popular myths. The important point is that such power is unequal. The concept of power assumes reciprocity, but there is always a difference between the power of one actor and another. Obviously all elites are to some extent limited by their assumptions about mass reactions to their politics, but an oligarchy is characterized by the *preponderance of power* it enjoys. Oligarchy, then, assumes inequality of power, nothing more.

Oligarchy is apparent in the fact that decisions in big organizations are usually made by a minority. When organizations become large, communication is difficult and the power of decision tends to be restricted to a few leaders. Some elites enhance their power by concealing information; but in any event the problems of disseminating information and of providing for widespread participation present almost insuperable obstacles. The pressure of demands for quick decisions often makes consultation impracticable. The highly technical character of many decisions tends furthermore to limit participation to those who have the requisite skills and knowledge—this despite the fact that the ramifications of the decision may extend throughout the organization. Thus the intensity of oligarchy probably increases in some sort of geometric ratio to organizational size. We know, for example, that the atomization of stock ownership encourages oligarchy. The more dispersed the stockholders become, the greater the power of the controlling minority. And it is control, not ownership, that counts in modern organization.

Robert Michels, a very distinguished student of oligarchy, found that it was characteristic of *big* organizations rather than of all.[2] In his view, organizations become oligar-

[2] *Political Parties* (Glencoe, Illinois: The Free Press; 1949). Almost a half century after Michels wrote, C.P. Snow found oligarchy to be similarly characteristic of contemporary organizational life: "One of the most bizarre features of any advanced industrial society in our time is that the cardinal choices have to be made by a handful of men: in secret: and, at least in legal form, by men who cannot have a first-hand knowledge of what those choices depend upon or what their results may be. . . . And when I say the 'cardinal choices,' I mean those which determine in the crudest sense whether we live or die. For instance, the choice in England and the United States in 1940 and 1941, to go ahead with work on the fission bomb: the choice in 1945 to use that bomb when it was made: the choice in the United States and the Soviet Union, in the late forties, to make the fusion bomb: the choice, which led to a different result in the United States and the Soviet Union, about intercontinental missiles." *Science and Government* (Cambridge: Harvard University Press; 1960), p. 1. The dynamics of oligarchy are similarly apparent in the experience of the Communist party in Russia, which before 1917 functioned with a large central committee. Once the revolution was successful, however, the need for control, action, and dispatch thrust power into pitifully few hands. As Barrington Moore says: "Just before the November Revolution on October 23, 1917, a small nucleus was created with the Party Central Committee at the suggestion of Dzerzhinsky, later chief of the secret police. The original members were Lenin, Zinoviev, Kamenev, Trotsky, Stalin, Sokol'nikov and Bubnov. The main task envisaged at this time appears to have been little more than the management of the details of the November uprising. Nevertheless, the idea of concentrating decision-making powers in the hands of a very few leaders persisted, owing to the continuing need for immediate and far-reaching decisions in the crises directly following the Revolution. By March 1919 the Eighth Party Congress set up, as a permanently acting body, a Political Bureau consisting of five members, who were 'to decide on questions which do not permit delay,' and to report bimonthly on all its work to a regular plenary session of the Central Committee. At that time the Politburo consisted of Lenin, Trotsky, Stalin, Kamenev and Bukharin. At no time during the period from 1919 to 1946 did the membership of the Politburo, including candidates, ex-

chic for technical and psychological reasons. The sheer number of members prohibits communication; and the resulting ignorance and inertia encourage direction by the few. Meanwhile, specialist claims increase the tendency toward oligarchy, because new skill groups gain access to strategic points in the hierarchy and acquire an impetus to rule. Public relations men, for example, are now among the top policy makers in most organizations. Thus size, numbers, and the need for expertise are among the technical reasons for minority control.

These "causes" of oligarchy are reinforced by psychological factors, including the desire for power encouraged by the dominant values of our society. Although oligarchy is often justified by the need for control and the pressure for action, it also reflects individual drives for power. The fulfillment of this drive is often encouraged, furthermore, by the "true believer's" need for some omnipotent leader or myth. That is to say, many subordinates need the man of power to displace the burden of individual responsibility and to receive in return the benefits of certainty. Although its psychic nuances cannot be treated here, a significant by-product of oligarchy must be mentioned: the selective process in big organizations brings the power seeker to the top. Moreover, power and its dividends increase as one ascends the hierarchy.

While the logic and rewards of organization encourage the drive for power, its criteria of selection ensure that those who rise possess an exceptional urge to dominate. The implications for responsibility are sharpened by Michels' conclusion that control of any elite can come only from *outside* the organization.

Michels developed his "iron law of oligarchy" by observ-

---

ceed seventeen individuals. . . . its functions covered almost the entire scope of political, economic, social and cultural problems in Soviet life." *Soviet Politics: The Dilemma of Power* (Cambridge: Harvard University Press; 1950), p. 141.

ing socialist political parties in western Europe. Despite their lip service to equality, he found them oligarchic in operation. Power was centered in a core of permanent officials who made policy and presented it full-blown to the members for ratification. It is similarly ironic that big organizations in the United States also exist in a democratic context and employ a liberal rhetoric, but are often nevertheless oligarchic. This is not only confusing but also somewhat inhibiting insofar as analysis is concerned. The problem of power is often ignored as an uncomfortable aberration. As a result, one must often cut through a haze of cheerful rationalizations concerning manifest power disequilibria. One such rationalization is the notion that authority in big organizations is essentially a matter of *consent*, depending upon the acceptance of those who are subject to it.[3] This view must be qualified, however, mainly because it fails to ask *why* authority is accepted. When this question is asked, the problems of learned deference to authority, to influence, and to sanctions are raised, and the motives for "acceptance" become clearer.

Obviously, individuals "accept" authority for many reasons and many possible reactions exist, ranging from eager cooperation to reluctant obedience. Confronted with an order, the average individual will estimate the consequences of various alternatives and adopt the one that seems in his own interest, insofar as he is able to identify it. In this restricted sense authority is no doubt "accepted." But to suggest as this thesis does that it is commonly within the individual's range of discretion either to accept or to reject is misleading. Rejection is usually impractical. Moreover, such a view fails to recognize the propensity to obey induced by socialization and by hierarchy, both of which tend to institutionalize obedience and to redefine "acceptance" by creating an expectation of compliance.

Hunter's study of power in Atlanta, Georgia, suggests the

[3] Chester I. Barnard: *Functions of the Executive* (Cambridge: Harvard University Press; 1938).

locus and the tactics of oligarchy.[4] While Atlanta may be unique, and while more recent research raises questions about elitist assumptions of community power structure, this remains an impressive study. He found a weblike pattern of power and influence ultimately residing in a half dozen members of an old-family elite. Viewed from the outside, power appeared to be more widely diffused, since many of its agents were obviously not members of the inner circle. But this illusion reflected the need to organize and to delegate power, particularly the need for a means of enlisting the energies and great expectations of those at the periphery. The vital decision to act or not to act remained in the inner circle, although the responsibility for organizing, articulating, and carrying it through was necessarily shared with others. The latter exercised influence, it is true, but theirs was a borrowed, temporary influence. In effect, this group *administered* the power of the industrial, banking, legal, and social elite, and enjoyed the façade of power that such participation gave them.

The structure of oligarchy thus consisted of an inner elite supported by an aspiring, co-opted outer circle which dealt with an apathetic ratifying majority. Although the inner elite

[4] Floyd Hunter: *Community Power Structure* (Chapel Hill: University of North Carolina Press; 1953); on oligarchy, see also Robert and Helen Lynd: *Middletown*, rev. ed. (New York: Harcourt, Brace & Co.; 1959); and F.A. Stewart: "A Sociometric Study of Influence in Southtown," *Sociometry*, Vol. 10, pp. 11-31, 273-86; D.B. Truman: *The Governmental Process* (New York: Alfred A. Knopf; 1951), pp. 139-55; this is an unusual analysis in which the author begins by specifically rejecting Michels: "Because of some serious limitations in his method, Michels derived from his evidence a series of implications concerning political leadership that are *largely untenable* . . ." (p. 140; italics added), then presents a summary of empirical research by Michels, Garceau, Berle and Means, Ross, Gray, MacIver, Millis and Montgomery, Cleveland, Brooks, McKean, Herring, Kile, Masland, and Myrdal that reinforces Michels' thesis. To say that delegation from the "active minority" to the rank and file is never complete or that oligarchy is a "matter of degree" (p. 142) is no doubt both inevitable and valid, but this hardly vitiates Michels' hypothesis.

remained behind the scenes, reaching policy decisions at informal meetings, respondents were apparently able to differentiate nicely between the "real" power holders and the contenders at various levels. While a recent New Haven study found little overlap between political and economic elites, and no generalized community power structure,[5] Hunter found (as the Lynds, Warner, Hollingshead, and Baltzell had found) that the elite influenced various kinds of decisions and was homogeneous, since the wealth, social

[5] R.H. Dahl: *Who Governs? Democracy and Power in an American Community* (New Haven: Yale University Press; 1961). Dahl concludes: "We shall discover that in each of a number of key sectors of public policy, a few persons have great *direct* influence on the choices that are made; most citizens, by contrast, seem to have rather little direct influence. Yet it would be unwise to underestimate the extent to which voters may exert *indirect* influence on the decisions of leaders by means of elections," p. 101. (Italics in original.) Dahl also documents the importance of specialization in maintaining a pluralistic leadership structure in New Haven, pp. 181-2. Indeed, to some extent, the three key policy sectors used in the study may inadvertently provide for a built-in specialization. Certainly the sector of party nominations for office is limited to a minority of political professionals, few of whom would presumably overlap with leaders on other substantive issues. Nevertheless, the specialization that characterizes our society insures that leadership and decision making will be somewhat diffused. Although organizational elites can often hire the many talents needed to make wise decisions, it is unlikely that one or a few men will possess the skill and information required to direct all the disparate activities of a large organization or a community. However, such qualifications of Michels' thesis are perhaps challenged by community leadership research which finds that even though specialization encourages pluralism, the *total* proportion of community members who are active in *all kinds* of decisions is extremely small. As L.C. Freeman, *et al.* found: "Less than three-tenths of one per cent of the adult citizens of the Syracuse area participated in a direct way in the making of these 39 community decisions." *Local Community Leadership* (Syracuse: University College; 1960), p. 26. The author found similarly in two New York communities of 6,000 and 9,000 each that a total of only 37 men in community X and 35 men in community Y were actively involved in local decisions, as measured by their participation in five important community decisions in each of the two communities. Robert Presthus: *Men at the Top: A Study in Community Power* (New York: Oxford Univ. Press, 1964).

position, and organizing skills of the minority were similar. While an outsider might occasionally be co-opted, usually through a romantic or a pecuniary nexus (and these were not necessarily exclusive), admission to this circle was extremely limited.

A similar tendency toward oligarchy is visible in most large groups, regardless of their function and ideology. In Congress, for example, party control is much stronger in the House than in the Senate, in part because the House is five times as large. Within Congress the selection and the influence of committees encourage government by minority. As one observer concludes:

> Congressional committees have lacked any definite responsibility. Their control over legislation submitted to them has been almost unlimited. They can amend or rewrite bills to suit themselves. They can report bills or pigeonhole them. They can initiate measures they desire and bury or emasculate those they dislike. . . . In short, congressional government is government by the standing committees of Congress.[6]

Perhaps the most powerful of such committees is the House Rules Committee which mainly determines the form and content of legislation that reaches the floor of the House of Representatives. Here again, the size variable is critical, for it is generally agreed that in the Senate, only one-fifth as large, committees are less powerful and legislation coming from them is subject to a much more incisive scrutiny. An example of the oligarchic power enjoyed by the Rules Committee is its handling of the 1961 federal aid to education

[6] George B. Galloway: *Congress at the Crossroads* (New York: Thomas Y. Crowell Co.; 1946), p. 184; consult also *The New York Times* summary of President Kennedy's difficulties during the first session of the Eighty-seventh Congress, in which "most of the Administration's major setbacks came in House committees, several of which . . . bottled up a number of high-priority Administration bills and drastically modified some others." Then follows an account of the Rules Committee's part in the defeat of the school-aid bill, September 28, 1961, p. 32.

bill. On the pretense that the bill would be released when legislation to provide aid to parochial schools was given to the Committee, the bill was bottled up to prevent debate and voting on the floor. But even when a parochial aid bill got to the Rules Committee, no action occurred. Finally, by an 8-7 vote, in which the deciding ballot was cast by a member from a Catholic constituency in Brooklyn, the Committee voted to shelve all pending federal aid to education bills. According to *The New York Times,* "after the meeting the New Yorker reiterated his contention that the Administration's school-aid bill constituted 'discrimination' against parochial schools because it would authorize grants for public schools only." [7] The *Times* called the Committee's action a "betrayal" of the long-range interests of the country, and found it tragic that "the straightforward political issue of Federal aid to the public schools has been distorted and envenomed by the divisive and emotional issue of Federal aid to parochial schools." [8]

In such ways, minority control and traditional organizational alignments in Congress permit strategically placed individuals to block legislation. In this instructive case, five Republicans, two conservative Democrats, plus the Democratic member cited above, were able to hamstring the entire House. The final hope of getting school-aid legislation during the current session was thus placed upon a chief executive whose razor-thin election victory had so far kept him from "stepping in emphatically . . . to rescue the bill that means so much to his reputation and to the country." [9]

Although the locus of their power is state and local rather than national, our political parties are similarly controlled by a professional minority.[1] Even a casual appraisal of the pre-

[7] *The New York Times* (July 19, 1961), p. 28.

[8] Ibid.

[9] Ibid.

[1] On the character of party organization, M. Duverger concludes: "The organization of political parties is certainly not in conformity with orthodox notions of democracy. Their internal structure is essentially

liminary tactics of presidential nominating conventions reveals the power of the active minority. Here again there is little despotism, although exhibitions such as the Democratic convention of 1960 suggest that the line is at times rather finely drawn. Ordinarily the will of the rank and file will not be flagrantly violated, and self-interest alone insures that the nominee will be broadly representative. Nevertheless, in the 1960 Democratic convention a handful of big-city and state leaders in New York, Pennsylvania, Ohio, Illinois, and California were able to push through without serious opposition a candidate whose popular appeal was certainly less impressive than his campaign organization and unlimited resources. In sum, such conventions are often the mere formalization of extended, preliminary, behind-the-scenes caucusing by innumerable combinations of influence and interest, reflecting bargaining among big-city, state, and national party leaders. And such bargaining is almost entirely restricted to a professional party elite, however sensitive it may be to great social and economic interests.[2] As Erwin D. Canham said in 1961: "Party organization, county, state, and national committees, should be made less oligarchical." But here again the majority plays its traditional role, namely, the ratification of choices made by others.

---

oligarchic; their leaders are not really appointed by the members, in spite of appearances, but co-opted or nominated by the central body. They tend to form a ruling class, isolated from the militants, a caste that is more or less exclusive. In so far as they are elected, the party oligarchy is widened without ever becoming a democracy." *Political Parties: Their Organization and Activity in the Modern State* (London: Methuen and Co., Ltd.; 1954), p. 422. See also, M. Ostrogorski: *Democracy and the Organization of Political Parties* (New York: The Macmillan Co.; 1902), Vol. 2, Chs. 6, 7. The foreign scholars upon whom I mainly rely in this chapter may lack the fullest sensitivity to the American political milieu, but they escape the "situational determinism" that inevitably colors the analyses of American social scientists.

[2] Even so sympathetic an observer of the American scene as D.W. Brogan states: "The basic defect of the Convention system is the imperfect representative character of the assembly. The delegates represent at least as much the wishes of the political leaders, pressure groups,

Similar behaviors appear in academic and professional associations, in labor unions, corporations, and universities. The "causes" are the same: the need for the organizing skills of permanent officials; the development of bureaucratic systems of leadership, before which the unorganized majority is virtually powerless; and the size and specialization of contemporary groups, reflecting modern innovations in political tactics and communication. The desire for power and the discipline of those who hope to rise, as well as the apathy or disenchantment of the majority, are also at work.

The role of *co-optation* in enhancing organizational discipline and continuity must also be emphasized. As Michels said, co-optation is the process by which those in power designate their successors. This prerogative is part of the monopoly of scarce values that hierarchy assigns to the organization's elite. Since such successors are chosen by existing elites, it can be assumed that they will personify traditional values. In this way sanctioned behaviors and expectations are transmitted through agents selected after what tends to be (given the remarkable tenure of oligarchs) a lengthy apprenticeship. Meanwhile the impact of co-optation extends beyond those immediately affected. Each promotion and its rituals provide an opportunity to dramatize the terms under which rewards are given. The indexes of success are reaffirmed, and the upward-mobiles receive another impetus to rise. For various reasons, including the desire to preserve internal unity and discipline, *loyalty* seems to have become the main basis for bureaucratic succession. Like seniority, loyalty enjoys the advantage of wide acceptance, for it is a quality almost everyone can aspire to.

---

city, county, and state 'machines' as they represent the wishes of the rank and file voters." *Politics in America* (New York: Harper & Brothers; 1954), p. 220. One may recall too Bryce's conclusion as to why great men are not chosen president which rests in part upon this facet of our political system, i.e., "the method of choice does not bring them to the top." *The American Commonwealth* (New York: The Macmillan Co.; 1907), Vol. 1, p. 84, pp. 78-85 *passim*.

Oligarchy and co-optation are apparent in union leadership, which becomes a sinecure despite periodic elections and an emphasis upon democratic values. Samuel Gompers served a thirty-eight-year term as president of the AFL. After his death in 1924 the reins were held by William Green for almost three decades. Daniel Tobin led the Teamsters for virtually half a century; Hutcheson led the Carpenters for thirty-five years and, upon retirement, was succeeded by his son. John L. Lewis was president of the UMW for over forty years. Such tenures and the resulting control of policy make possible tremendous concentrations of power. As Kermit Eby said:

> The modern trade union, like the modern corporation, is monolithic; one huge human shaft of power directed from the top. Its conventions are attended by professionals—"pork choppers"—whose present and future security depends on the maintenance of the power hierarchy. Decisions which affect the rank-and-file worker are increasingly removed from his hands in both time and space. The decisions which must be made are technically so complicated that only the expert or the leaders advised by the expert are competent to make them.[3]

Oligarchy as an "organic necessity" is the result of technical demands for internal direction, unity and consistency, control of market conditions, leadership skills, public relations, and lobbying. It is rendered necessary, in short, by the need for someone to give coherence and continuity to the vague, often conflicting aspirations of the majority. Given the role of unanticipated consequences in human affairs, the implications of oligarchy may come as a shock to those who exercise it, assuming that such considerations ever arise. Doubts, however, are probably resolved by the assumptions of infallibility that characterize most oligarchs; self-images which are nourished by their isolation and power.

[3] Kermit Eby: "The Drip Theory in Labor Unions," *The Antioch Review*, Vol. 13, pp. 95-102.

Power to initiate, to communicate, to reward, to sanction, to shape public opinion—these are the prerogatives and tactics of oligarchy. As a result, policy and orders flow from the top downward, limiting the rank and file to an essentially negative role. Having neither the power of initiation, which permits the oligarchy to decide what shall be done and when, nor of choosing the avenues of consultation, which can be used to ensure favorable reactions to their policies, nor the control of patronage, which ensures discipline, the majority can only ratify. When such actions sharply violate their expectations, the mass may exercise a veto power, but such contingencies are remote since they occur only if the minority loses the tactical skill that brought it to power in the first place.

In democratic societies the tendency toward oligarchy stands out most sharply in crises, when the use of arbitrary methods for democratic ends becomes acceptable. An obvious example is the way in which military and security imperatives are accepted during wartime. Most of us regard such invasions as a temporary inconvenience, a necessary tribute to national survival. Similarly, during wartime certain groups shelve ideals which previously had seemed irreducible. For example, physical scientists made great contributions during and after World War II through their research on new weapons. It is well known that their professional ethic centers on individual independence, on the free exchange of information, and on a rigorous disavowal of authority as a basis for truth. These values, moreover, are not merely desirable; they are supposedly among the essentials of scientific progress. Yet apparently they could be set aside. We find, for example, that during World War II the 30,000 scientists in the Office of Scientific Research and Development were controlled by about "thirty-five men in senior positions." [4] This minority assigned research, established policy vis-à-vis the military and the public, and generally ran

[4] Vanevar Bush: *Modern Arms and Free Men* (New York: Simon and Schuster, Inc.; 1949), pp. 6-7.

things according to "convenient, authoritarian military liaisons." [5]

Hierarchy and oligarchy seek *rationality*, another common structural characteristic of large-scale organization.[6] Rationality may be defined as the capacity for objective, intelligent action. It is usually characterized by a patent behavioral nexus between ends and means. While rationality is always limited by human error, inadequate information, and chance, within these limits the rational person applies intelligence, experience, and technical skills to solve his problems. In an ideal-typical organization rationality is sought by organizing and directing its many parts so that each contributes to the whole product. Specialization, careful recruitment, job analysis, and planning are among the obvious means to this end.

We assume that society tends to produce individuals who possess its dominant characteristics. The rationality of the big organization is similarly instilled in its members. Not only are its structure and procedures designed to enhance predictability, but individuals too become, insofar as possible, animated instruments. Individual discretion is limited by regulations and precedents that cover all anticipated events, and such regulations tend to become ends in themselves. As a result, individuals try to find written authority for every action and to avoid action when such cannot be found. The very interpretation of rules and the search for authority to act (or not to act) become valued skills. Knowledge of the rules and how they can be bent gives the individual security and a share of organized power. He thus develops a vested interest in preserving the rules against change.

Rationality is also sought through the division of labor

[5] "The Great Science Debate," *Fortune* (June, 1946), p. 236.

[6] The following comments on rationality and specialization in organization are based mainly on Weber: *Theory of Social and Economic Organization* (Glencoe, Illinois: The Free Press; 1957); and Merton: "Bureaucratic Structure and Personality," *Social Forces,* Vol. 17, pp. 560-8; Gerth and Mills: loc. cit.

and through recruitment on a scientific basis. Job requirements, including both technical skill and emotional qualities, are determined by men selected for their ability to determine such qualifications. Skill and character are matched with such specifications, insuring that placement is as objective as possible. This rational distribution of human effort is reinforced by the fact that organization units are also set up on a specialized basis. Such specialization enables the individual (and the organization) to develop exceptional skill.

Even the specialist's isolation contributes to his skill because he finds satisfaction in the complete mastery of his role. Denied an understanding of the larger scheme, he magnifies the limited insights and satisfactions that are within his grasp. He is, as it were, driven to this end. Objective, impersonal standards become all the more acquisitive because he is often unaware of their implications. He thinks everyone lives that way. One is reminded of the Prussian staff officer who spent a lifetime seeking ways to reduce mobilization time by one half-hour. As Merton and others have shown, certain dysfunctions follow, including a resistance and an inability to change.[7]

Another significant by-product occurs: the decision-making process becomes highly diffused, the product of an organizational mind. Organized irresponsibility follows. Decision making in the big organization becomes vague and impersonal, the instrument of an anonymous, fragmented intelligence.[8] Each decision is the result of various technical and personal considerations, the sum of the contributions of everyone involved in the deciding process. This diffusion means that "everyone" (i.e., no one) is responsible. In extreme cases the condition may lead to arbitrary and immoral behavior, particularly when compounded by intense per-

[7] Merton: op. cit.

[8] This aspect of bureaucratic systems is compellingly portrayed in the novels of Franz Kafka: *The Castle* (New York: Alfred A. Knopf, Inc.; 1941) and *The Trial* (New York: Alfred A. Knopf; 1957).

sonal identification with the state, the party, the church, or the "organization." In every case, the probabilities that the organization may act unjustly are increased by the weakening of individual responsibility. Only "the system" is responsible.

The modern culmination of this system was seen in the Nazi apparatus. "The crime is handed down from chief to sub-chief until it reaches the slave who receives orders from above without being able to pass them on to anybody. One of the Dachau executioners weeps in prison and says, 'I only obeyed orders. The Fuhrer and the Reichsfuhrer, alone, planned all this and then they ran away. Gluecks received orders from Kaltenbrunner and, finally, I received orders to carry out the shootings. I have been left holding the bag because I was only a little *Hauptscharfuhrer* and because I couldn't hand it on any lower down the line. Now they say that I am the assassin.' "[9] This suggests why the big organization more often causes a crime of logic than one of passion, to use Camus' phrase.

Such procedures and attitudes are often necessary to handle the volume and diversity of activity in big organizations. Methods for handling each type of problem are prescribed, with each specialist contributing to the decision on the basis of his skill and jurisdiction. This overriding technical ethos increases the probability that personal factors will be minimized. Ideally, there is no way that such elements can affect the decision process. The specialist's loyalty is to the work process and to his own technical skill, rather than to any mitigating aspects of a case. As Weber shows, to do otherwise would evoke considerable anxiety, so strong are the demands of precedent and procedure.

The organization, in sum, is rationally planned to achieve its ends. Like the human organism, it has a directing center that transmits cues to the entire organization. Authority, rewards, and sanctions are allocated in ways that ensure that

[9] Albert Camus: *The Rebel* (New York: Random House; 1959), p. 182.

its members work together. As we have seen, hierarchy and oligarchy are perhaps the main instruments for so doing. The first assigns authority, responsibility, status, income, and deference in a descending scale from top to bottom, providing a chain of graded interpersonal relationships that insures the delegation of all sanctioned impulses. Oligarchy makes its contribution by monopolizing power and the distribution of the organization's scarce values. Men work for status, recognition, and security; oligarchy permits the organization's elite to determine the conditions under which such values are allocated.

All this is highly idealized, of course. Informal centers of power compete with the elite for influence in determining how resources are to be distributed. Unanticipated consequences subvert the organization's formal goals. Individuals persist in giving their latent objectives priority over organizational claims. Nevertheless, in organizations with high morale, i.e., those in which the legitimacy of means and ends is widely endorsed, the image is generally accurate. The resulting bond between the elite and the rank and file ensures identification, consensus, and even a sense of real participation among the latter.

We conclude this chapter by considering two common assumptions about big organizations: that they are characterized by *"efficiency"* and *"freedom from conflict."* Both assumptions need to be qualified. Despite the fact that organizations exude an aura of "efficiency," being highly organized to achieve their goals by means of the structural characteristics outlined above; and despite the fact that individuals, hired on the basis of training and expertise, pursue their specialties with authority and discretion and in accordance with prescribed rules; and despite the fact that everyone is briskly competent and appears to know exactly what he is doing; the belief in the "efficiency" of bureaucratic organization is almost impossible to sustain. Not only is the very concept of "efficiency" virtually impossible of definition, except in some gross, tautological sense such as "the achievement of organizational goals with the minimum expenditure of resources," but no competent research exists demonstrating the "efficiency" of the bureaucratic model compared with some alternative. While some of its characteristics, such as specialization and oligarchy, probably increase productivity and discipline, it is fair to conclude that a rigorous demonstration of its "efficiency" has not yet been made.

As Karl Mannheim has said, the advantages of modern organizations lie mainly in their tendency to increase group rationality by placing power and authority in relatively few hands.[1] This permits the organization's major policies to be determined with limited conflict and great finality. Once this has been done, the energies of the entire organization can be devoted to the task of carrying them out. Centralized authority and the conclusive resolution of the essential value question, "What is to be done?" is the major operational advantage of the bureaucratic model. But even this impressive advantage leaves unanswered questions about the effect of oligarchic decision making upon morale, and about the caliber of decisions reached without full participation.

A related characteristic often imputed to the bureaucratic model is its "conflict-free" nature. This assumption is rarely analyzed, yet it is directly related to whatever "efficiency" the model achieves. The declining market value of conflict in contemporary society is surely related to the dysfunctions of conflict as a personal bureaucratic skill. If one assumes that centralized authority is required to achieve order and continuity in the organization, it follows that conflict must be muted and confined to the organization's elite. Once decisions are reached at this level, further argument is prohibited. As in the British Cabinet, an administered consensus occurs, ensuring "collective responsibility" and a united front before the organization and the outside world. That executives who disagree strongly with policy decisions must re-

[1] Karl Mannheim: *Man and Society in an Age of Reconstruction* (New York: Harcourt, Brace & Co.; 1941), pp. 244, 293-5.

sign if they feel unable to accept the institutional decision suggests the intensity of this demand for consensus. The "conflict-free" assumption also provides psychological gains, reinforcing authority by the implication that the revealed decision is the "one best way," scientifically achieved in line with the experience, inside information, and knowledge possessed by the organization's leaders. Patent conflict, by contrast, suggests that since equally wise and expert men can disagree on an issue, there is some question about the very existence of objectively superior alternatives, and of the organization's ability to discover them. In this sense, the very premises of organizational logic are challenged by conflict.

The strategic advantages of conflict repression are also apparent in the internecine struggles among competing units of the organization. Here, too, dissent is confined within the unit, enabling the latter to present a united front in its endless competition with other units for a larger share of the organization's resources. Elites have a direct stake in such consensus because any inability to maintain equilibrium and its attending competitive advantages brings disapproval from higher echelons which also desire on their own part to convey upward an image of cohesion within their larger sphere. The weight of such expectations is shown by the fact that the gravest offense in bureaucratic society is to go over the head of one's superior, to reveal conflict to outsiders.

The "conflict-free" assumption is undercut by the inherent tension between authority based upon hierarchy and that based upon the expertise of the many specialists found in the typical big organization. Understandably, each element tends to define its own role as the ultimate basis for authority. Those in hierarchical positions will insist that final authority must reside at the top, because the disparate skills, training, and professional introversion of specialists require some disinterested and superior co-ordinating influence. On the other hand, specialists will rarely grant that those in formal positions of authority fully merit the authority, power, and income which they usually enjoy. While the intensity of this conflict varies, it is in some degree a built-in characteristic of all big organizations. In view of this, it seems that instead of defining the bureaucratic model as "conflict free," we ought to regard it as a system in which conflict is inherent. At the same time, there are no doubt significant operational gains coming from the kind of centralized authority which enables modern organizations to administer consensus through the means outlined in this chapter.

We have now analyzed the major structural characteristics of big organizations, including *size, specialization, hierarchy, status, authority, oligarchy, co-optation, rationality* and "*efficiency.*" These characteristics constitute the *bureaucratic model,* an ideal type of all large-scale organizations. Such organizations provide a distinctive work environment for their members. Behavioral expectations are clearly prescribed, and interpersonal relations are structured by nice distinctions among the authority, status, and rank of those concerned. At the same time, conflict is always present. This reflects the tensions between those in hierarchical positions, who monopolize organizational power and rewards, and those in specialist roles. In the next chapter we shall trace the historical developments which culminated in the organizational society.

CHAPTER 3

TOWARD THE ORGANIZATIONAL SOCIETY

When Henry Adams returned to America in 1871, he remarked that size and "an increased facility of combination" had become striking characteristics of the economy. Although the emerging pattern was clearest in industry, the bureaucratic model and its values also invaded other areas, extending the control of both human and material resources. By the 1930's the trend had culminated in the "organizational society." In economic terms, competitively determined prices, wages, and production had been displaced by an imperfect market, a market characterized by government intervention, negotiated decisions between labor and management, "sticky prices," and relatively few sellers in basic sectors of the economy such as automobiles, steel, and oil. A similar trend occurred in nonindustrial sectors. Power and security provided common motives, and the means of achieving them became increasingly alike.

Thus a "prebureaucratic" society of small organizations and unbridled competition was replaced by a more rational bureaucratic society. Obviously, complete rationality and control did not follow. In fields such as retail sales where capital requirements remained small, many small units flourished and competition remained lively. In all areas, the unanticipated consequences of human behavior remained as numerous as their intended objectives; and chance, error, and irrationality still influenced events. But, broadly speaking, the calculated direction of social affairs increased steadily from 1865 to the present. The federal government's manipulation of consumer and commercial credit suggests the expanding periphery of control over matters once left to chance. The obsolescence of the "laws" of supply and demand was dramatically revealed in 1961 by the indictment and conviction of several General Electric executives for overt collusion in submitting identical "competitive" bids to governmental agencies. Similarly, the molding of public opinion and the manufacture of favorable popular images by advertising and public-relations firms marks the advance of calculated operations. The development of integrated enterprises, mainly in steel and oil, which controlled their product from raw material to consumer, is another example of the trend.

As a result, traditional ideals and theories became dated. In economic analysis, for example, the laissez-faire ideal of the competitive, self-regulating economy remained viable long after our major economic areas (investment banking, steel, copper, oil, automobiles, rubber tires, aluminum, tin containers, as well as liquor and cigarettes) had become typically oligopolic. A few sellers possessing vast financial and technical resources dominated a vast market. The myth of the typical American as an independent, self-employed, profit-making individual persisted, largely unaffected by evidence that size and technology had greatly increased the proportion of *employees* in the labor force. Despite the rise of national unions, the fiction of the individual worker bargaining for himself, moving about freely seeking a higher wage, remained current.

The laissez-faire model, based on certain eighteenth-century assumptions of Smith, Ricardo, and Bentham, was strained in an attempt to explain the facts of "imperfect competition." If price competition was outlawed by tacit agreement, brand and advertising competition (based on technical advance and a great deal of pure rhetoric) was enlisted to reinforce the limping theory. The depression of the 1930's brought the first systematic modification when Chamberlin and Robinson analyzed the disparity between the model and the real world. Two decades later, however, it still could not be said that their theory of imperfect competition dominated popular economic discourse in the United States.

The iconoclasm of Keynes, who gave government an equilibrating role in economic affairs and demolished some of the central assumptions of classical theory, was reluctantly accepted. Some economists insisted that the model had been misused, that it was never meant to describe actual conditions but merely to ease analysis and prediction. Although a model is by definition a caricature, however, its task is nevertheless to help us understand reality. If it fails to do this, its validity must be questioned. Others maintained that even though the economy was no longer competitive, everything worked out as well as if it had been.

Laissez-faire economic theory was of course more than an economic philosophy. It was the unifying element in the American scheme of values. And since values are usually impervious to facts, popular views were little affected by the economic revolution. Certainly among the public and in those areas where few sellers and many buyers had become typical, and where demand and production had little to do with price, the pure theory of competition remained vigorous. Only a few professional economists faced the implications of the new economic structure for traditional theory and analysis. The dominant myths began to be questioned, however, by young university graduates whose career preferences revealed their own acceptance of the organizational society. Increasingly they chose security in one of the depression-proof giants.

This chapter is concerned with our evolution from a primarily rural, agricultural, competitive, and rather individualistic society to an urban-industrial complex whose major social activities are carried on by huge bureaucratic structures. Although each will be handled separately, there was a similar pattern of bureaucratic development among all the great interests, industry, labor, government, mass communications, and so on. The politics of survival demanded that each close ranks against the other contenders for power and plan its strategy accordingly. This competition partly explains the ubiquity of big organizations.

In the formative years of American capitalism, extending roughly from 1865 to the turn of the century, business enterprise was typically owner-operated and controlled. The system was highly personalized. The owner risked his own money, played an active role in management, and competed whole-heartedly with his rivals. Neither through control of production, price, markets, large-scale operation, nor virtually unlimited capital and technical resources could he significantly influence the market. Although the early history of Standard Oil indicates that such efforts were made, the conditions permitting a fully administered economy did not as yet exist. Such an economy first appeared after the panic of 1873 when railroad consolidations were followed by widespread mergers.

An organizational society, however, requires concentrated power in various social areas. This rough equilibrium was not achieved until the 1930's when agriculture and labor gained the political strength that allowed them to manipulate their economic environment. Nor did these achievements result in more than a temporary equilibrium, since new conditions soon changed the balance of power. For example, financial interests suffered because the taxation and investment policies of big government reduced sharply their influence over industry by permitting corporations to set aside sufficient profits to meet their capital needs for expansion and replacement. Similarly, the alliance between government and labor during the New Deal period was shattered by the return of conservative government following World War II, as symbolized by the Taft Hartley and Landrum Griffin Acts.

The formative period from the Civil War to the first great merger movement, from 1897 to 1904, began with an economic revolution. Before the war our economy was one of merchant capitalism. From 1820 to 1860 the first small factories appeared and manufacturing got its start with the use of coal for steam power, with the rise of railroads, and with the integration of factory units. But this was still the age of the speculative capitalist rather than of the manufacturer. Moreover, during the entire period from the Revolutionary War to the Civil War, agriculture dominated the economy. Manufacturing was done in the home by the "putting-out" system, or less frequently, in the small shop. Labor was provided by the family or by the proprietor and a few apprentices. The present factory system, depending on machine power tended by wage earners, is a post-Civil War phenomenon. Not until 1890 did the value of manufactures equal that of agriculture, but in another decade its value doubled that of its chief rival. Natural increase and immigration provided the manpower necessary to feed the growing economy. From 1820 to 1860 our population grew from about 10,000,000 to 31,000,000. Of equal significance for industrial development, the proportion of the urban population rose from five per cent to over sixteen per cent. From 1860 to 1870 manufacturing establishments increased by almost eighty per cent.

This emerging capitalism was dominated by a few entrepreneurs who possessed unusual skill in finance and integration. Carnegie in steel, Rockefeller in oil, Armour in packing, Stanford and Harriman in railroads, and Morgan in finance were among some of them. While their part in building industry has probably been overdrawn (without the rich human and natural resources of a young nation such progress would surely have been impossible), their philosophy and tactics set the pattern for the organizational society. Their careers symbolized the single quality most responsible for American industrial vitality, a freedom from tradition that welcomed technological change. Their genius for integration, their demonstration of the versatility of finance capitalism, their insight into the advantages of the oligopolic market—all provided a guide for those who followed.

Despite its survival as a symbol, laissez faire existed for only a brief time. Our industrial revolution began after the Civil War, yet within thirty years the first great merger movement had begun. By 1897 consolidation to avoid ruinous competition and to capture market control and provide huge capital resources had become common. Thus the period in which the typical enterprise was operated in a competitive milieu by a single entrepreneur or family existed only briefly. The succeeding corporation era encouraged the development of big organizations by making capital accumulation easier, by permitting risk sharing, and by divorcing ownership from management.

The architects of consolidation were versatile. Several variations on the corporation theme appeared between 1865 and 1900. The panic of 1873 brought the first great combinations in the form of "pooling" agreements by the railroads to ease the sharp competition that had brought on the debacle. Survival was ensured by dividing up the market. When pooling was declared illegal by the Interstate Commerce Act of 1887, an alternative was found in the form of "trusts." Here stockholders turned over controlling blocks of securities to trustees, receiving in exchange trust certificates. Enjoying absolute power, trustees created monopolies in sugar, lead, whiskey, and oil. However, successful prosecutions in New York and Ohio in 1890 and 1892 foreclosed this form of combination too. The court decisions demonstrated again the subtleties of the law by voiding trusts on the grounds that charter rights had been violated, rather than on the grounds that monopoly violated the public interest.

Corporations next resorted to the "holding-company" device. This made possible the great mergers which occurred between 1897 and 1904 and as a device continued unchanged until the Holding Company Act of 1935. Under this scheme, which is used by our major corporations today, control of several companies is centered in a single organization. Despite possession in some cases of only a small proportion of its operating subsidiaries' stock, the holding company can appoint the subsidiaries' directors and officers, allocate their profits, and maintain general policy control.

The scope of operation and control made possible by the holding company is illustrated by Standard Oil of New Jersey.[1] Note how it conforms to the bureaucratic characteristics outlined in the preceding chapter. This vertically integrated giant has over 250 subsidiaries scattered throughout the world. With total assets of nearly four billion dollars, it has 500,000 employees working in 140 countries and producing seventeen per cent of the world's oil. The holding company for this industrial empire, the Jersey Company, includes 1,300 executives and staff. The Jersey Company has experienced a series of antitrust suits under the Sherman and Clayton Acts. According to the Department of Justice, the Company's alleged illegal practices have included international cartel agreements for price fixing and the dividing of markets and production control. On the domestic front the charges include concentrated pipeline control, which permits the Jersey Company to influence the price of crude oil by controlling its supply; "price collusion"; tying-in contracts with service stations requiring the latter to carry only one brand product while permitting the Jersey Company to cancel the agreement on short notice; and the substitution of advertising competition for price competition. As Eugene Rostow, Dean of the Yale Law School, observed after a study of the industry: "The manifest wastes of such behavior raise the question of whether in many cases monopolistic competition

[1] The following comments on Standard Oil of New Jersey are from G. Burck: "The Jersey Company," *Fortune,* Vol. 44 (October, 1951), pp. 98-113.

may not be more costly to society than monopoly itself." [2] In 1942, following government action, the Jersey Company agreed that all affiliates in which it owned fifty or more per cent of stock would stop any practices that conflicted with the antitrust laws.

The board of directors and executive committee of Standard is composed of fourteen "autonomous and self-perpetuating" executives. "The directors run the company. . . . For the power of stockholders is only potential and has not recently been wielded in sufficient concentration to bother management at all." [3] The board controls its empire by supervising administrative and financial matters and providing advice. Since it appoints all the major executives of its affiliates, one may safely assume that such "advice" will be accepted. "The affiliate does what it thinks best, [but] if it turns out that it has made a bad mistake, why we may try out a new man." [4] Periodic review of the budgets and capital spending of the subsidiaries, and the Jersey Company's role as lender, provide the main financial controls. Insofar as policy and advice are concerned, the Jersey Company apparently attempts to centralize major policy decisions and to push operating decisions down to the subsidiaries.

The control made possible by these bureaucratic relations between parent and offspring seems clear enough. Certainly on policies affecting production, prices, and wages, the Jersey Company is supreme. "The parent's marketing principles closely correspond to those of Esso Standard Oil, its largest

[2] Eugene Rostow: *A National Policy for the Oil Industry* (New Haven: Yale University Press; 1958), p. 76; Rostow's conclusions on the size of the units in the industry are germane: "In the oil industry, as in many others, the large size of the corporate units of ownership and management is not a necessity, based on technological imperatives; nor on balance does the large size of the business unit result in important technological advantages. . . . The bigness of the big integrated oil companies . . . has substantially nothing to do with their efficiency or their costs," pp. xiii-iv.

[3] Burck: loc. cit., p. 103.

[4] Ibid., p. 176.

subsidiary."[5] Co-optative appointment of its own members and of the top-level personnel of its operating companies gives them another control instrument. Such control is reinforced by a policy of exchanging executives between headquarters and field. In a larger sense, the control of executive careers throughout the empire by means of the power to reward and to punish must mean that the Company's will looms large.

Its role as banker also gives the Jersey Company disproportionate influence. As Gilbert Burck concludes, the needs of the oil industry for venture capital are greater than those of most industries, and the money is provided by Standard at less than going rates. Approval of the purpose of a loan is undoubtedly a prerequisite of favorable action by the Jersey Company. In its financial relations with subsidiaries, the Company's influence must be at least as great as that of the financial interests upon whom the industry once relied for capital, and who usually demanded in return a voice in operating policy. While good management requires that operating decisions be decentralized, policy framework is always determined by the parent company.

Although the Jersey Company is not entirely representative, being among the largest of some seventy billion-dollar U.S. corporations, most big corporations comprise similar vertical and horizontal integrations, with objectives that include controlling marketing conditions from raw material to finished product; gaining the advantages of diversification; finding new investment opportunities for excess capital; and generally remaining flexible in a changing economy. The huge scale of operations, the highly centralized policy control, and the resulting bureaucratic management practices (e.g., control from the top down) are most germane to our study of organizational society.

The huge size of the early corporations nicely suited the American milieu. A continental land-mass, fertile and rich in mineral wealth, provided a basis for expansiveness. An

[5] Ibid., p. 181.

endless frontier had provided endless opportunity, and the shock of its eventual passing was cushioned by new technological frontiers. Wealth was still there for the taking, and men of vision and strength, imbued with an intensely pragmatic outlook, took it. Individualism and social mobility flourished, and size itself became an honorific item in the national scheme of values. A spirit of optimism that equated change with progress because change often *was* progress achieved religious sanctity. While occasional protests arose from Populists and Progressives in the late nineteenth century and brought the Sherman and Interstate Commerce Acts, the power and technical efficiency of the industrial giants overcame most fears. In the main, not until the impact of war and depression after 1930 was there any serious questioning of the dominant laissez-faire theory or its corporate instruments.

It gradually became clear, however, that a basic change had occurred. As Calvin Hoover, President of the American Economic Association, concluded: "We can say that by the beginning of World War I our economy had become sufficiently characterized by concentration in industry, imperfect competition, oligopoly, administered industrial prices, price leadership, and other departures from or modifications of the rule of the free, fully competitive market for us to consider the change fundamental."[6] Economic change was reflected in both social and organizational change. A society in which economic and social power were rather widely diffused (and certainly not widely sought or understood) was replaced by one in which power steadily became more concentrated and desired.

The equalization of power increased bureaucracy, i.e., administration by rules, as self-conscious groups began to demand legal recognition of their work status. When, for example, trade unions insisted on contracts, a variety of informal conditions and practices, such as the ubiquitous

[6] C.B. Hoover: "Institutional and Theoretical Implications of Economic Change," *American Economic Review*, Vol. 44, p. 10.

coffee break, had to be covered specifically in the work bargain. Jurisdictional disputes similarly illustrate labor's new concern with legal relationships, and both labor and management began to operate in terms of *rules*. As a result, a whole new field of labor law evolved and unions were obliged to secure the legal and financial skills that would permit them to bargain intelligently with industry.

Traditional ideals were modified by the changing economic structure with its attending conditions of participation. Social mobility and economic independence, basic American values, were challenged by the restricted access to capital and raw materials that accompanied a concentrated, vertically integrated industrial economy. Inevitably, opportunities for self-employment declined as huge aggregates of capital and technical resources became necessary for entry and survival. From 1940 to 1950 the labor force increased by over ten million, yet the number of self-employed workers and proprietors remained almost the same. Work specialization and the separation of the worker from his tools increased dependence and made centralized authority more necessary. Owner-operators were replaced by professional executives whose behavior reflected their scientific-management, hired-hand role. Stockholders, the absentee landlords of the twentieth century, were remote and uninterested, playing the only part that atomized ownership permitted, the calculation of dividends. Power shifted to those who could operate large-scale enterprises rationally and with proper regard for the new art of human relations, which became more important as organizations became more impersonal.

Social change created new skill groups, while others became obsolete. The risk-taking owner-operator of the nineteenth century was replaced by the general manager surrounded by technical staff and advertising man, who boasted (and often proved) that he could create effective demand. It was price "leadership," excess-profits taxation, and "fair-trade" legislation that brought the research laboratory and the advertising agency into existence. The new "public-interest" rationale of industry created the need for yet another skilled functionary, namely, the public relations expert. He was living proof that the creative role of ideas is equalled by their rationalizing function. Such innovations characterized the transformation of social organization and market conditions during this century.

Several indications show the trend. In the field of labor, the rise of national industrial unions, the change in make-up of the labor force, the successful resort to politics under the New Deal, and the effort to influence the election of political candidates, marked the arrival of a new contender for social power. In agriculture, the indications include more effective use after 1933 of a built-in political advantage (rural over-representation in state and national legislatures), the changing pattern of farm size and ownership, the cultivation of a national image of the farmer as the symbol of Jeffersonian virtue, and the steady advance of mechanized farming. Like labor and industry, agriculture's political tactics enabled it too to frustrate "economic law." In industry, indications include the smaller number and larger size of firms, the increasing difficulty of entry, the frequent mergers, the increasing proportion of total business held by one of a few firms, and the declining rate of survival among small enterprises.

At the outset it is useful to review the general pattern of corporate holdings during the first half of this century. The classic source of information here is the Temporary National Economic Committee which found in 1934 that the 200 largest financial corporations held about half the national industrial wealth.[7] About the same time Berle and Means found that less than one per cent of some 300,000 nonfinancial corporations controlled about half the total corporate wealth. Nearly half the corporate wealth in the United States was in the hands of 200 corporations, one of which, the American

[7] *Temporary National Economic Committee Monograph,* No. 11, pp. 4-5.

Telephone and Telegraph Company, controlled "more wealth than is contained within the borders of twenty-one of the states." Berle and Means concluded: "A society in which production is governed by blind economic forces is being replaced by one in which production is carried on under the ultimate control of a handful of individuals." [8]

Such concentration was achieved mainly through industrial and financial mergers. As we have seen, the first great combinations occurred from 1897 to 1904. World War I was followed by another wave of consolidation, and the prosperity following World War II again brought a similar development. Mergers occur, apparently, in good times when conservative public opinion eases antipathies toward monopoly and encourages corporations to protect their gains or to spread their risks by merger. The first merger period, from 1897 to 1904, aimed at vertical integrations in order to control the market. By 1904, 318 industrial combinations had been formed, capitalized at about seven billion dollars and comprising 5,288 plants. According to the U.S. Industrial Commission on Trusts and Industrial Combinations, the mean share of the total domestic market controlled by twenty-two of the most important mergers was seventy-one per cent.

After World War I a significant revival of consolidation occurred. From 1919 to 1930 nearly 12,000 public utility, banking, manufacturing, and mining concerns disappeared. The total number of mergers was about 2,100, five times the number during the period from 1877 to 1904. By 1925 the sixteen largest public utilities controlled over fifty per cent of the total national generating capacity.[9] In 1921 the total number of banking establishments was over 30,000; ten years later the number had been reduced by almost one third. At

[8] A.A. Berle, Jr., and G.C. Means: *The Modern Corporation and Private Property* (New York: The Macmillan Co.; 1933), p. 46.

[9] Federal Trade Commission: *Electric Power Industry*, 70th Congress, 1st Sess., Senate Doc. 46, p. 176.

the same time, an urge to expand appeared in other fields such as retailing. The A. & P. chain, which had some 5,000 stores in 1922, had added 12,500 more by 1928.[1]

The conditions that had encouraged earlier merger movements were again in evidence following World War II, namely, prosperity, conservative government, apathy or disenchantment toward antitrust legislation, in addition to a rather sophisticated justification of bigness. In this environment the postwar merger movement was bound to surpass its predecessors. *Fortune* magazine estimated that during the period from 1945 to 1953 there were 7,500 mergers important enough to be noted by the financial journals. The value of the companies involved was about ten per cent of total corporation assets. As William B. Harris said: "It is certain that the merger movement has resulted in whittling down the population of independent corporations in the one-million-net-worth league and in increasing the size of larger companies."[2] Meanwhile, in January, 1955, the trend was dramatized by the merger of the Chase National Bank and the Bank of the Manhattan Company, two giants in commercial banking. The resulting enterprise became the nation's second largest bank with resources of about $8,000,000,000 (California's Bank of America being first with combined assets of ten billion dollars). Labor too contracted the merger fever, and a long-heralded fusion of the AFL and CIO occurred in 1955.

The reasons for such combinations emphasize both the advantages of big organization and the social changes outlined in this chapter. As Harris concludes, since market conditions favor size, an incentive is always present for firms to expand by new acquisitions both horizontally and vertically. In a society where size qua size is highly valued, consolidation for sheer growth will always be a powerful motive.

[1] H.W. Laidler: *Concentration of Control in American Industry* (New York: Thomas Y. Crowell Co.; 1931).

[2] This and the following comments on mergers are mainly from "The Urge to Merge," *Fortune*, Vol. 50 (November, 1954), p. 102 and *passim.*

Horizontal mergers reflect the fact that growth in a given business or industrial area must end when that field is exhausted. Thus successful firms look for new areas to conquer and for ways of diversifying risk. Excess-profits taxes also encourage mergers by providing "cheap dollars" for such investments. Meanwhile, small companies confronted by three or four giants, the typical pattern in basic industry today, may feel that their survival chances are increased by merger.

The current wave of mergers is also motivated by the desire to gain access to new markets. Buying into an existing enterprise that produces the same commodity or provides an attractive new market has become common practice. New products such as television and frozen foods will also attract the attention of established corporations who wish to share in the advantages of technical change. In this context, small firms (like minor political parties) often play an innovative role, developing new products or techniques that are coopted by larger firms once their feasibility is proved.

The most spectacular mergers have occurred in the automobile industry. In 1955 the number of independent companies was cut in half by the merger of Nash-Hudson (American Motors, Inc.) and Studebaker-Packard. The survivors, however, were confronted by the sobering fact that two firms (Ford and General Motors) now produced about eighty per cent of all passenger cars. These mergers resulted in inquiries by the Attorney General to determine "whether this pattern is nothing more than the consequence of competitive forces at work, or whether . . . collusion or the suppression of competition has been at work." For our purposes, however, the knotty question of the effect of mergers on competition is secondary. The main point is that mergers tend to increase concentration, which in turn tends to increase big organizations and bureaucratic conditions of work. In a word, our primary interest is in size per se rather than in the effects of size and concentration upon "competition."

On a common-sense basis, mergers seem to increase concentration. This is not always so, however, because as in the case of U.S. Steel the size of the total market may become so large that even a rapidly growing firm may over a period of time control less of the market. Nevertheless, when two or more firms merge, both concentration and size have probably increased, in the short run at least. A related factor is the high survival value of size. In most industries the failure rate among giants is substantially less than that among small and medium-sized firms. There is evidence too that after an initial shakedown period our economy has achieved considerable stability in basic areas such as steel, oil, and electrical equipment. Among the hundred largest corporations in the period from 1909 to 1948, for example, sixty-three disappeared during the first twenty years, but only six disappeared during the following eighteen years.[3] Huge capital resources, experience, and good will enable established firms to survive. Failure rates support this interpretation, showing that small firms have a very high failure rate, while big enterprises rarely fail. In time such a pattern probably increases concentration.

Concentration is certainly apparent in the structure of our major basic industries. In most industries three or four giants account for about one half of total production, while a substantial number of small firms share the remaining output.[4] The resulting market situation is neither purely competitive nor purely monopolistic, but lies somewhere in between. Chamberlin called the attending economic behavior "imperfect competition," and it has since become known as "oligopoly," or competition among the few. With minor exceptions such as soft coal, such quasi-competitive relations are the rule in basic industry and are also characteristic of cigarettes, motion-picture production, and commercial aviation. In 1947, for example, the three largest firms in auto-

[3] M.A. Edelman: "A Note on Concentration and Merger," *American Economic Review,* Vol. 44, pp. 392-3.

[4] J.K. Galbraith: *American Capitalism* (Boston: Houghton Mifflin Co.; 1952), pp. 39-44.

mobiles, agricultural machinery, rubber tires, meat products, liquor, cigarettes, copper, tin containers, and office machinery did two thirds or more of all business in their respective fields. A high degree of concentration also exists in steel, glass, dairy products, industrial chemicals, gasoline, cement, fertilizers, and milk distribution.

While it is difficult to prove, it seems that concentration is increasing still, in view of the wave of mergers since 1945 and the restriction of entry by huge capital requirements and the experience of established firms. Where penetration has occurred, e.g., in aluminum, in automobiles, and in steel, the capital and the impetus were provided by *government*, which alone had the capital and risk potential. After examining twenty large, basic industries, Joseph Bain concludes: "Absolute capital requirements for an efficient plant in all the manufacturing industries examined are large enough to restrict seriously the ranks of potential entrants."[5] Bain's calculations as to the capital required for "one efficient plant" are as follows: steel, $265,000,000 to $665,000,000; petroleum refining (including transportation facilities), $225,000,000 to $250,000,000; automobiles, $250,000,000 to $500,000,000; tractors, $125,000,000; tires and tubes, $25,000,000 to $30,000,000; cement, $20,000,000 to $25,000,000; and cigarettes, $125,000,000 to $150,000,000. The smallest amount required was $500,000, in shoe manufacturing. These figures, moreover, do not include "shakedown losses" that may be "large and prolonged."

Although industry was the first group to gain decisive na-

[5] "Economics of Scale, Concentration, and Entry," *American Economic Review*, Vol. 44, p. 37; for a recent analysis, see Ralph L. Nelson: *Merger Movements in American Industry* (Princeton: National Bureau of Economic Research; 1959). Unfortunately, the author offers few conclusions about the effects of mergers on concentration even though his analysis covers the three great merger movements which occurred from 1895 to 1956. He does show, however, that the number of firms disappearing as a result of mergers increased from an annual average of 289 in 1943-54 to 387 in 1954, 525 in 1955, and 537 in 1956, pp. 123-4.

tional power through consolidation and political influence, other interests soon adopted similar tactics. A survey of labor, agriculture, and government suggests the way in which a rough power equilibrium was attained by the nineteen-thirties.

The trend in all areas was toward scientific, technical, semiskilled, and clerical employment, with a *relative* decrease in the "skilled" and "self-employed" categories. A persistent anomaly followed. The economic values of a society composed mainly of wage-earning employees were expressed in terms of "profit making." Meanwhile the number of small stockholders in our population and the decline of entrepreneurial status indicate that "profit making" is actually a highly restricted activity. In 1953 the total labor force, consisting of 63,000,000, included only four million entrepreneurs (excluding farm proprietors), while only 6,500,000 persons owned stock in publicly held companies. Moreover: "More than half of the total marketable stock owned by private investors . . . [was] held by a very small percentage of the population."[6] The fidelity to the *rentier* ideal seems mainly to have been due to great expectations.

An analysis of the labor force reflects the changes taking place, particularly in the development of industry and manufacturing, in the growing role of science and technology, and in the rise of big organizations in business, finance, agriculture, and labor. The trends can best be shown statistically. (All data are from *Statistical Abstracts of the United States*, for the years cited.) In 1870 our total population was 40,000,000; by 1950 it had risen to over 150,000,000. Beginning with 1870 when, as we have seen, the present industrial society began to take shape, agriculture dominated the economy with 6,730,000 workers of a total labor force of 12,920,000. Manufacturing and hand trades were a poor second with 2,130,000, while educational and professional services required only

[6] J. Keith Butters, *et al.*: *Effects of Taxation on Investment by Individuals* (Cambridge: Harvard Business School; 1953), p. 26.

330,000. Trade, including finance and real estate, employed 850,000. Transportation (including public utilities) with 580,-000 employees was also insignificant.

By 1900, however, a new trend had appeared. Of a total labor force of 29,000,000, agriculture still dominated with 9,500,000, but manufacturing had sharply risen to 6,250,-000. Trade now involved 3,000,000, and professional services had increased to over 100,000,000. Transportation and other public utilities had also increased to 2,000,000.

By 1930 agriculture had lost its lead, having declined to only 10,480,000 in a labor force of 48,000,000. Manufacturing, with 10,990,000, now surpassed agriculture. Trade had doubled its numbers. Educational workers had increased to 1,650,000, while other professional services numbered 1,760,-000. By another decade the disparity between agriculture and manufacturing had increased further. In 1940 gainful workers numbered 53,000,000, of whom agriculture took only 9,000,000, a decrease of one and one-half million during the depression decade. Meanwhile, manufacturing continued its gains, employing almost 12,000,000 workers. Among other categories, only professional services and trade increased significantly during this period.

Agriculture, in sum, suffered a relative decline from 1870 to 1940 as shown by her declining share of the total labor force. The dividing point for agriculture is 1870; before this time she had always provided at least one half of the total working force. Although her relative position had declined steadily, in 1870 agriculture still retained fifty-three per cent. By 1940 her proportion had fallen to only seventeen per cent. Put another way, whereas agriculture had provided fifty per cent of the labor force in 1870 and manufacturing only one sixth, by 1940 agriculture's share had decreased to about one sixth, while manufacturing had increased to over one quarter.

The changing occupational structure that followed these economic changes is apparent in the following table:

Socio-Economic Groups in the Labor Force*

			Proprietors, Managers, Officials					
YEAR	TOTAL	*Profs.*	*Total*	*Farmers*	*Non-Farm*	*Cler-ical*	*Skilled*	*Semi-skilled*
1910	37,317	1,632	8,578	6,132	2,446	3,804	4,363	5,489
1920	41,236	2,049	9,180	6,387	2,792	5,682	5,570	6,631
1930	48,598	2,945	9,665	6,012	3,652	7,936	6,282	7,972
1940	52,020	3,381	9,233	5,274	3,958	8,923	6,104	10,918
1950	56,239	4,910	9,327	4,309	5,018	10,820	7,782	11,146
1960	68,579	7,162	9,903	2,898	7,005	9,768	8,870	12,363

* *U. S. Statistical Abstracts* (Washington, D.C.: U.S. Government Printing Office), see vols. for the years cited. For "skilled" workers I have used the "craftsmen, foremen, and kindred workers" category from the *Abstracts;* for "unskilled" the "operatives and kindred workers" category is used. While there will be disagreement about these selections, they do reveal the secular trend which is my major concern.

The most dramatic changes are the sharp increase in professional, clerical, and managerial jobs, and the striking decline of farm proprietors. In 1910, over twenty-three per cent of the labor force was self-employed, but by 1959 this proportion had fallen to only fifteen per cent. Meanwhile, the huge increase in semiskilled, clerical, and professional jobs reflected the demands of big organizations for more white- and blue-collar workers. The turn to machine power and the reduced need for craftsmen was mirrored in the relatively slower increase of skilled workers after 1920. This trend was accompanied by a rise in the proportion of semiskilled workers, from fourteen per cent of the labor force in 1910 to twenty-one per cent in 1940, levelling off at about eighteen per cent in 1960.[7]

[7] W.S. Woytinski and Associates: *Employment and Wages in the United States* (New York: Twentieth Century; 1953), pp. 274, 763. Such changes were attended by a vast increase in administrative workers. During this century, while production workers in American manufacturing industry increased by 87 per cent, those in administrative kinds of work increased by 244 per cent, S. Melman: "The Rise of Administrative Overhead in the Manufacturing Industries of the United States 1899-1947," *Oxford Economic Papers,* Vol. 3, p. 62. F.W. Ter-

Thus by mid-century only about fifteen per cent of Americans worked for themselves; the remaining eighty-five per cent were *employees*. Roughly half of them, perhaps 25,000,000, worked in enterprises that can be called "big organizations." The conditions of their working environment included size, standardization, impersonality, exquisite specialization, hierarchy, and dependence. Such organizations, moreover, can buy the research and management skills that intensify these conditions still further.

The bureaucratized labor force is spread around the economy. Its members include some 11,000,000 public servants, civilian and military, in local, state, and federal governments. Some 9,000,000 of them work for our 500 largest industrial corporations, eleven of which have over 100,000 employees and one of which, General Motors, has 625,000. Many work for private utilities like American Telephone and Telegraph, whose assets of fourteen billion dollars and 745,000 employees overwhelm the others in its field. They also work in the transportation industry, mainly for big railroads like Pennsylvania with 113,213 workers, New York Central with 81,552, and Southern Pacific with 79,143.

Some are found in great financial houses like California's Bank of America, New York's Chase Manhattan, and The First National City Bank of New York, each of which is capitalized at over eight billion dollars and has 15,000 or more workers. Others serve the giants of life insurance, where the fifty largest firms do over eighty per cent of the business, leaving the remainder to be shared by 1,000 other companies. Of these fifty, two giants, Metropolitan and Prudential, have combined assets of thirty-two billion dollars and a labor force of over 100,000. Yet others are clerks in vast retail empires, including Sears Roebuck (185,000), A. & P. (135,000), Woolworth's (87,500), and J. C. Penney

---

rien and D.L. Mills: "The Effect of Changing Size Upon the Internal Structure of Organizations," *American Sociological Review*, Vol. 20, pp. 11-13.

(75,000). A few work for the twenty largest universities, which have 400,000 students or over twenty per cent of the total. In rough terms these statistics suggest the extent of bureaucratization in our society.

Since the number of proprietors remained almost the same, while the number of workers increased substantially, the size of organizations obviously increased. In agriculture, for example, the average size of farms increased steadily during this century, while the total number decreased slightly. As *The New York Times* reported in 1955, "The traditional family-type farm is disappearing rapidly and is being replaced by large-scale and highly mechanized projects."[8] In 1900, there had been 5,737,000 farms, which increased to 6,560,000 by 1916, and to 6,812,000 by 1935, the high point in our history. By 1945, however, this number had decreased by about one million. Five years later the total number of farms had declined further to 4,884,818. During this time our population increased from 76,000,000 to over 150,000,000. The farm-production index increased by almost fifty per cent, from eighty-five (1910) to 123, while gross farm income rose from $7,352,000,000 to $25,432,000,000.

Here again technology and the capital required for highly mechanized, commercial farming brought results similar to those in basic industry. In 1949, for example, 484,000 farms, less than ten per cent of the total, produced over fifty per cent of all farm products, and nine per cent of the nation's farms earned more than the remaining ninety-one per cent.

Meanwhile, the size of farms increased steadily. In 1920 farms of 1,000 acres and over numbered 67,405; by 1940 they had increased to 100,531, and by 1945 to 112,899. The trend toward size is also apparent in the next smaller category, farms from 500 to 1,000 acres. In 1920 the number had been 149,819. By 1940 such farms numbered 163,694, and by 1945, 173,777. Hired workers on all farms during this quarter of a century *decreased* from 2,883,000 to 2,117,000. Thus

[8] *The New York Times* (December 20, 1955), p. 22.

the family-type farm, which had produced the Jeffersonian ideal of the sturdy yeoman, faded before the big corporation farm, often owned by an absentee landlord who sought a place in the country and perhaps a way to take advantage of generous tax write-offs by refurbishing a rundown farm.

Another incentive was the price-support program of the government which guaranteed farm prosperity. Despite the disapproval of agricultural economists and the dismay of the neo-classical theorists, support at fairly high levels began to look more and more like a permanent policy. Commercial farmers made it clear that the government "ought" to help them in this and other ways. Here again the disparity between economic fact and economic theory was strange and wonderful. The spectacle of the farmer competing successfully with business in the struggle for subsidies violated liberal economic theory, but the lessons of organization had been well learned.

The increase in union membership (18,000,000 in 1960, five sixths of whom were affiliated with AFL-CIO) and the rise of a huge, monolithic structure in labor also confirm the advance of big organization. Survival in a managed economy required collective discipline, the de-emphasis of the individual worker, the turn to government, and "cooperation" with industry. Although membership fluctuated with changing economic conditions, with labor legislation, and with the impact of war, from 1900 the trend was upward, amounting to about five per cent increase annually.[9] In 1900 only three per cent of a labor force of 29,000,000 was unionized. By 1935 membership had risen to almost nine per cent while the total labor force had increased by less than half. By 1953 the proportion of union members to total working force reached almost twenty-seven per cent. In round numbers, the totals were as follows: 1900, 791,000 members; 1935, 3,728,000; and in 1953, between sixteen and seventeen million.

[9] I. Bernstein: "The Growth of American Unions," *American Economic Review*, Vol. 44, p. 305.

The causes of this growth were varied. The economic cycle was basic, with membership usually rising in good times and decreasing during periods of unemployment. Exceptions occurred, however, and doubts came to be raised about the old theory that the business cycle was *the* independent variable insofar as union membership was concerned. Unionism suffered its worst decline in the eminently prosperous years from 1921 to 1923 and was fairly stable during the period from 1927 to 1929. Allied with economic conditions was sympathetic legislation such as the National Labor Relations Act. When this Act was passed in 1935, union membership was less than 4,000,000; two years later it had more than doubled. By 1941, even before the war-inspired spurt, membership had jumped to 10,489,000. From 1942 to 1945 union membership increased from 10,762,000 to 14,796,000, a gain of about thirty-six per cent. Since 1930, it seems, unions have benefitted most from emergencies, such as war and depression. Once crisis provided an opportunity for entry, they consolidated their gains, which included not only increased numbers but also a foot in the door that served them well as time and organization brought new opportunities.

Big government also symbolizes the era of the organizational society. The trend is apparent in the number of public servants, in the size of the national budget, and in the magnitude of public indebtedness. It can be shown that public employment has increased at a disproportionate rate. In 1870 there were only 49,000 federal employees. By the turn of the century the number had increased to 256,000. With the exception of sharp rises during World War I, growth from this time until the early nineteen-thirties was steady but unspectacular, with employees approximately doubling from 1901 to 1930. The great depression, however, brought a sharp upsurge which was further accelerated by World War II. During the nineteen-thirties public employees doubled from about 550,000 to over one million. But this increase was far surpassed during World War II, which began with 1,370,000 civil servants and ended with 3,569,000. After 1945, however, federal jobs (excluding the military) declined steadily and have now apparently been stabilized at about 2,250,000.

This vast number of employees underscores government's expanding role during our lifetime. War, depression, and the threat of war have combined to project government into practically every aspect of national life. The erosion of laissez faire by big agriculture, by big labor, and by big industry has been accelerated by big government's efforts to control the economy. The great depression brought great popular disenchantment with laissez faire and an unprecedented acceptance of economic planning. The change has been somewhat obscured by the use of an "emergency" label, and by our national tendency to regard what has become permanent and normal as an aberration. But as the French say: "There is nothing so permanent as that which is temporary."

Public spending also dramatizes changing popular expectations. In 1860 total federal expenditures were only $63,000,000, but by 1870 the Civil War and increased veterans' benefits had brought the national budget to $309,000,000. This was the high point of federal expenditures for thirty years, finally exceeded in 1890. From that time on expenditures climbed steadily, and 1917 brought the first billion-dollar budget. The cost of modern war was reflected in a twelvefold increase in 1917 and 1918, rising to a total of $18,514,000,000, an amount not to be exceeded until World War II. By 1945 public spending reached the staggering total of over one hundred billion dollars. Following the war some retrenchment occurred: the budget was cut to $60,000,000,000 in 1946; to $39,000,000,000 in 1947; and to $33,000,000,000 in 1948. Subsequently, however, the consensus that Russia was not prepared to meet the conditions of peaceful coexistence, in addition to the need of sustaining a purchasing power equal to the fifty-per-cent increase in productivity since 1939, brought rearmament and foreign aid programs that boosted expenditures sharply.

Given hindsight, we can now see that depression spending,

which was widely heralded as the beginning of the end, was actually mild. The national debt, which had been $24,000,000,000 in 1924, increased to only $28,900,000,000 in 1935, the middle of the depression. The grand expenditures began in the late nineteen-thirties with rearmament. But even these amounts, reaching $40,000,000,000 in 1939, appear relatively insignificant beside subsequent wartime spending. In the four years from 1942 through 1945 the debt rose as follows: to 72 billion; to 136 billion; to 201 billion; and to 258 billion dollars. Moreover, the demands of defense and debt service (around nine billion dollars per year) have now raised the figure to $280,000,000,000. Since we have enjoyed unequalled prosperity and are still unable to reduce the debt, it can be assumed that it will remain near this figure indefinitely. In sum, throughout the entire period war and defense have been the principal factors in high public expenditures and indebtedness.

The size and concentration that have marked government and the major economic sectors have invaded "noneconomic" sectors as well. Since some of these latter activities, such as the mass-communication media, are actually profit-oriented, or like art, music, and higher education are at least affected by economic considerations, the term "noneconomic" is not entirely accurate. Perhaps their proper distinction is that they have a special "public-interest" quality. In contrast to other forms of endeavor, they are probably more "personalized," depending more upon human talent than upon machine power and capital resources. Certainly, in their creative function of providing the information that makes democracy possible, such "noneconomic" activities are unique and vital. The nature of their products provides another rough distinction. While durable goods are the major product of basic industry, intangibles such as emotional experience, information, and opinion are the main products here. This distinction is tenuous, however, since industry also produces expendable commodities, while the mass media produce "opinion commodities" that have permanent impact on individual personality. In any case, we now turn to those areas whose objectives and resources might seem less amenable to organizational logic.

Here too the imperatives of advancing science and changing economic values have made a revolution. Newspaper ownership, for example, reveals a secular trend toward size and combination similar to that in basic industry. From 1909 onward the number of independent dailies steadidly declined. Despite the increase in literacy and in population, the number of dailies reached its peak fifty years ago. From 2,600 in 1909 the number has been reduced to about 1,600. Only one city out of twelve having daily newspapers can show competition in this field; only in our large metropolitan centers do readers enjoy the diversity of opinion that competition brings. Once again, the owner-operator was replaced by new corporate forms, this time by nation-wide newspaper chains. Such chains, including the Hearst, Scripps Howard, and McCormick Patterson interests, now control 53.8 per cent of total newspaper circulation.[1] The difficulties of entry and the resulting concentration are suggested by the fact that between five and ten million dollars are required to launch a big city paper. In a medium-sized city of 50,000 the investment required is around $750,000.

These financial demands mean that newspaper publishing has become big business, but at the high cost of editorial freedom and citizen education. Although the quantity and coverage of news production is excellent, access to the public media has been curtailed, and the press no longer serves as a marketplace for opposing ideas. As the distinguished Committee on Freedom of the Press concluded: "The owners and the managers of the press determine which persons, which facts, which versions of the facts, and which ideas shall reach the public."[2]

[1] Commission on Freedom of the Press, Robert D. Leigh, ed.: *A Free and Responsible Press* (Chicago: University of Chicago Press; 1947), p. 43.

[2] Ibid., p. 16.

Opinion uniformity in the newspapers is increased still further by their invasion of the radio field. About one third of 1,000 stations are now controlled by newspapers, and in a hundred smaller communities the only newspaper owns the only radio station.[3] This means that essentially the same news menu is served by each medium, both of which depend upon the major news services for national news. A stereotyped product is an almost inevitable result.

News distribution also became structured as a few major news services assumed control of selecting, writing, and disseminating national and international news. Standardized opinion received another fillip as the same story with the same interpretation appeared in newspapers across the country. The resulting decline of individual criticism and expression was aggravated by the syndicated columnist whose interpretations provided a predigested opinion for million of readers. Both diversity and quality languished under a system that featured manufactured news and mass appeal. Reporters understood the realities of power, and the expectations of their publishers were clear enough. The dominant rationale held that since the publisher owned the newspaper, which was after all a business, its editorial policy was properly his to determine.

Radio and television followed the trend as the major networks, their clients, and the advertising agencies dominated local stations, aided by the latter's need for "name" programs and advertising revenue. Almost 800 of the country's 1000 radio stations are affiliated with one of the four major networks. Here again, programming reflected science, specialization, and the pecuniary nexus. Responsibility was atomized, masked, and unequally shared by clients, agencies, and networks. Television, which was hailed as a new opportunity for experimentation, quickly fell into the organizational mold. John Crosby, whose frank and intelligent critiques of radio and television make him unique among his guild, has

[3] Ibid., pp. 43-4.

commented on this development: "Television is suffering from the same ailment that afflicts the rest of the country—bigness. Today three networks control what 180,000,000 people are going to look at. Even if the propram heads who wield this vast power were all high-minded, this would be a narrow bottleneck through which to pour all the creative energy of the country. But they're not high-minded men. . . . When an independent producer brings a show to a network, the network's first query is: "What's my cut?" The going rate is thirty per cent. If the producer doesn't cut the network in for that much, he's not likely to get air time." [4]

Although such practices indicate that programming responsibility is shared among sponsors, advertising agencies, and networks, it is not equally shared. The advertising agencies, which are the least visible to the consumer, have the most control over program content. As early as 1930 "much of the original glamour and mystery of radio had vanished, and men had to take a more realistic approach. The Ayer firm [number ten among the top advertising firms mentioned below] rapidly developed the view that an agency must start with the client's sales program, determine whether radio could help, and then devise a program which will achieve specific ends in terms of sales." [5]

The volume and concentration of advertising billings and the attending influence of relatively few agencies and sponsors are suggested by the following data. Among the three big networks in 1944, C.B.S. had thirteen clients who bought over $1,000,000 of time each; and of these, three spent over $4,000,000. N.B.C.'s million-dollar clients numbered eleven; A.B.C.'s, nine; and M.B.S.'s, three. Among the advertising agencies. J. Walter Thompson bought over $13,000,000 worth of time from the three networks; Young and Rubicam bought $10,034,731; and Dancer, Fitzgerald, $7,062,811. Three agencies that is, bought one fourth of the total

[4] *New York Herald Tribune* (July 29, 1960).

[5] Quoted in L. White: *The American Radio* (Chicago: University of Chicago Press; 1947), p. 56.

time sold by the three major networks. In 1945, moreover, only seven sponsors and six agencies provided fully one half of C.B.S's $65,724,362 billings.[6]

By 1958 the pattern had changed. The advent of television, with billings something like ten times those of radio, radically altered the distribution of media advertising. Some 507 advertising agencies handled a total of $1,970,000,000 worth of billings in radio and television. Of these agencies, the sixteen largest did $955,000,000 worth of billings, almost fifty per cent of the total. A relatively small number of sponsors continued to dominate media advertising and to share with the agencies the major responsibility (or lack of it) for program content. The hundred leading network-television advertisers did 93.4 per cent of total 1958 billings, which amounted to $527,641,094. Moreover, the first ten among them accounted for forty-two per cent of this huge sum. As one might expect, the first position was held by soap companies, followed by the big firms in food products and automobiles.[7]

The effects of such structural variables on program content and the shaping of American values seem clear enough. Since the advertising agencies' aim of maximizing the audience is shared by the sponsor who provides the money, programs were bound to be standardized. The networks, licensed to control the air in the public interest, in effect sublet their concession to unknown occupants, the agencies, who assumed the major role in program design. Here again the scientific paraphernalia (market research, program ratings, motivational research, etc.) of a new bureaucratic skill group exerted its influence. Although the sponsor would not buy any "package" indiscriminately, his main objective was to increase sales, and it was the "engineers of consent" who told him how. Their consumer research proved that comedians were preferable to symphony; so the same en-

[6] Ibid., pp. 57-8.

[7] *Broadcasting*, Yearbook Issue (1959), pp. D62-D74; *Printers' Ink* (October 30, 1959), pp. 304-5, 361-2.

tertainers labored the same tired routines for decades. Here the lack of competition was painfully apparent. Although critics insisted that radio had not had a new idea in twenty-five years, the success of the existing formula provided little reason for change. Thus the pecuniary values, the harnessing of social science to merchandizing, and the resulting search for standardized commodities seen in newspaper publishing were duplicated in radio and television.

In motion pictures a succession of antitrust suits aimed mainly at block booking indicated that the managed market existed there also. Control of the environment from producer through consumer was achieved through vertical integration and through the shaping of consumer demand by unrestrained advertising. Under the block-booking system, the theater owner was obliged to contract for films in groups, sometimes forty to fifty at a time. In effect, to qualify for a few "A" films he must accept several "B" pictures or worse.

Insofar as content was concerned, the labored, tasteless repetition of themes based on a few primeval values was amply apparent. The molding of opinion by socially validated beliefs was demonstrated by constant oversimplification in a world of black and white in which truth and beauty always triumphed. Only the most intrepid director would violate the stereotype of the happy ending. The film as an "art" form embodying reality became the antithesis of art. It became a mere escape mechanism, a means of providing emotional satisfactions that life failed to provide. As the *New Yorker's* reviewer concluded, in giving up his job, "Ninety percent of the moving pictures exhibited in America are so vulgar, witless, and dull that it is preposterous to write about them in any publication not intended to be read while chewing gum."[8]

While television is changing the film industry's structure in undefinable ways, motion-picture ownership has been highly concentrated, with five major companies enjoying

[8] Quoted in Ruth A. Inglis: *Freedom of the Movies* (Chicago: University of Chicago Press; 1947), p. 8.

an "overwhelming superiority" in capital resources, volume, profits, and power. Before 1940 the "Big Five"—Metro-Goldwyn-Mayer, Paramount, R.K.O., Twentieth-Century Fox, and Warner Brothers—"controlled seventy per cent of first-run theaters in the ninety-two largest cities." [9] The "majors" also include Columbia, United Artists, and Universal. In 1938 these companies were sued by the Department of Justice which charged them with monopolistic practices, citing their vested interest in both production and distribution and their ownership of theaters. In addition to block booking, their offenses included blind selling, overbuying, and clearance protection. Blind selling is related to block booking; the exhibitor contracts to buy films which are often not yet produced. Overbuying also attended block booking because the exhibitor was obliged to contract for many films, sometimes including short subjects and newsreels in order to secure those he wanted. Clearance protection sets time limits before pictures shown by a certain type of house can be shown by others in the same zone. This system protects the first-run theaters, which are eighty per cent affiliated and are often owned or controlled by the major film companies. Following extensive litigation, these practices were modified under a "consent decree."

While the court decisions of the past two decades "have destroyed the nationwide combination that controlled the motion picture industry," [1] the decisions did not provide for sustained regulation of relations between those who make, those who distribute, and those who show its product. Some observers fear that the industry, which in the words of one judge, has "shown a marked proclivity for unlawful conduct . . . ," may resume its old ways once the courts' watchdog role, established in the *Paramount* case, comes to an end.[2] Market structure and the pattern of film allocation remain

[9] Ibid., pp. 36-51.

[1] M. Conant: *Antitrust in the Motion Picture Industry* (Berkeley: University of California Press; 1960), p. 218.

[2] Ibid., p. 209.

far from the competitive model. Distributors retain potential monopoly power through their copyright of popular films. The circuits of motion-picture houses, some of which were divorced from producer ownership, were not broken into small enough units. United Paramount theaters, for example, retained some 500 houses, while National Theaters and Stanley Warner emerged with 300 each. When such circuits are concentrated in specific areas, as the larger ones tend to be, they may again permit strong bargaining for preferential treatment.[3] As Michael Conant concludes: "The circuits should have been destroyed."

This brief account of "noneconomic" areas indicates similarities between the structure and tactics of the mass media and those of the major basic industries. Vertical integration in order to control production, distribution, and demand is a common feature, attended by size and concentration. The planning and effort required to gain such control is an impressive tribute to human ingenuity. But the imperatives of economic organization, such as the need to secure a safe return on a huge, fixed capital outlay, encourage violent standardization and a pervasive "don't-take-a-chance" mentality. A related dysfunction is the high money costs of maintaining the overhead necessary to control such complex systems. In reply to the claim that high labor costs are driving the United States out of some world trade markets, Cameron Hawley has said, "Our inability to compete in world markets today is much less a matter of higher labor costs than it is of the excessive load of overhead with which so many American corporations have burdened themselves."[4]

In this chapter we have traced the emergence of the bureaucratic model as a major organizational form in our society. Beginning about 1875, social, economic, and political trends in the United States prepared the way for the "organizational society," characterized by large-scale bureaucratic institutions in practically every major social area.

[3] Ibid.

[4] Cameron Hawley: *Life*, Vol. 50 (June 2, 1961), p. 57.

The major trends included the separation of ownership from management; increasing size and concentration in business, industry, and even eleemosynary fields; the decline of competition; the development of a political economy; and the emergence of an *employee* society. We now turn to the social basis of personality as a preface to an analysis of individual behavior in this changed organizational context.

CHAPTER 4

THE SOCIAL BASIS OF ORGANIZATIONAL PERSONALITY

WE MUST now consider how personality is formed through the process of socialization. Once this process has been examined in a broad social context, its formulations will be applied to the typical big organization, which we have defined as a miniature of the larger social system. For this purpose we shall rely mainly upon Harry Stack Sullivan's interpersonal theory of psychiatry and the two disciplines upon which it rests, namely, social psychology and cultural anthropology.[1]

There are of course many psychologies and many theories of personality, each differing somewhat in its conception of the critical variables that shape personality and human behavior. Sullivan's interpersonal theory, however, provides a most fruitful basis for examining behavior in a bureaucratic setting. What follows depends explicitly upon his formulations, particularly those dealing with anxiety, authority, and the social and developmental basis of personality. The utility

[1] Harry S. Sullivan: *Interpersonal Theory of Psychiatry*, H.S. Perry and M.L. Gawel, eds. (New York: W.W. Norton & Co., Inc.; 1953), pp. 16-18.

of these concepts for organizational analysis should become clear as they are applied in this and subsequent chapters.

A major assumption of interpersonal theory is that man is a social product; his motivating values and behavior are mainly determined by the dominant values of a given society. This cultural matrix outlines his aspirations and provides the very symbols and concepts with which he thinks. Although the notion that mind possesses supersensory powers is as old as Plato, who denied that sense perceptions were real, medical research has shown that mind is actually the product of a particular state of knowledge at a given time. As F.S.A. Doran concludes: "Mind is an expression of brain function. . . . Its contents are largely determined by the social force of tradition, and by the fears, beliefs, prejudices, and values of those with whom it comes in contact." [2]

In sum, social conditions define knowledge. Men do not think in a vacuum; reason occurs instead within a given framework of cultural values that is rarely questioned, because it is the only reality one knows. This framework becomes a cherished emotional and intellectual repertory and will be so retained until shattered by powerful conflicting experiences. Such personal and social value systems give meaning and order to the phenomenal world. They play a labor-saving role by providing "givens" that facilitate perception and appropriate behavior. Such value systems are systematically instilled by society, which employs compelling rewards and sanctions to insure that individuals internalize them.

It is a major assumption of this study that we may validly conceive of big organizations as microcosms of the larger social system. This formulation permits us to apply the concepts of socialization and interpersonal psychiatry to the analysis of organizational behavior. Organizations are indeed miniatures of society. They have a hierarchy of status and of roles, a system of myths and values, and a catalogue of ex-

[2] F.S.A. Doran: *Mind: A Social Phenomenon* (New York: William Sloane Associates; 1953), p. 169.

pected behaviors. They are probably more significant than most associations because of their concern with economic and status needs, and with the discipline that results. Big organizations, then, are defined here as miniature social systems that meet many of the most basic needs of their members and expect in return loyalty and conformity.

A caveat is required. Although the values inculcated by society and its many competing organizations are perhaps inevitably conflicting, we shall confine ourselves here to an analysis of the socialization *process* itself, and to the kinds of values that seem functional in terms of *work* organizations. In later chapters we shall consider the problem of value incongruity and attending personal strains, as seen for example in the conflict experienced by middle-class children who are taught to be aggressive and competitive outside the home while remaining generous and co-operative within the family.

In essence, Sullivan's interpersonal theory is concerned with individual and group relations, their social context, and their critical role in shaping personality. Whereas psychiatry in the past had focused primarily upon the unique individual, Sullivan conceived of personality as mainly the result of *social interaction.* "Psychiatry is the field of interpersonal relations under any and all circumstances."[3] Similarly, "Personality is manifest in interpersonal relations, and not otherwise."[4] This conception was based upon two decades of experience with neurotic and schizophrenic patients, which convinced him that "not sick individuals but complex, peculiarly characterized *situations* were the subject matter of research and therapy."[5] Essentially, personality and mental aberrations were the result of the individual's pattern of accommodation with people who were significant to him. Psychiatry was compared and linked with social psychology.

[3] H.S. Sullivan: *Conceptions of Modern Psychiatry* (New York: W.W. Norton & Co., Inc.; 1953), p. 4.

[4] D.R. Blitsten: *The Social Theories of Harry Stack Sullivan* (New York: William-Frederick Press; 1953), p. 58.

[5] Ibid., p. 21.

Psychiatry, however, approached the study of human behavior through aberrant behavior, which Sullivan insisted was usually an example of extreme or "unduly prolonged instances of relatively universal behavior."[6] Psychoneuroses were merely an exaggerated manifestation of conventional behavior.

Although a member of the "cultural" school of psychiatry, Sullivan built into his interpersonal theory the biological elements of personality. This is clearly apparent in his developmental conception of personality in which unfolding biological needs, such as the sex instinct during adolescence, bring about significant modifications of personality. But the expression of such needs is always largely determined according to existing social values *imposed through interpersonal contacts.* In this conclusion he followed Mead, Cooley, and Simmel, who found earlier that "personality traits are determined in large measure by sociological and cultural conditions."[7] His psychiatry, then, is essentially a cultural psychiatry, drawing upon social psychology and anthropology which had demonstrated the critical role of given social values and institutions in shaping personality.

In the present analysis organizational behavior is similarly viewed as the result of interpersonal liaisons in a "complex, peculiarly characterized [bureaucratic] situation." For our purpose, then, Sullivan's conceptions of anxiety, social determinism, and personality formation seem especially fruitful.

From birth onward the individual is subjected to group norms that over a period of time mold his personality. Personality is defined as a consistent way of reacting or accommodating to interpersonal situations. The reduction of anxiety by compliance with the perceived wishes of authoritative persons such as parents, teachers, and superiors, is a critical mechanism in this process. Interpersonal psychiatry asserts that most behavior is the result of the individual's search for

[6] Ibid., p. 23.
[7] Ibid., pp. 19-20.

relief from tension by conforming to authority. Anxiety is seen as the most compelling of such tensions, and much of behavior is explained by efforts to escape its painful effects. Apart from certain psychological needs, the bases of tension are socially derived. The child learns that "good" behavior is rewarded, while "bad" behavior is punished. He learns to seek the sanctuary of approval because anxiety evoked by the disapproval of authority figures is unpleasant. Such learning and reinforcement are most clearly seen in childhood when parents manipulate their affection to control him. Although it is sometimes difficult to decide just who is manipulating whom at this stage, the parents usually win out. "Socialization" has occurred; the child has learned the culture; he accepts socially approved patterns of behavior.

The end result of the process by which individuals learn to maintain security in interpersonal relations is called the "self-system." This system may be defined as a characteristic way of reacting to others. Unlike needs based upon the physiochemical structure of the individual, the self-system "is derived wholly from the interpersonal aspects of the necessary environment of the human being; it is organized because of the extremely unpalatable, extremely uncomfortable experience of anxiety; and it is organized in such a way as to avoid or minimize existent or foreseen anxiety." [8] The self-system, however, does not necessarily guarantee functional accommodations. Its characteristic security operations may result in failure. A peculiarity of the self-system is its resistance to experiences that are incongruent with its current organization. Such dysfunctional accommodations are characteristic of our ambivalent type.

Because the socialization process is essentially a function of learning, we must briefly consider learning theory. Here again an outsider must decide which specific theory is most useful for his purposes, for as in the case of psychology, there

[8] Sullivan: *Interpersonal Theory of Psychiatry*, p. 190.

are several theories of learning. In what follows, the work of so-called SR theorists such as Thorndike, Pavlov, Skinner, and Mowrer will be drawn upon.[9] These men believe that the learning of anxiety follows a basic Pavlovian principle: an individual associates a given stimuli with a certain response. They also stress the reduction of anxiety as a reward or reinforcement for certain kinds of learning. Both concepts seem useful in explaining behavior in the authority-structured bureaucratic situation.

Learning may be defined as a modification of the nervous system resulting from exposure to a certain kind of stimulus. Its effectiveness depends upon the number and strength of existing habits, upon one's perceptual facility, and upon the strength of the drive or need evoked by the stimulus. *Perception* is the process of becoming acquainted with the environment. Its basic motive appears to be curiosity, but anxiety and an apparently instinctive tendency to use our sense organs are also involved.[1] Observation suggests that we appraise new situations in an effort to orient ourselves, to decide what role is appropriate. Our perception defines the behavioral limits of a situation in the sense that its accuracy determines the effectiveness of our response. Evidence will be presented later to show that a certain level of anxiety facilitates perception. However, as Sullivan and others have shown, anxiety may also distort perception, culminating in exaggerated, "neurotic" responses.

It is clear that perception is affected by the environment which provides the potential stimulus field. In some situations stimuli are obvious and highly differentiated. There is little ambiguity, therefore, about the behavior expected. The bureaucratic situation has these characteristics, and a major assumption based on experimental psychology can now be stated: *in big organizations, both perception and condition-*

[9] B.R. Bugelski: *The Psychology of Learning* (New York: Henry Holt & Co., Inc.; 1956), Chs. 1, 4, 5.

[1] S.S. Stevens: *Handbook of Experimental Psychology* (New York: John Wiley & Sons, Inc.; 1951), pp. 357-8.

ing are sharpened by the manifest, authoritative nature of the stimuli. The bureaucratic situation will therefore be called a "structured field."

Reinforcement is also vital to learning, since it eases conditioning through rewards and punishment. We know that reinforced responses will be quickly learned and will, over a period of time, change one's personality. Individuals develop certain tensions (anxieties) that reflect needs for food, water, sex, recognition, power, and security. Actions that satisfy these needs are reinforced because they reduce tension generated by the need. The reduction of anxiety is thus an unusually powerful reinforcement. Learning is also affected by attitudes, i.e., by predispositions to act in certain ways. We learn things that agree with our preconceptions (our personality) much more easily and retain them longer than those that seem alien.

The psychological field of organization and the way it affects behavior can be suggested by two classic studies. Pavlov and Skinner have shown how problem solving in dogs and rats can be conditioned through the manipulation of stimuli and through the use of rewards and punishments.[2] Pavlov's classic experiments demonstrated the conditioned response by adding a new stimuli, a bell sound, to the usual situation causing salivation in dogs. Normally dogs salivate only upon seeing food, but after the bell was rung several times just before feeding, Pavlov found that the sound itself caused salivation. The animal had become conditioned to the bell sound.

Skinner's experiments suggest the importance of *reinforcement* (using the reward principle) in learning. A hungry rat, placed in an empty box equipped with only a lever, will in time depress the lever. Since this releases food, the consequent reduction of hunger increases the chances that the rat will repeat the action, illustrating the need-reduction princi-

[2] I.P. Pavlov: *Conditioned Reflexes* (London: Oxford University Press; 1927); B.F. Skinner: *The Behavior of Organisms: An Experimental Analysis* (New York: Appleton-Century-Crofts, Inc.; 1938).

ple in behavior. Reinforcement and motivation, building upon needs and satisfactory ways of meeting them, thus lead to learning and to habit formation.

Different patterns of learning (socialization) result in different modes of perception. The bureaucratic situation, for example, is not "seen" in the same way by all its members. While some individuals perceive the organization as a favorable place in which to assert their career claims, others view its systems of authority and status as threatening. Each structures reality into a discrete mold. As our three modal types suggest, each adopts interpersonal accommodations that meet his own needs.

Socialization, however, is more than a process; it is also a system for inculcating certain approved values and excluding others. Both the process and the values have a lasting influence upon personality. Margaret Mead found a striking example in the Balinese custom of teasing and playing with the child until it became excited, whereupon the mother breaks off play without further gratification. This practice produced withdrawn adults, unable to achieve close emotional relations with others.[3] Kardiner found similarly that the mother is a frustrating object to the child in the Marquesian and Alorese societies.[4] Neglect and rejection characterize mother-child relations among the Marquesians; but since the father assumes a protective role, the children develop independent, outgoing personalities. In Alor, however, both parents reject the child, a practice which apparently accounts for the suspicion and hostility of the Alorese. Among the Comanche, on the other hand, parental care was found to be consistently sympathetic, resulting in self-confident, co-operative adults.[5]

[3] Margaret Mead: *From the South Seas* (New York: William Morrow & Co.; 1939).

[4] A. Kardiner: *The Psychological Frontiers of Society* (New York: Columbia University Press; 1945).

[5] Ibid.

The effect of social structure on personality is suggested by Fromm's analysis of German character in *Escape From Freedom.*[6] He maintains that dislocations following World War I prepared German society for totalitarian government. Highly respected institutions, the army, the patriarchal family, political control by military and upper-class elements, and a rigid class system collapsed following the war. The democratic Weimar Republic, inflation, impoverishment of the middle class, the growing political influence of the working class, mass unemployment, the father's inability to support the family, the defeat of the hallowed army, all brought the disintegration of old values and a state of psychological shock that resulted in a desire "to escape from freedom." Submission to the political and racial myths of Hitler provided the major avenue.

Not only was the individual German's personality shaped by such values, but German institutions reflected and reinforced them. The well-known German respect for authority molds and reflects an authoritarian social structure. Such social influences were reinforced by the individual's projection of his conscience upon German institutions. Money-Kyrle argued (on the basis of interviews following World War II) that the German bureaucrat's idealization of the state indulged his own authoritarian inclinations.[7] His dependency permitted him to accept its directives even when they were immoral. At the same time, the rigid class system nourished power-oriented attitudes that well suited the demands of the state. The individual's subordination to such imperatives as racial purity, and the feelings of helplessness

[6] Erich Fromm: *Escape From Freedom* (New York: Rinehart & Co., Inc.; 1941). The extension of the family system to political systems in non-Western cultures is analyzed in R.A. LeVine: "The Role of the Family in Authority Systems: A Cross-Cultural Application of the Stimulus-Generalization Theory," *Behavioral Science,* Vol. 5, pp. 291-6.

[7] R.E. Money-Kyrle: *Psychoanalysis and Politics* (New York: W.W. Norton & Co., Inc.; 1951).

that followed, were compensated for by dividends of shared power.

American values and institutions also shape personality in distinctive ways. There have, of course, been many analyses of the so-called American character; those by foreigners such as Bryce and Tocqueville may be best because they are less culture-bound. Although cross-cultural generalizations are always subject to error, societies are different; and such differences mean, as Newcomb said, that "there are many aspects of personality which are, so to speak, standard equipment in one society." [8] In our culture such equipment includes a distrust of theory, considerable respect for size and quantitative standards, respect for power, an unchallenged belief in a high degree of social mobility (based upon the ideal of equal opportunity), great disparity in consumption levels (validated by *personal* success or failure), and a pragmatic ethic that often makes success the test of truth. Although often regarded by Europeans as the product of considerable naïveté, these values probably reflect our youth, wealth, and relative freedom from intense religious and political differences. These conditions provide an objective basis for our well-known optimism.

More important, they are bound up with a pervasive *need to be liked.* This single impulse, it seems, explains much about our affinity for group action. We are trained to get along with others and to honor this value highly. Exceptionally sensitive to majority norms, we are good at co-operation, although this fact is somewhat obscured by the rhetoric of competition and by the notion that we are unusually "individualistic." Here our emphasis upon competitive athletics probably has a myth-fulfilling function, sustaining a faith that has become tenuous in more important areas. In major industries such as steel, automobiles, and electrical equipment, a competitive shadowboxing goes on; but con-

[8] T. Newcomb: *Social Psychology* (New York: Holt, Rinehart and Winston; 1950), p. 340.

centration and difficulty of entry have culminated in a watered-down advertising competition among firms that produce commodities similar in both quality and price.

These changing terms of competition among organizations have changed the terms of competition *within* organizations. Personal competition remains lively, but it is worked out in an organizational context which requires different values and behavior. An obsolescence of individualism is apparent in a general preference for conformity and adaptability. Well-rounded men who can "play on the team" are sought in most fields,[9] including the universities, where one might have thought that diversity would have been nourished.[1] This condition is aggravated by hierarchy, which insures that one's career chances are mainly dependent upon his immediate superior. Needless to say, the latter's judgment is always an amalgam of personal, technical, and professional considerations, including such subjective indexes as loyalty, dependency, and conviviality. The typical American is assumed therefore to be a group-oriented individual, anxious to be liked and afraid to be different. With some exceptions to be noted later, socialization tends to produce individuals who function well in group situations.

The manipulation of affection and approval begun by parents is continued by the school, the church, and the professional association. Each invokes the mechanisms of learned behavior and anxiety to cash in on its claims. Over a period of time, the characteristic ways of accommodating to such claims shape the individual's personality. The intensity of needs for approval vary individually, just as the values that evoke anxiety vary within cultures in terms of class, vocation, religion, and race. But everyone develops certain satisfactory methods of accommodation, of avoiding anxiety, and of gaining approval.

9 William H. Whyte, Jr.: "The New Illiteracy," *Saturday Review Reader*, No. 3 (1954), p. 160.

1 For academic stereotyping, see T. Caplow and R. McGee: *The Academic Marketplace* (New York: Basic Books, Inc.; 1959).

Anxiety is among the most compelling human drives. As Sullivan maintains: "I believe it fairly safe to say that anybody and everybody devotes much of his lifetime, and a great deal of his energy . . . to avoiding more anxiety than he already has, and, if possible, to getting rid of some of this anxiety."[2] Although anxiety is a hypothetical construct, because we can only infer that it "causes" behavior, the present analysis rests squarely upon this conception of anxiety's role. The internalization of approved values creates a built-in capacity for anxiety as the desires of the individual collide with society's expectations.

Abnormal or neurotic anxiety, however, is different from the fairly common kind of uncomfortable, often unspecific feeling that all of us have when we lack adequate control of situations that are important to us. Anxiety occurs along a continuum ranging from incapacitating, free-floating dread to mild uneasiness. In the present analysis our main concern is with *functional anxiety*, a moderate degree of tension or sensitivity that tends to sharpen the individual's perception of behavioral alternatives appropriate to a given situation and to their probable consequences. In big organizations functional anxiety insures greater sensitivity to the nuances of interpersonal situations and to the varied roles demanded by the nice gradations of status and authority in the bureaucratic work place.

Anxiety appears when something threatens the individual's relations with persons important to him. Sullivan insists that anxiety is so pervasive that our interpersonal relations are always affected by it. Social psychologists, too, recognize the central role of anxiety in explaining behavior and personality, since the threats and uncertainty associated with it evoke powerful motivations. Among successful business executives, for example, the fear of failure often leads to compulsive attempts to achieve security by controlling

[2] H.S. Sullivan: *Interpersonal Theory of Psychiatry*, p. 11; Sullivan: *Conceptions of Modern Psychiatry*, pp. 19-23.

one's environment and by achieving ever greater success.[3] Cultural psychologists believe that western society and its major values aggravate anxiety. Erich Fromm contrasts the individual security of the preindustrial era, when status relations were clearly defined, with the uncertainty attending capitalism and its breakdown of family and community stability. Self-alienation often followed because interpersonal relations were colored by an exploitative motive, while the success theme encouraged a certain moral nihilism. Sullivan and other cultural psychologists, including Fromm, Horney, and Thompson, believe that contemporary society represses some of the potential "good" in the individual, while encouraging certain destructive behaviors and unrealistic ambitions. Rejecting the "adjustment" ethic of modern education, their indictment centers on the loss of spontaneity and of self-realization attending society's acquisitive demands for conformity. Western man, they say, is so educated that the mere assertion of a personal point of view brings guilt feelings.

The weight of social expectations is increased by the inability of the immature child to judge their validity; he necessarily accepts prevailing values on the basis of faith. During this stage, Sullivan maintains, the child "learns to chart a course by the anxiety gradient." Such interaction with society and its authority figures results in a "self-system" developed in an attempt to reconcile individual needs with those of society. As a style of behavior that evokes the approval of authority figures, this system becomes a way of meeting interpersonal situations with a minimum of strain. The resulting image is of an individual constantly seeking equilibrium and developing stereotyped patterns of accommodation. A continuous reinforcement occurs as functional

[3] B. Gardner: "What Makes Successful and Unsuccessful Executives," *Advanced Management*, Vol. 13, pp. 116-25; W.L. Warner: *American Life: Dream and Reality* (Chicago: University of Chicago Press; 1953), pp. 188-9.

methods are retained because they reduce anxiety, while dysfunctional ones are discarded.

The mechanisms used to reduce anxiety include avoiding responsibility by dependency upon one's superiors. In studying anxiety among nurses in a large, seven-hundred-bed hospital, I.E.P. Menzies found: "Tasks are frequently forced upwards in the hierarchy, so that all responsibility for their performance can be disclaimed. . . . We are struck repeatedly by the low level of tasks carried out by nursing staff and students in relation to their personal ability, skill, and position in the hierarchy." [4] The patent authority structure of the organization encourages this type of accommodation. This defense is often dysfunctional, however, because it reduces the ability of the nurses to handle anxiety realistically. Excessive dependence and evasion result instead of an ability to tolerate and to deal more effectively with anxiety.[5] The resulting pressure toward regressive, childlike behavior makes some of the best students stop their training because they are "distressed about the inhibition of their personal development." [6] Insofar as authority relations are concerned, bureaucratic conditions of subordination and dependency may encourage infantile behavior.

The link between childhood experiences and organizational behavior is explicit in the following psychiatric study by M.B. and R. A. Cohen.

> An adult person is seen as responding to people and situations in the present on the basis of modes of reaction which have been established in him at an early period in his life and which are relatively fixed and unchanging. In persons who have had favorable life experiences, the modes of reaction are, on the whole, rational and realistic. In those who have had unfavorable experi-

[4] "A Case Study in the Functioning of Social Systems as a Defence Against Anxiety," *Human Relations,* Vol. 13, pp. 95-121.

[5] Ibid.

[6] Ibid., p. 117.

ences, the modes of reactions are less rational and less realistic. For example, an employee may be observant of the way in which his boss greets him at the start of each day's work. If the boss smiles and speaks in a friendly tone, the employee feels that all is right with his world; he can now get down to work and look forward to a good day. If, however, the boss ignores him, or greets him with a preoccupied smile, the employee may interpret this as being due to the fact that the boss has a hangover, has quarrelled with his wife, is thinking hard about how to make a sale to an important customer; or he may interpret it as meaning something is wrong in the boss's attitude toward him. The more rational person will, perhaps, look back over his performance record of the past few days to see if the boss has had any cause to feel unpleasant toward him; not finding anything outstanding in the way of cause for criticism, he concludes that the boss has something on his mind which is no concern of his. The less rational person will tend to conclude, without weighing the pros and cons, that the boss is dissatisfied with him; he will seek for the cause, and perhaps find some more or less trivial complaint which might be made against him. He will then decide that this is the reason for the lack of friendliness in the greeting.

The more rational person's thinking is based on a good general estimate of his own worth as an employee and a fairly accurate working knowledge of his boss. He would, for instance, have concluded from his past experience with the boss that he was a fair-minded person who did not tend to ride his employees for minor errors. The less rational employee does not have the same accurate estimation of his own worth (even though it may be high), nor is he able to see the boss in terms of his previous experience with him. Instead, his evaluation of the current situation is distorted by the effects of early life experiences with arbitrary and unreliable authority figures (chiefly, of course, his parents) which have led him to conclude that all authority figures whom he meets will behave similarly. In these early relationships, the person may have developed such techniques of dealing with these unreliable authorities as overemphasis on perfect performance, or the assumption of an attitude of compliance designed to placate them. In situations where the superficial manner of the boss reminds him of his extremely painful and unpleasant childhood experiences the defensive operations which were devised to take care of the childhood situation may be automatically evoked without the person's first stopping to determine whether the boss is, in fact, similar in attitude and behavior to the earlier authority figure. Because the employee's observation of the current person with whom he is in relationship is subordinated to the necessity to use these well-established defenses, his ability to learn or to convince himself that the boss is not like that is seriously impaired.

From this example, two of the basic propositions of interpersonal psychiatry can be seen. First, present day attitudes are based on previous experiences with people important in the person's life; second, where early experience has aroused severe anxiety, defense reactions take precedence over learning from new experiences. One final point: It is a well documented fact that no one in our culture is free from experiences which have caused severe anxiety and which have therefore led him to develop a certain number of defensive ways of dealing with others which protect him from awareness of anxiety. However mature and rational a person may be, there are always to be found such areas of difficulty; in such areas one will not accurately size up the problem he is faced with or communicate adequately with the others involved, or handle the situation with maximal intelligence and foresight. This necessarily affects the performance of all of us when we are dealing with other people, and the way in which it affects our performance will have profound influence on the other people in their turn. In particular with the administrator, whose job is to a large extent concerned with dealing with others, certain kinds of anxiety-driven behavior will have important effects on the way the job is done.

We offer four examples of the way in which personality structure affects administration. They are, naturally, oriented around the difficulties which arise because of some aspect of the administrator's character. There is one exception (Case A) in which the specific limitations of the administrator's character tend to make her a good administrator, at least within certain limits. Some, but not all of these examples, came from people who were patients. However, they were all successes in terms of doing their work, making their living, and so on.

Case A was a liaison officer between two agencies. She operated on a high level, participating in policy-making as well as in carrying out various projects. Her administrative contacts were largely with superiors and equals. Because of her special knowledge, she frequently suggested and sold ideas to her superiors and then sold them to those who were to carry them out. Her job did not carry a great deal of direct authority, but rather this was exerted through her superiors. Her job was largely determined by her own abilities. In fact, she had developed it far beyond any of her predecessors. Her particular ability was that of finding out what people wanted and then selling their ideas to others (or even to themselves). She seldom originated an idea; her greatest interest was focussed, not on the work itself, but on what those with whom she worked would think of her, and, indeed, her whole working day could be considered as a continuous effort to elicit approval from the people around her. Actually, she was a favorite daughter of a number of the superiors with whom she worked. Their attitude can be expressed: 'What would we do without A? She is so willing, so friendly, so hard-working, so reliable.' Her relationships with her equals were not very close or warm. They, of course, suffered from contrast with this paragon, and there was some tendency on the part of A to help her superiors to notice this contrast. Naturally, since A's interest was so centered on approval, she did not have time for casual friendly contacts with her colleagues; also she feared their envy, and sensed that she deserved it. Occasionally, she was much in the limelight as the result of being singled out for recognition. Such situations gave rise to feelings of fear almost to the point of panic, since she dreaded the resentment both of those she outcompeted among her equals, and those she overtook among her superiors.

To cite a specific example of the way in which A functioned: A community project was proposed by one of the departments with which A was connected. She was acquainted with several of its originators, whom she regarded as deserving of considerable respect. She did not, however, know anything about the project itself except its vague general purpose. The project ran a year, and when the proposal to renew the funds was considered, it was turned down. The project became the focus of considerable controversy, some members of the department being strongly in favor of it and others strongly opposed. Its adherents decided to try to get the money for it from another department, with which A was also connected. None of this went through A, who had no official function in regard to the work. However, when it was mentioned to her, she immediately concluded that the project ought to continue—on the basis of her respect for the workers and her desire for their approval, not on the basis of any knowledge of the validity of this particular work. She promptly went to the key man, spoke exactly the right words, and the whole turmoil disappeared. The project was approved and the money was found. She had recognized correctly that the key man was prejudiced against the particular kind of project which was being carried on and that he was suspicious of the kind of controversy which was raging about the issue. She therefore spoke to him in terms of the worth of the work and the useful results and increased prestige for the department which were to be expected from it. The primary need of building up the man's feeling of confidence or belief in the project—still without any information, but on the basis of a calm, soothing, confident manner—was met. A's own need for approval sensitized her to quick recognition of the reasons for the other person's lack of approval for the project, and her skill in setting up situations where she would be approved of made her a good protagonist for the project.

This interest in and skill at eliciting approval dated from her childhood. Her mother was a severely critical, demanding person who was always in the limelight at home. She used such tactics as illness and depression, as well as the emotional dependency of the children upon her, to force the whole family to give her constant cheerful attention, approval, openly demonstrated affection, and reassurance. The needs of A were disregarded, both by the mother who dominated her and by the father who was forced to ignore her through fear of the mother's jealousy.

In her administrative work, A was occupied, first, with trying to please the superiors and, in a sense, to get from them the approval she failed to receive at home; second, with placating the always threatening figure whose good-will might be but an evanescent thing, which could give way to rage and attack; third, with avoiding any serious threat to the superior in the way of knowing more or having any greater ability. She both sought the limelight, for the reassurance it gave her of being approved of, and feared it, for the retaliation it brought from the envy of others.

It can be seen that A's approach to her work had one serious defect. While she did an outstanding job, what she did depended to a dangerous extent on her immediate superior. She tended to take up and carry out any ideas presented to her by a person whose approval she valued whether it was good or bad, practical or not. The combination of her great energy and selling ability on the one hand, and her lack of critical judgment resulting from her dependency on approval on the other hand, resulted in the danger of unleashing this dynamo of energy in a direction which might be shortsighted or even harmful.

Case B was, again, a government official who had held a variety of administrative positions. He had been at the head of a staff of perhaps one hundred and fifty workers, being in turn responsible to a higher departmental head. He then became something of a management expert, and revised the procedures of a whole department, involving many thousands of workers. A comment of one of his fellow workers was illustrative of his difficulties in the latter job: 'B, you are always getting new ideas, writing them up, selling them, and then going on to something else without following them through.' A further side light on B's problems came from the fact that this comment seemed funny to him, an expression of his fellow worker's jealousy. The trouble with B as an administrator was that he was not interested in administration; he was not concerned with the work itself, or with the comfort or efficiency of his subordinates, or with the recognition of his superiors. His concern was with showing how clever he was. If he were cleverer than his fellow worker or his boss, that made him feel good, and he seldom hesitated to let the other person in on it. Since he was in actuality an exceedingly intelligent and able chap, he had a good deal of success. But as he moved up in the hierarchy of administration, his lack of genuine interest in the work introduced an increasing deficiency.

An example in point was illustrated by his transfer to a new job. At the time of the change the reorganizational work mentioned above had arrived at the stage of being completed on paper. It had not yet been put into operation, tested, revised, and tested again. Yet B was unaware that this could be thought of as part of his responsibility, and quickly turned to developing great new ideas for his new job. Yet it was a vital part of his responsibility for the old job to follow up on the reorganization plan because it was actually his brain child, had been carried out against the opposition of many conservatives in his department, and without his active interest had every chance of disappearing in the files. There was no one to replace him in the task of pushing the reorganization through, and, as a matter of fact, this absence of a replacement can itself be attributed to B's personality, in that he had not trained or interested anyone in so doing.

His performance in his work was also clearly derived from his childhood experience. His father was a clever ne'er-do-well, full of bright ideas and ingenious schemes; his mother was a martyred soul who earned the family's living and tried to elicit from B some of the dependability and affection the father lacked. The boy found his life at home so painful that he managed never to be around. He worked on the school newspaper, played in the band, went out for baseball, joined the Boy Scouts; and since his afternoons and evenings were filled with such activities, he was seldom at home. In this way, he did not have to take part in the struggles between the parents and spared himself the painful emotional demands of the mother, while acquiring considerable feeling of achievement from his scholastic abilities and the prominence that his activities brought him. In his current life too, the great defect was his inability to tolerate emotional relationships with others; he was not a filial and co-operative subordinate, a friendly and companionable fellow worker or husband, or a kindly and concerned superior. He was, rather, a clever and isolated person, full of bright ideas and unaware of his emotional emptiness.

The third illustrative case, C, was a top-level administrator in a government agency. Despite his high position, he had two major weaknesses as an administrator. First, he was unsure of his authority and tended to regard differences of opinion as insubordination. Instead of permitting open discussion by his staff which could finally culminate in a considered decision by him, he became tense and angry and ended discussion with an arbitrarily stated edict often arrived at too hastily. Second, he was exceedingly anxious to be a well-liked boss and this need made him too readily inclined to listen to one person's point of view and agree with it even though it might not correspond with his better judgment. The overauthoritative behavior occurred when a difference of opinion arose in a group; the overagreeable behavior, when he discussed a problem with just one other person. C's conflictful attitudes obviously put a premium for his staff on making private arrangements with him rather than decisions in which the whole administrative group participated. This, in turn, led to lack of communication from one co-worker to another, as well as to a somewhat inconsistent collection of projects and plans, not all of which were compatible.

To illustrate the kind of difficulties C's conflict gave rise to: His executive assistant came to him to discuss the problem of a junior technician in the agency, a personable young man who seemed to be a constant focus of dissension among the clerical staff and also among his fellow technicians. It appeared that he was actively involved in flirtations with two of the stenographers, and in addition he went to considerable trouble to charm all of the young and attractive girls in the office. He played the two whom he was involved with off against each other, with the result that they were not speaking and refused to co-operate in their work. Several of the less involved girls had taken sides, and the morale and efficiency of the office had dropped considerably. The young man's fellow technicians were angry with him and collaborative work between them suffered. C's assistant suggested that the young man be discharged; C agreed, expressing his confidence in his assistant's judgment and his feeling that the decision was wise.

Immediately after he was told of his discharge, the young man came to see C. With his usual charm and plausibility, he told his side of the story, and C succumbed to his appeal and reversed his assistant's decision. This, of course, meant a serious blow to the assistant's pride and, as well, an undermining of his prestige with the workers whom he supervised. Perhaps most serious of all was the doubt which he now had of the advisability of taking the responsibility for making decisions in the future which might expose him to a repetition of this rebuff.

C was the only child of a stiff and reticent college professor and a socially prominent mother who was cold, authoritarian, and yet overindulgent to her son. Association with his father's intellectual friends, his mother's society friends, and great emphasis in his rearing on his special destiny combined to set him apart from his juvenile confreres. He did not have the experience of group life and give-and-take with equals which would have given him some idea of the place he could win in a group by virtue of his own ability. He came to think of himself as destined to do great things, while he lacked the self-esteem upon which leadership must be based. His conception of leadership had the connotation: a leader must be able to make himself obeyed. It also had the connotation: a leader must be loved by his men. To combine authority with friendliness requires that a person be able to tolerate differences of opinion and resentment when the subordinates are not pleased with his decisions. Made anxious by differences of opinion, which called into question his intellectual ability, his worthiness in the eyes of his father; made anxious also by others' resentment of his authority, which stirred up frightening echoes of his resentful feelings toward his mother's authority—he was unable to find any securely consistent position which would enable him to deal with such conflicts. His own feelings of loneliness and isolation led him into the pseudointimate twosomes with his staff. Those who treated him as though they liked him were most successful in winning their points, yet when they did, it was necessarily with the knowledge that the next to confer with the boss might well come out with a new and totally contradictory point won.

Case D, again a government administrator in charge of several hundred workers, was handicapped by the dislike which his subordinates and, to some extent, his equals and superiors felt for him. While he was a person of outstanding ability, perhaps the most gifted of the four mentioned, he had been the least successful in his work. His assistants were not motivated to please him or to make the activities that he planned and directed into successes; some of them, indeed, probably rejoiced in seeing this haughty and distant man defeated. His superiors were inclined to judge him according to the strict letter of the law, and when an error occurred, saw to it that he took the consequences.

The dislike for him was based on his arrogant, superior manner. He felt that each should do his work according to the rules and that there was no excuse for sloppiness, inefficiency, or any personal element. If the rule is that employees are to get to work at 8:30, then arriving at 8:31 is an infraction which carries consequences. He felt that if one does good work, that should be its own reward and there should be no need for praise.

Despite these consciously held ideas, D was extremely sensitive. When he was not appreciated by his superiors or when his subordinates disliked him, he felt hurt and could not understand it. He wished his subordinates to consider him a good leader, and had difficulty in recognizing that this required some evidence of concern for them on his part.

To illustrate with an example: Over a period of a year he had become increasingly critical of the attitudes of his subordinates, even though their performance equalled or excelled that of a parallel unit. He felt that they had become too self-centered since the war; they demanded too much for themselves and did not recognize their place in the scheme of things as *he* had done when on *his* way up the ladder. Finally, when the employees organized a grievance committee, which was an accepted practice in other similar units, D became incensed, refused to recognize the committee, and became so bitter in word and action that the efficiency level of his unit fell to a very low ebb.

Some of D's difficulties can be traced back to the way in which the problem of affection was handled in his upbringing. He was the elder of two sons of a very stern, forceful, and reserved father and a somewhat passive, ailing mother. An outstanding athlete in his youth, his father had suffered an industrial accident which to most men would have been severely disabling. However, instead of accepting a pension, or even a more sedentary inside job, the father had bulled his way to success in a job calling for hard physical exertion. D was reared in this Spartan tradition, and accepted as his own his father's standards of grim persistence and acceptance of fate, even at the expense of suppressing artistic and creative interests of his own. D had a younger brother who did not adhere to the father's standards—instead he was lazy and self-indulgent. When refused a request by the father (a request which D would never dream of making), he would throw a temper tantrum so violent that the sick mother would intervene to have his request granted. Thus the brother was granted much for which D had longed as a youth. But instead of feeling envious of the brother and resentful of the inconsistency of his parents, D felt rage at the younger brother whom he regarded as too self-centered, demanding, and lacking in respect and consideration for his elders. In other words, he was unaware that he, too, craved affection and indulgence as his younger brother did. . . .

In concluding, two points derived from the psychiatric study of administrators seem to . . . warrant considerable further study.

First, those who choose administrative work for a career and who succeed in it seem to have certain personal motivations for making the choice and certain personal traits which account for their success. (We are not including in this statement those who become administrators by chance or by outliving their competitors.) The motivations have something to do with deriving a sense of well-being and security from knowing how to get others to do things that one decides are worth doing. Success in achieving this has something to do with finding out in the early years, when dealing with parents and siblings, how to get other people to want to do what you wish. It is easy, for instance, to think of the contrast between the stereotype of the college professor, a person who is highly intelligent and capable of formulating excellent plans but who has not a ghost of a notion as to how to go about interesting or inducing anyone else to carry out his ideas; and another kind of person who handles with ease and spontaneity the problems of relationship with those who are involved in the work. This personality difference is what

> we refer to as having been in large part determined by the nature of a person's early relationships. . . .
>
> The second point is that success in administration on higher levels has one significant difference from that on lower ones—namely, that there is no superior to please or to manipulate when one reaches the policy-making top. Therefore, for the top man, the motivations and skills must be at least in some ways different from those of the men who work under him. He must, for one thing, have a considerably greater degree of maturity and independence of judgment. There is a large, and open, question as to whether these traits will be found at the top in the event that they are lacking on the way up the ladder. Further, as illustrated by Cases A and B, there is considerable doubt whether the personality characteristics contributing to success in climbing up the ladder, are always conducive to good leadership once a man has arrived at the top.[7]

These cases indicate the links between childhood experiences, personality, and organizational adjustment. They illustrate Sullivan's interpersonal theory as a way of explaining organizational behavior. In his view, interpersonal relations are largely a function of individual needs to reduce anxiety. Thus the objective situation is only one part of the field; individual perception and personality always play their part in determining how a given situation will be handled. But perception is the product of a "self-system" reflecting the individual's experience from childhood onward.

Interpersonal theory, then, emphasizes the interplay between the social situation and personality. The situation, however, plays the major role. As Sullivan concludes: "The human organism is so extraordinarily adaptive that not only

[7] M.B. Cohen and R.A. Cohen: "Personality as a Factor in Administrative Decisions," *Psychiatry*, Vol. 14 (1951), pp. 47-53. By special permission of the William Alanson White Psychiatric Foundation, Inc. Copyright by the William Alanson White Psychiatric Foundation.

could the most fantastic social rules and regulations be lived up to, if they were properly inculcated in the young, but they would seem very natural and proper ways of life."[8] Certainly it is clear that man can live under many different ethical and political systems. Cultural anthropology has revealed the range of behavior that characterizes so-called instinctive drives. It is not surprising therefore that Sullivan and the others should build their theory around its major assumptions.

Anthropological research destroyed some cherished illusions. Freud's theory was shown to depend in part upon his definition of certain sexual behaviors and attitudes as being *instinctive*, when in fact they reflected his own nineteenth-century, European, middle-class values. Similarly, the competitive impulse that most Americans accepted as primeval was shown to be culturally determined. The Hopi, for example, exhibited none of the so-called competitive instinct, and a similar "aberration" was found in Japan following World War II when school children resisted competitive innovations. In regard to pugnacity, the Arapesh and Dobu tribes were sharply different, suggesting again the weight of social structure in shaping "inherent" tendencies. The only universal instinct seemed to be man's effort to elevate his own values into a system of cosmic validity.

Man's susceptability to socialization is in part explained by the individual's long period of biologic and economic immaturity. While lower animals become self-sufficient shortly after birth, western man is dependent for some two decades before he strikes out alone. During this time he is dependent upon those who provide his emotional and physical sustenance. At the same time, it appears that even as a child he becomes conscious of his power. When toilet training, walking, and speech begin, he learns that he can defy his parents in matters that are obviously important to them. Here again we see that biological impulses are always con-

[8] Sullivan: *Interpersonal Theory of Psychiatry*, p. 6.

ditioned by cultural patterns that differ from society to society. Even the Oedipus complex, which Freud believed to be instinctive, is now thought by some anthropologists to be culturally specific, the result of a monogamous, patriarchal family structure.

The family and other authority figures measure the individual's "growth" largely in terms of his adjustment to social norms. Such norms include national traditions and mythology, religious beliefs, economic and political values, in fact, the whole cultural web that sustains us throughout life. These norms include the parents' perception of the kinds of skills and attitudes required by children for success in our organized society. As a result, individual personality tends to reflect the social structure. The dominant values of society become a superego controlling the individual through approval and anxiety. As Fromm observes: "Society must tend to mold the character structure of its members in such a way they will want to do what they have to do under the existing circumstances." [9]

As we have seen, the individual's successive experiences with authority figures result in a "self-system," a way of relating himself to the world. This system becomes a framework for accepting or rejecting the vast number of stimuli that impinge upon him. Millions of sensory fibers transmit such stimuli through his nervous system. Certain reflexes become reinforced and linked together, providing the basis for habitual patterns of behavior. *Both an individual's perceptions and his behavior become, so to speak, structured.* He develops a time-tested way of organizing reality, and his reactions become stabilized accordingly. This relatively consistent pattern of behavior is commonly defined as "personality." Moreover, the personality continually reinforces itself by a selective process that tends to accept only approved impressions which are in turn incorporated into the existing value system. Conflicting stimuli are rejected, and

[9] Erich Fromm: *Man For Himself* (New York: Rinehart & Co., Inc.; 1947), p. 241.

when an individual rejects all conflicting stimuli, we say that he has a low tolerance for ambiguity.

How this process of organizing reality becomes stereotyped is suggested by the so-called "authoritarian-personality" type, i.e., one who scores high on a scale of attitudes that include racial prejudice, militarism, chauvinism, antiradicalism, exceptional conventionality, deference for authority, a poor view of human nature, belief in force and "toughness," and a general power orientation.[1] The well-known California F scale, which measures authoritarian attitudes, includes nine attitudinal categories and several descriptive statements of each. The "authoritarian personality" is one who selects a large proportion of such statements as being compatible with his own attitudes. For our purposes the significance of the scale is that many of these attitudes seem congruent with those of the upward-mobile type.

AUTHORITARIANISM SCALE[2]

CONVENTIONALISM: *Rigid adherence to conventional, middle-class values.*

Obedience and respect for authority are the most important virtues children should learn.

[1] Among others, T.W. Adorno, *et al.: The Authoritarian Personality* (New York: Harper & Brothers; 1950); Fromm: op. cit.; J. Jahoda and R. Christie: *Studies in the Scope and Method of "The Authoritarian Personality"* (Glencoe, Illinois: The Free Press; 1954), pp. 226-75; J. Block and J. Block: "An Investigation of the Relationship Between Intolerance of Ambiguity and Ethnocentrism," *Journal of Personality*, Vol. 19, pp. 303-11; A.H. Maslow: "The Authoritarian Character Structure," *Journal of Social Psychology*, Vol. 18, pp. 401-11; R. Christie and J. Garcia: "Subcultural Variation in Authoritarian Personality," *Journal of Abnormal and Social Psychology*, Vol. 46, pp. 457-69; M. Rokeach: "Generalized Mental Rigidity as a Factor in Ethnocentrism," *Journal of Abnormal and Social Psychology*, Vol. 43, pp. 259-78; M. Rokeach: "Narrow-Mindedness and Personality," *Journal of Personality*, Vol. 20, pp. 234-51; M. Rokeach: "Prejudice, Concreteness of Thinking and Reification of Thinking," *Journal of Abnormal and Social Psychology*, Vol. 46, pp. 83-91.

[2] T.W. Adorno, *et al.:* op. cit., pp. 248-50. Used by permission.

A person who has bad manners, habits, and breeding can hardly expect to get along with decent people.

If people would talk less and work more, everybody would be better off.

The businessman and the manufacturer are much more important to society than the artist and the professor.

AUTHORITARIAN SUBMISSION: *Submissive, uncritical attitude toward idealized moral authorities of the in-group.*

Obedience and respect for authority are the most important virtues children should learn.

Science has its place, but there are many important things that can never possibly be understood by the human mind.

Every person should have complete faith in some supernatural power whose decisions he obeys without question.

Young people sometimes get rebellious ideas, but as they grow up they ought to get over them and settle down.

What this country needs most, more than laws and political programs, is a few courageous, tireless, devoted leaders in whom the people can put their faith.

No sane, normal, decent person could ever think of hurting a close friend or relative.

Nobody ever learned anything really important except through suffering.

AUTHORITARIAN AGGRESSION: *Tendency to be on the lookout for, and to condemn, reject, and punish people who violate conventional values.*

A person who has bad manners, habits and breeding can hardly expect to get along with decent people.

What youth needs most is strict discipline, rugged determination, and the will to work and fight for family and country.

An insult to our honor should always be punished.

Sex crimes, such as rape, and attacks on children, deserve

more than mere imprisonment; such criminals ought to be publicly whipped, or worse.

There is hardly anything lower than a person who does not feel great love, gratitude, and respect for his parents.

Most of our social problems would be solved if we could somehow get rid of the immoral, crooked and feeble-minded people.

If people would talk less and work more, everybody would be better off.

Homosexuals are hardly better than criminals and ought to be severely punished.

ANTI-INTRACEPTION: *Opposition to the subjective, the imaginative, the tender-minded.*

When a person has a problem or worry, it is best for him not to think about it, but to keep busy with more cheerful things.

Nowadays more and more people are prying into matters that should remain personal and private.

If people would talk less and work more, everybody would be better off.

The businessman and the manufacturer are much more important to society than the artist and the professor.

SUPERSTITION AND STEREOTYPE: *The belief in mystical determinants of the individual's fate; the disposition to think in rigid categories.*

Science has its place, but there are many important things that can never possibly be understood by the human mind.

Every person should have complete faith in some supernatural power whose decisions he obeys without question.

Some people are born with an urge to jump from high places.

People can be divided into two distinct classes: the weak and the strong.

Some day it will probably be shown that astrology can explain a lot of things.

Wars and social troubles may someday be ended by an earthquake or flood that will destroy the whole world.

POWER AND 'TOUGHNESS': *Preoccupation with the dominance-submission, strong-weak, leader-follower dimensions; identification with power figures; over-emphasis upon the conventionalized attributes of the ego; exaggerated assertion of strength and toughness.*

No weakness or difficulty can hold us back if we have enough will power.

What youth needs most is strict discipline, rugged determination, and the will to work and fight for family and country.

An insult to our honor should always be punished.

It is best to use some prewar authorities in Germany to keep order and prevent chaos.

What this country needs most, more than laws and political programs, is a few courageous, tireless, devoted leaders in whom the people can put their faith.

People can be divided into two distinct classes: the weak and the strong.

Most people don't realize how much our lives are controlled by plots hatched in secret places.

DESTRUCTIVENESS AND CYNICISM: *Generalized hostility, vilification of the human being. Human nature being what it is, there will always be war and conflict.*

Familiarity breeds contempt.

PROJECTIVITY: *The disposition to believe that wild and dangerous things go on in the world; the projection outwards of conscious emotional impulses.*

Nowadays, when so many different kinds of people move around and mix together so much, a person has to protect himself especially carefully against catching an infection or disease from them.

Nowadays, more and more people are prying into

matters that should remain personal and private.

Wars and social troubles may someday be ended by an earthquake or flood that will destroy the whole world.

The wild sex life of the old Greeks and Romans was tame compared to some of the goings-on in this country, even in places where people might least expect it.

Most people don't realize how much their lives are controlled by plots hatched in secret places.

SEX: *Exaggerated concern with sexual "goings-on."*

Sex crimes such as rape and attacks on children deserve more than mere imprisonment; such criminals ought to be publicly whipped, or worse.

The wild sex life of the old Greeks and Romans was tame compared to some of the goings-on in this country, even in places where people might least expect it.

Homosexuals are hardly better than criminals and ought to be severely punished.

When combined with certain other typical values and behaviors of successful executives isolated by Gardner, Henry, and Warner, the "authoritarian personality" findings provide a highly tentative but suggestive hypothesis, namely, that bureaucratic structure and its behavioral demands provide a sympathetic environment for the authoritarian type, who may, in turn, be equated with the typical upward-mobile. For example, note the similarity between the following values found to be characteristic of successful business executives, and the items included in the F scale: low identification with one's mother and close attachment to one's father; condescending attitude toward subordinates and a close positive identification with superiors; admiration for powerful, decisive, and prestigeful superiors.[3]

As suggested, the conditions of participation in big or-

[3] Warner: op. cit.; Gardner: op. cit.; W. Henry: "The Business Executive: The Psychodynamics of a Social Role," *American Journal of Sociology*, Vol. 54, pp. 286-91.

ganizations place a high value upon power, status, prestige, order, predictability, easy acceptance of authority, hard work, punctuality, discipline, and conventionality. The authoritarian personality scale reveals several categories and their definitive attitudes that are correlated with such values, including the following:

Conventionalism: "Obedience and respect for authority are the most important virtues children should learn." "If people would talk less and work more, everybody would be better off."

Authoritarian Submission: "What this country needs most, more than laws or political programs, is a few courageous, tireless, devoted leaders in whom the people can put their faith."

Authoritarian Aggression: "What youth needs most is strict discipline, rugged determination, and the will to work and fight for family and country."

Anti-Intraception: "The businessman and the manufacturer are much more important to society than the artist or the professor."

Power and "Toughness": "People can be divided into two classes: the weak and the strong." "No weakness or difficulty can hold us back if we have enough will power."

The significance of the authoritarianism research is that certain individuals have personality needs that include dominance, submissiveness, and rigidity. Our analysis suggests that such individuals have an affinity for big organizations. We also know that values are related to occupational preference. In a word, to some extent individuals are attracted by vocations that suit their personality.

Such alignments are suggested by research showing that men can be divided into two broad categories, extravert and introvert. William James called these "tough-minded" and "tender-minded," for reasons which will soon become apparent. Not only are traits in each category surprisingly uniform, but they reflect vocational interests. Extraverts are usually realistic in their perception and adjustment to events. They accept conditions as they are, believing that existing values and institutions are necessary and proper. They accept the rationality and legitimacy of the existing system. In general, they are oriented toward absolute categories, custom and ceremony, hierarchy, and obedience.[4]

On the other hand, the introvert has rather different values. He tends to measure institutions by some ideal standard, and to believe that human intelligence can remove their inadequacies. Having an optimistic view of man, he prefers an "open society" to one where status is determined by birth or tradition. He prefers complexity in geometric and art forms and regards problems as multifaceted rather than as simple and clear cut. Not only is the world seen as unordered, but its values and institutions are relative and changing. Unlike the extravert who is outward looking both in conception and interest, the introvert is highly self-conscious. Emotionally and artistically oriented, he often rejects majority norms. According to Jung, this dichotomy is also apparent in the kinds of mental illness to which each type is susceptible. The extravert is subject to hysteria and psychopathy, disorders that have few moral implications; the introvert's illnesses include anxiety, depression, and compulsion, which mirror value conflicts.

Such conclusions enable us to define personality types and to trace the relation between society, personality, and vocation. We turn first to personality traits and job preference. The German psychologist, Spranger, suggested that individuals could be divided on the basis of interest into several categories.[5] Two of these are useful for our purposes, the

[4] H.J. Eysenck: *The Psychology of Politics* (London: Methuen; 1954); *The Structure of Human Personality* (London: Methuen; 1953); T.W. Adorno, *et al.:* op. cit.

[5] E. Spranger: *Types of Men,* 5th German ed. (New York: Hafner Publishing Co., Inc.; 1928), cited in Eysenck: *The Psychology of Politics,* pp. 159-61.

theoretical and the *economic.* The theoretical person, who resembles the introvert, is empirical, rational, and critical, mainly concerned with discovering truth. Vocationally, he is a scientist, philosopher, or academic. Opposed to this is the economic type, a utilitarian, who honors that which is useful. Consequently, he tends to reject art, theory, and esthetics. The successful administrator is usually the pragmatic type, since he must to some extent view individuals as means to organizational ends.

Spranger's theory provided the basis for linking occupation with values. H.E. Brogden, for example, found a consistent dichotomy between "practicality" and "idealism," which conformed nicely with the "tough-minded" and "tender-minded" categories.[6] "Idealistic" items include a preference for reading the lives of Plato, Aristotle, and Socrates, rather than those of Alexander, Caesar, or Charlemagne. The idealist would rather be a politician, mathematician, or minister, than a businessman or sales manager. His friends are introspective and interested in social questions rather than industrious, practical, or endowed with leadership qualities. On the other hand, the "practical" individual accepts a business society's terms, placing a low value on theoretical and esthetic activities. Unlike the "idealist," who is concerned with how things "ought" to be, he accepts things as they are and works out a scheme of action within this framework.

This dichotomy between the practical and idealist types carries over into vocational preferences, as demonstrated by the Strong Vocational Interest Inventory. The Strong test assumes that individuals who succeed in certain occupations have similar interests and values. *Ability* is not a factor in the test; *interest* is the main consideration. Patterns of interest for many vocations have been established, with the result that one can determine which he fits. Once the

[6] H.E. Brogden: "Primary Personal Values Measured by the Allport-Vernon Test, 'A Study of Values,'" *Psychological Monographs,* Vol. 66, No. 16, pp. 1-31, cited in H.J. Eysenck: *The Psychology of Politics,* p. 163.

vocational patterns were analyzed, several conclusions emerged. Thurstone, for example, found four major interest factors: science, language, people, and business. Interest in business was characteristic of the "tough-minded," while interest in people-oriented vocations characterized the "tender-minded." A positive correlation was thus found between values and vocational preferences.

A related study may now be mentioned. Barron found that "yielders" (those who conformed to group opinion) preferred simple designs, whereas "nonyielders" (those who retained their opinions regardless of majority pressure) preferred complexity in designs.[7] In this study the idealist-complexity independents (introverts) had the following traits. They valued creative work, original ideas, the individual, integrity over personal appeal, some uncertainty, and free communication of inner feelings. They disliked taking orders, integrating with a group, discipline, or devotion to a leader.

While conclusions drawn from such disparate studies must be highly tentative, they do suggest a basic personality difference between an idealistic type and a pragmatic one. Applying this hypothesis to the bureaucratic situation, we assume that the idealistic personality tends to avoid structured, collective situations in which personal or hierarchical authority is the source of legitimacy. His value preferences seem inapposite to typical organizational demands such as uncritical acceptance of the organization's manifest goals, structured interpersonal relations, collective decision making, and diffused responsibility. Bureaucracy's twin imperatives, obedience and manipulative personal relations, seem equally unappealing.

On the other hand, we can assume that the bureaucratic situation provides a sympathetic work place for the pragmatic type who seeks accommodation through certainty and power. Obviously, organizations include other types, and a definite range of behavior characterizes this particular

[7] Barron: "Complexity-Simplicity as a Personality Dimension," *Journal of Abnormal and Social Psychology,* Vol. 48, pp. 163-72.

type; but the upward-mobile will probably find the bureaucratic milieu generally compatible. In Sullivan's terms, his self-system and its time-tested security operations prove functional in the "complex, peculiarly characterized" interpersonal relations that occur in big organizations. Such upward-mobile types personify organizational values. The true "bureaucratic personality," they accept the organization's latent goals of power, growth, and survival. They define and express its values to the outside world. Although other members may reject its collective values, the upward-mobiles are deeply committed to them. If they are to succeed, they must accept such values uncritically. They are intensely subject to organizational discipline. If, as the Indian proverb says, to be free is to be without desire, they are not free, because they desire power and its derivative rewards.

While the extent to which individuals legitimize organizational claims varies considerably, the pragmatic type seems well adapted to such accommodations. Certainly his easy acceptance of authority is functional. Such claims are reinforced by the organization's "conditional love," which (like parental love) is often contingent upon obedience. Here again the anxiety mechanism seems basic. Approval and acceptance are exchanged for loyalty and conformity. Deprivations may occasionally be required, but such expectations are usually met on the basis of tacit understanding. Accommodation is also eased by middle-class child-raising practices and extended education, which honor authority and self-discipline.

As suggested earlier, the pragmatic type has high dominance and submission tendencies, exceptional conventionality, and a low tolerance for ambiguity. He believes in firm leadership, in differentiating the weak from the strong. He honors respect for parents and obedience in children. Having this orientation, he believes that most problems can be solved by vigorous action. Here again, it seems, the bureaucratic situation provides an appropriate milieu for individuals with some of his tendencies. His dominance-submission needs, for example, enable him to play the dual role of deference to those above and dominance toward those below. As Gardner, Henry, and Warner found, *successful executives have an intensely personal attachment to their superiors, accompanied by a detached and impersonal feeling toward their juniors.*[8] They also have a common fear of failure. Such attributes seem functional in the bureaucratic arena.

While the pragmatic type's style of accommodation increases his life chances, we can assume that the idealist has lost ground. His toleration for ambiguity and preference for personal autonomy have proved less amenable to organizational demands. The scientist, technician, engineer, scholar, and artist, i.e., the professional-employee class, are now directed by the upward-mobile. His values are critical because they shape the ends and conditions under which their skill and knowledge are expressed. Since elite values tend to become bench marks for popular behavior, the upward-mobile's influence seems bound to increase. Here again social theory may be applied in an organizational context. Riesman and Hoffer have suggested the decline of individualistic, "inner-directed" man in favor of an "other-directed" personality strongly motivated by the need for group approval and thus intensely subject to conventional values of success and power.[9]

Significantly, this perception of the changed conditions of occupational success directly influences socialization. The family now receives many of its child-rearing cues from organizational elites whose influence and life styles provide the daily fare of the mass media. These individuals most dramatically personify the change from an economy of saving to one of consumption. They validate the "success" aspirations of our society. While training in such values may occur almost

[8] W. Warner: op. cit., pp. 188-9; Gardner: op. cit.; W. Henry: op. cit.

[9] David Riesman: *The Lonely Crowd* (New Haven: Yale University Press; 1950); E. Hoffer: *The True Believer* (New York: Harper & Brothers; 1951).

unconsciously, it is often systematically built into the child's personality by parents whose education, insight, and expectations give them an awareness of functional norms and behaviors in a bureaucratic society. As Miller and Swanson found, urban child-rearing practices directly reflect existing social and economic organization:

> Bureaucratic parents train their children for this new world and treat them in terms of its values. For most parents this will not be a matter of self-conscious planning. Their methods of child care will simply reflect the values these fathers and mothers have learned from living in a bureaucratized society. . . . The confident, smooth relations of the great organization of which he must become a part will require him to get along well with other people and to take their feelings as well as his own into account with skill and confidence. . . . [The] child will need to be taught that superiors are not hateful figures to be challenged, but men of skill and feeling whom he should emulate.[1]

In this chapter we have traced the molding of personality by social values and socialization. In stark form, the following developmental process tends to occur. Socially validated beliefs and behavior are instilled in the young through the anxiety-conformity-approval syndrome. In this way "culturally defined and interpersonally imposed patterns of behavior come to motivate human beings as imperiously as biologically determined requirements."[2] This process, moreover, persists throughout life as the socialization role of the family is reinforced by the small group, the school, and the church. Success now requires extended university training, and such training is the prerogative of middle-class families who employ child-rearing practices that give their children the inside track by emphasizing striving, punctuality, and

[1] D.R. Miller and G.E. Swanson: *The Changing American Parent* (New York: John Wiley & Sons, Inc.; 1958), p. 55.

[2] Blitsten: op. cit., p. 53.

the suppression of unprofitable emotions. These attributes prove functional in big organizations, now the main sources of status and prestige. As a result, those who possess these attributes assume power and replace themselves with men who reflect their own image. In such ways the socialization process is tuned to the organization's demands for consistency, conformity, and the muting of conflict.

CHAPTER 5

THE PSYCHOLOGY OF BIG ORGANIZATIONS

WE NOW turn to the psychological bases of organizational behavior. How are individuals conditioned to accept the legitimacy of authority? What are the conditions of participation set down by the organization for its members? In this chapter the essential proposition is that the bureaucratic situation constitutes a "structured field," comprising three discrete systems: *authority, status,* and *small groups.* Psychologically, a structured field is one in which stimuli are patent, stable, and compelling. Such a field eases perception and learning by providing cues that guide and limit individual choices. The individual's learned deference toward authority is evoked and interpersonal relations are ordered in ways that honor organizational claims for loyalty, consistence, and dispatch. Organizations are composed of a congeries of small groups that have a similar influence on behavior. They inculcate majority values in their members; they reward compliance and punish those who resist their demands. In many cases, group values contribute to the organization's manifest goals. In others, they conflict with them. But in every case, small groups have a pervasive socializing function. In sum, the three systems of authority, status, and small groups provide the major conditions of participation.

Here, an important qualification must be made. In addition to the systems just mentioned, every bureaucratic situation includes a fourth system, namely, that of technology. This system consists of the technical process that participants must use to achieve their purpose. Consider for example the operating room in a hospital where a group of specialists is about to perform an operation. Factors of authority, status, and small groups are obviously at work, but these are augmented by technical imperatives, the "laws of the situation," which govern perhaps even more imperiously the behavior of doctors, anesthesiologists, nurses, and so forth. Similar task requirements provide the framework for most interpersonal contacts in modern organizations. Despite the difficulty of separating this technical system from the other systems, the major focus of our analysis is upon the latter; the inherent technical context is treated as a "given."

We saw earlier that big organizations are systems of roles graded by *authority*. Ideally, there is very little ambiguity in interpersonal relations. Each position is differentiated by fairly precise assignments of authority and prestige. Such assignments outline the repertory of expected behaviors attached to each position. While personality differences will obviously affect the resulting accommodations, these conditions encourage stereotyped responses. The authority system is a critical factor in this context.

Authority can be defined as *the ability to evoke compliance*. Unlike power, which is a broader concept with connotations of force and the ability to impose one's will regardless of opposition, authority usually rests upon some official position. Although it has several bases of validation, authority is typically legitimated by formal, hierarchical position.[1] It has been argued by Chester I. Barnard that

[1] For an analysis of authority in a bureaucratic environment, see Robert Presthus: "Authority in Organizations," in S. Mailick and E. Van Ness:

authority must be "accepted" by those who fall within its penumbra. This conception of authority is useful, but one must note that the word "acceptance" has many meanings, and that "acceptance" is only the final expression of many complex motivations, affected by the bureaucratic situation and the personality of the individuals concerned. The question remains, why does the individual "accept" bureaucratic authority.

To say that authority is defined by "acceptance" suggests that the individual has a real choice between acceptance and refusal, that authority is an "either-or" proposition. But this assumes too great a degree of free will and too simple a social situation. As we have seen, the individual is trained from birth onward to defer to authority. He develops a generalized deference to the authority of parenthood, experience, knowledge, status, and so forth. If he is lucky, there may be an occasional situation in which his judgments are authoritative, although for most of us this luxury is confined to one's role as parent and less frequently, in American society, as husband.

Moreover, in any given authority situation, factors other than the immediate interpersonal relationship are involved. So many degrees of compliance exist, ranging from enthusiasm to resignation, that explicit rejection becomes a crude and unlikely alternative, particularly among highly socialized individuals. (Parenthetically, bureaucratic individuals will often be highly socialized, i.e., sensitive to the built-in expectations of interpersonal situations, because of the extended education required to acquire the necessary technical skills.) We can assume that compliance will be normal. In organizations, people rarely withhold consent. Rather, they evade, procrastinate, "misunderstand," "forget," or pro-

---

Concepts and Issues in Organizational Behavior (Englewood Cliffs, N.J.: Prentice-Hall, Inc.; 1962), pp. 186-95; on the nature of power in its many forms, see Charles E. Merriam: *Political Power* (New York: McGraw-Hill Book Co.; 1934); and Richard A. Schermerhorn: *Society and Power* (New York: Random House; 1961), Ch. 1.

ject the unwelcome task upon someone "better qualified."

For these reasons, the probability of hierarchical authority being rejected is remote. Indeed, in big organizations where authority and its symbols are organized and obvious, and where sanctions exist to encourage "acceptance," we have left the level of mere "influence" for a more authoritative level. The essential distinction is one of *sanctions:* bureaucratic authority is reinforced by rewards and punishments, while mere influence operates without such sanctions. This difference underlies the assumption that bureaucratic interpersonal relations are more often "authoritative" than "influential." This is not to say that organizations do not use influence. With the possible exception of the military, authority usually has a façade of permissiveness, but those concerned are rarely unaware of the structure of authority in a given situation. Moreover, aside from other motivations such as ambition, the need to reduce anxiety, and the desire for group approval, the mere fact that an order emanates from a superior tends to induce "acceptance" based on an assumed legitimacy of his role. Thus the very structure of big organizations creates a tendency to comply.

Authority does not always operate hierarchically. In addition to informal centers of power, there is the fact that technical skill demands recognition. A superior may defer to a specialist when technical questions are conclusive. Yet, as the experience of the atomic physicists suggests, the control of specialists in terms of recruitment, rewards, and programs is usually exercised by those in hierarchical positions.

Any appraisal of authority must also note that big organizations are composed of many subhierarchies, each bound together by authority, interests, and values in a way similar to the total organization. Each has its power structure headed by a leader who is decisive within his own system, but who is a subordinate when viewed from the perspective of the larger hierarchy. This devolution of power has important consequences. It insures discipline since the life chances of those in each subhierarchy are determined through representations made to the elite on their behalf by such subleaders. As a result, an upward-looking posture characterizes the whole organization. Moreover, the will of the elite is transmitted downward through the organization by the subleaders, again reinforcing their authority and status within their own subsystems.

Here, the ambiguity of goals in organizations may be seen. To retain his position and preserve the hope of future rewards, each subleader must honor organizational values and at the same time retain the loyalty of his own group by defending their interests against competitors within the system and against neglect by the elite. Although he is torn between such conflicting demands, his own career is in the hands of his superiors, and we can assume that he will give priority to their claims. They will measure him by the loyalty, dispatch, and affirmation with which he carries out their policies. Thus the price that the subleader pays for marginal power and great expectations is loyalty upward.

In considering the different premises underlying bureaucratic promotion, Henri de Man reveals other tensions of authority. While employees prefer that their superior be chosen on the basis of technical skill and bargaining ability, the manager who delegates authority has quite different qualifications in mind. "In large-scale industries . . . characterized by extreme division of labour, he usually knows little about the craft competence of the worker he promotes to a foreman's job. What he wants is a "trusty" man, this meaning one whom he can regard as being devoted to the profit-making aspect of the undertaking and fully convinced of the importance of maintaining the employer's authority. [This system] rests on the psychological assumption that bureaucratic and quasi-military discipline is the best sort of discipline for an industrial enterprise." [2]

Organizational authority, in sum, is composed of legal, moral, psychological, and skill ingredients, whose relative

[2] Henri de Man: *Joy in Work* (London: Kegan Paul; 1929), pp. 204-5.

weights vary in terms of how manifest and compelling the stimuli are in a given situation. Big organizations are systems in which stimuli are exceptionally patent and compelling. In addition, they are relatively constant. Authority and its symbols are hierarchically structured so that the individuals who personify authority may change, but the *system* of authority remains. Indeed, the organization may be defined as a relatively permanent system of authority relationships. As a result, there is little ambiguity about rights and obligations. In comparison with other forms of social power, which are often vague and transitory, bureaucratic power is obvious and definable. The principle of hierarchy ensures that it usually follows the formal structure of the organization. Moreover, insofar as organized behavior is group behavior, the weight of authoritative stimuli is increased by sheer numbers. The acceptance of organizational values by the majority fosters a consensus that makes dissent seem quixotic. Both the upward-mobiles who embrace such values and the indifferents who tolerate them become anchoring stimuli who encourage the acceptance of group norms. Only the ambivalents find authority threatening. This leads us to a major proposition: *reactions to authority constitute the most critical variable in organizational accommodation.* Each of our types reacts somewhat differently to authority, and these differences mainly account for their discrete patterns of adjustment and mobility.

Authority relationships thus mediate personality and the ability to estimate the consequences of alternative responses to organizational claims. Although attitudes toward authority are largely derived from early experiences with one's parents, cultural values provide the raw material from which socialization is built. In a patriarchal, highly structured society such as is characteristic of the Middle East, deference to authority becomes ingrained and automatic. In a more mobile and individualistic society, authority must rely to a greater extent on objective bases of skill and rationality to make good its claims. Here again, we see the weblike pattern of culture, family, and individual, each acting upon the other.

Despite the interplay of such situational, psychological, and cultural factors, we can assume that big organizations produce exceptional probabilities that individuals will defer to authority based on hierarchical position. We know that the formal possession of authority, the mere occupancy of a superior position, encourages deference in others. We also know that a positive assumption of authority on whatever grounds enhances compliance. Haythorn found that "when one member of a group was aggressive, self-confident, interested in an individual solution to a task, and showed initiative, the other members of the group showed less of such behavior than they normally did."[3] This tendency was based upon the group's desire to avoid conflict, as well as the common "levelling effect" of a group situation.

As Donald Calhoun has suggested, organizations try to establish their legitimacy by rationalizing authority in terms of ethical and ideological principles.[4] All organizations, of course, strive to find some basis other than sheer power for their authority. Evocative symbols and rituals, usually idealistic, patriotic, or "service-oriented," are enlisted to inspire loyalty to the organization. If loyalty is to be merited, the values, motives, and routine behavior of the organization must be seen as selfless; if possible the organization must appear as the embodiment of certain universal ideals that are beyond criticism.

Max Weber posited three bases of legitimacy for bureaucratic authority: legal, traditional, and charismatic. The first is based upon the assumption that the organization functions

[3] Cited in L.F. Carter: "Leadership and Small Group Behavior," in M. Sherif and M.O. Wilson: *Group Relations at the Crossroads* (New York: Harper & Brothers; 1953), p. 273.

[4] I am deeply indebted here to D.C. Calhoun's: "The Illusion of Rationality," in R. Taylor, ed.: *Life, Language, Law; Essays in Honor of Arthur Bentley* (Yellow Springs: Antioch Press; 1957); see also, H. Kaufman: *The Forest Ranger* (Baltimore: Johns Hopkins University Press; 1960), pp. 175-97.

impersonally in terms of duly enacted laws, rules, and regulations. As the term suggests, traditional legitimacy rests on the belief that the organization and its values are hallowed by age and experience and ought not be challenged by any time-blinded individual. Charismatic legitimacy is based upon an irrational faith in leaders who are assumed to have magical powers. The charismatic personality inspires among his followers a desire for sacrifice and devotion. Traditional and charismatic authority are essentially prebureaucratic; over a period of time, both tend to be replaced by legal norms.

Most organizations enlist all of these appeals in justifying their claims to obedience, and the appeals are usually articulated in terms of the general welfare. However, it is necessary for organizations and their elites to simplify what is really happening, since their objectives are actually more complex and less disinterested than this. While elites do seek to advance the common good, they are at least equally concerned with perpetuating the organization and its personal prerogatives and with mediating conflicting interests within it. However, as Calhoun says, if mass loyalty is to be maintained, all three activities must be rationalized in terms of the first objective. Since it is impossible to define the general welfare, much less to achieve it, the organization must invoke another ideological resource, the myth that it is founded upon unquestionable, unchanging principles. These principles are obviously superior to the individual claims of its members.

Once such principles are accepted, it becomes possible to attribute any patent shortcomings, blunders, and injustice to the organization's members, leaving its ideals intact. If an individual achieves something noteworthy, it is an institutional triumph; if he fails, it is a personal aberration. This behavior is seen in the dramatic "confessions" that occur in the Communist party, but sacrificial mechanisms that differ mainly in degree are evident in most big organizations.

Necessity demands that failures of theory and practice be personalized, projected on some individual in a way that shows human error was involved rather than organizational legitimacy. Certain highly self-conscious systems, among which one can safely include the Marine Corps, the medical profession, and the Foreign Service, exhibit this collective idealization, often evoking exceptional loyalty from enchanted members. By contrast the individual feels ineffectual. The continuity, power, and rituals of big organizations reinforce this self-perception.

As we have seen, this side of the bureaucratic coin appears to suit a pragmatic personality type who has unusual need for certainty, authority, and mystical helpers. "Science has its place, but there are many things that can never be understood by the human mind." "Every person should have complete faith in some supernatural power whose decisions he obeys without question." (Items from the Adorno authoritarianism scale.) The claims of the organization to legitimacy, rationality, and loyalty are reinforced by associating it with eternal wisdom. We saw earlier that the hierarchical distance between elites and the rank and file in big organizations encouraged a tendency to endow leaders with charismatic qualities. Elite monopolization of authority, status, and income reinforces this tendency.

Another psychological tactic of big organization is the promotion of an illusion of unanimity among its members. Internal differences of interest and opinion are muffled in an effort to present a public image of discipline and unity that will enhance the organization's authority and its competitive chances. Dissent and criticism are repressed or confined within the organization. Once a decision has been hammered out, everyone must accept it since further discussion would impair the desired solidity. In part, organizations restrict participation in order to avoid the appearance of internal disharmony that true participation often entails. The common requirement that speeches and publications be cleared through a "public-information" agency is germane. Unfavorable reports can easily be dismissed as irresponsible or unauthorized, the implication being that the organization's elites are its only responsible spokesmen. These are the priests who represent the organization before the public, interpret its catechism, and explain away any disparity between its high ideals of service and its daily behavior.

To increase the probability that its members will endorse the unanimity principle, various incentives are used. These include appeals to loyalty, sacrifice, perpetuation of the organization's ideals, etc. Negative sanctions, on the other hand, are powerful yet latent, depending upon the social sensitivity, the anxiety-reduction needs, and the ambition of the individual. Such mechanisms reduce the need for crude sanctions, and since the majority of members are "indifferents" who merely tolerate organizational demands, followed by the "upward-mobiles" who eagerly accept them, only a small residue of "ambivalents" remain as subjects for discipline. Moreover, since recruitment criteria now cover personal as well as technical qualifications, organizations will tend to recruit and retain members who can make functional accommodations.

Such accommodations have their basis in socialization. The successive authority relationships that begin in childhood and continue throughout one's life culminate in a "self-system" that normally includes a *generalized* deference toward authority. This pattern of behavior is continually reinforced because it reduces anxiety by insuring the approval of those who are important to us. Big organizations provide many opportunities for anxiety reduction through such deference. In the process certain typical values and forms of behavior are instilled in their members. Consider, for example, the universal values of professional military organizations and the stylized behavior of their members. Discipline, "honor," "obedience," respect for authority, castelike social distinctions (symbolized by such gems as "officers and their ladies, enlisted men and their wives"), an orientation toward physical power—*all are internalized and become personal norms of conduct.*[5]

The resulting pattern of "anticipated reactions" is the main basis upon which organizations function. An obvious (although rather extreme) example is the effect of rank insignia in the military. The mere sight of a high-ranking officer, identifiable at twenty paces, evokes a whole battery of conditioned responses from his subordinates. The accommodation is reciprocal, moreover, in that both parties know their proper roles. Levels of deference, degree of familiarity, tone of voice, indeed, the whole interpersonal situation is mediated with ease and dispatch by this single cue. The operational effect of such signals seems clear: the more patent and authoritative the stimulus, the more prompt and certain the response.

Anxiety's role in reinforcing organizational authority is explicit in Alvin Gouldner's account of the experience of a new plant manager.

> Before being handed the reins . . . Peele was called to the main office for a "briefing." The main office executives told Peele of his predecessor's shortcomings, and expressed the feeling that things had been slipping at the plant for some time. They suggested that . . . the former manager who had recently died, had grown overindulgent with his advancing years, and that he, Peele, would be expected to improve production. . . . Peele, therefore, came to the plant sensitized to the rational and impersonal yardsticks which his superiors would use to judge his performance. As a successor, Peele had a heightened awareness that he could disregard top management's rational values only at his

[5] G.D. Spindler: "The Military—A Systematic Analysis," *Social Forces,* Vol. 27, pp. 143-53; E.G. French and R.R. Ernest: "The Relation Between Authoritarianism and Acceptance of Military Ideology," *Journal of Personality,* Vol. 24, pp. 181-91; for a fascinating historical study of military organization and mentality, see C. Woodham-Smith: *The Reason Why* (New York: McGraw-Hill Book Co.; 1954).

peril, for his very promotion symbolized the power they held over him. Since he was now on a new assignment, Peele also realized that he would be subject to more than routine observation by the main office. As a successor, he was "on trial," and, therefore, he was anxious, and anxious to "make good." Comments about Peele's anxiety were made by many main-office personnel, as well as by people in the plant who spoke repeatedly of his "nervousness."

In turn, this anxiety spurred Peele to perform his new role according to main-office expectations. As one of the main-office administrative staff said, "Peele is trying hard to arrive. He is paying more attention to the plant." Peele also accepted top management's view of the plant out of *gratitude* for having been promoted from the smaller plant where he had been, to the larger one at Oscar Center. "I appreciate their confidence in me," he said, "'and I want to show it.'" [6]

An interesting latent consequence of such behavior is an exaggeration of authority demands, which is often dysfunctional since it aggravates the fear of action and responsibility often seen in big organizations. This distorted perception reflects the anxiety of the individual to please his superiors and his impression of being relatively powerless vis-à-vis the organization's leaders. Since the elite is remote and its will cannot always be definitely known, the individual attempts to anticipate its expectations. As a result such expectations may seem more compelling than they are meant to be. The individual is not inclined in any case to underestimate them for fear of impairing his career chances. In this way organizational claims may be expanded beyond reason. Here the federal government's loyalty-security pro-

[6] Alvin W. Gouldner: *Patterns of Industrial Bureaucracy* (Glencoe, Illinois: The Free Press; 1954), pp. 71-2; for additional evidence on the psychological bases of the anxiety-authority relation see J. Block and J. Block: "An Interpersonal Experiment on Reactions to Authority," *Human Relations*, Vol. 5, pp. 91-8.

gram is illustrative. The going rationale was, "Don't take a chance, kick 'em in the pants." This rule of exaggerated response is a major dysfunction of big organizations.

Similar compliance reactions based on authority occur in all social relations. Authority and prestige based on wealth, knowledge, technical expertise, social class, notoriety, or whatever the current values, elicit deference in all interpersonal situations. Communication between two individuals is always influenced by estimates of their relative status. In everyday affairs this is shown by the fact that the weight we attach to any opinion is largely a matter of the commentator's prestige. In organizations the tendency to defer exists simply because orders come from above, from superiors. By itself the formal distribution of authority creates a disposition to obey. Hierarchy, the isolation or remoteness of the organization's elite, and its power reinforce this tendency.

Despite some untenable consequences, such a psychological situation is generally economical, insuring discipline and the reduction of overt interpersonal conflict. The organization's task is simplified by the fact that the reactions it evokes are already deep-seated. Since birth the individual has been conditioned to operate in an environment structured by authority. Noncoercive influences, including custom, mobility expectations, and potential rewards, practically eliminate the use of gross instruments of control. Indeed, the organization's resort to formal authority and sanctions is almost a confession of failure. As will be shown later, the effectiveness of permissive measures is also a function of the social class and the anxiety potential of those concerned.

Because obedience becomes almost automatic, its significance is easily overlooked, or it may be repressed as an uncomfortable irony in a society where individualism is a pervasive ideal. Nevertheless, authority relations become institutionalized between parent and child, leader and follower, teacher and student, officer and enlisted man, etc. Over a period of time various stylized responses evolve, many of which have a remarkable survival value. For example, the contemporary military ritual whereby one moves two steps backward before turning away from a superior is apparently of feudal origin. Although such accommodations may be provoked by imperative cues, the mere presence of an authority figure is usually sufficient to evoke compliance. Since individuals become conditioned to whole classes of stimuli, the respect for authority initiated by parents is generalized to the whole range of authoritative stimuli. With the exception of the ambivalent type, the entire socializing experience of the individual seems to prepare him for an organizational role.

We can now consider the psychology of the *status system.* This system may be defined as a hierarchy of deference ranks. The deference that is ascribed to organizational positions may be called status or prestige. Sociologists define status as the *position* one holds and prestige as the deference attached to the position. We shall use status in its more popular connotation. While prestige is in part assigned to the person who occupies a given position, it is mainly ascribed to the position itself. We are concerned here with hierarchical status rather than with the status ranking attached to occupational roles of specialists. As noted earlier, status is disproportionately allocated in organizations. Its perquisites of income and prestige are concentrated at the top and decrease swiftly as one descends the hierarchy. Status gradations are highly visible. They are marked off by appropriate titles, offices, equipment, secretarial assistance, and degrees of accessibility. Relative amounts of authority further differentiate status ranks. The rationale for such a distribution system is that one's status is roughly equal to his ability and his contribution to organizational goals.

Hierarchical control of status rewards and resulting status anxiety encourage the cheerful acceptance of existing patterns of distribution. The use of the co-optation principle in appointing successors, and the fact that long tenure in a single organization is now the modal career pattern enhance dependency. The individual becomes extremely sensitive to the opinions of his immediate superiors, who control his life chances. In some bureaucratic situations, including academia, the apprentice must be sponsored by a patron who insures his advancement through assiduous (however muted) negotiations with other influential seniors. This system results in the somewhat anomalous spectacle of middle-aged men exhibiting dependency behavior quite similar to the mother-child relationship. Such sponsorships violate bureaucratic values of impartiality and impersonality because they may reflect personality, class, and religion. The resulting personal dependency is a function of the long training and the indoctrination characteristic of technical fields; of the natural insistence of elites that successors mirror their own values; and of individual needs for status and security.

Such dependency relations are remarkably similar to earlier patterns of individual experience. As we have seen, anxiety is an integral part of the child's developing relationship with his parents. After two decades of clinical experience, Sullivan concluded that anxiety is uniquely an interpersonal phenomenon, with its origins in the extreme dependence of the infant upon his mother. This learned tension becomes a critical mechanism in personality formation as the individual meets threats to his self-esteem by compliance, and receives reinforcement for such responses through the consequent reduction of anxiety. This early conditioning seems to be at work in the organizational situation where dependency is built into most interpersonal relationships by patent status differentiations. One's career mobility and the perceived atmosphere of his work environment are determined in part by the attitudes of his superiors toward him. In his routine work he must secure their approval in order to obtain the resources necessary to carry out any new program. Such conditions mean that the typical organization man will be disciplined, anxious, and sensitive in his relations with others. He will understand that mobility requires the support of prestigeful seniors, the gatekeepers who control the entrance to the avenues of authority, status, and income.

Emotional security is also among the rewards, since socialization insures that finding a validation of one's values in the group is a prerequisite of satisfactory personal adjustment. The number and diversity of social groups provide a broad range of individual choice and accommodation, insuring some compensation for the individual's restricted organizational role. Relative status within the whole society is apparently less vital than a recognized status position in one or more of such groups. Fortunately, there is a status hierarchy for everyone, ranging from honored professions to the underworld. Even within prisons a complicated and subtle hierarchy exists, in which forgers are near the top since they presumably work with their brains. Despite the variety of such indexes and the several roles that each of us plays as parent, citizen, marriage partner, etc., *occupation* has become the major status referent. Education, technical skill, and attending levels of consumption now seriously challenge property as status indexes. Since occupational roles are increasingly played in big organizations, as a result of the decline of the small entrepreneur, big organizations become important dispensers of status dividends. The status of one's occupation can be augmented by the status of the organization in which he works.

The status system, however, has other functions. *Perhaps the most important is to be seen in the fact that differential status allocations reinforce the authority of organizational leaders.* Whether the system is consciously directed to this end is not at issue. We are interested in its objective results. The motivation of those who control the distribution of status rewards is a highly subjective and unprofitable question. The status system ramifies authority by validating the right of elites to exercise it. "Insignia and titles of status have the effect of credentials." [7] The system fosters the as-

[7] Chester Barnard: "Functions and Pathology of Status Systems in Formal Organizations," in William F. Whyte, ed.: *Industry and Society* (New York: McGraw-Hill Book Co.; 1946). With characteristic insight, Veblen shows how "manners" are functionally related to status and

sumption that unequal rewards reflect objective differences in ability. Status thus honors the principle of hierarchy and its allocation of authority throughout the organization. In effect, the legal, rational basis of authority is reinforced by personal, charismatic qualities imputed to those who exercise most of it. We saw earlier that the distance between elites and the rank and file encouraged the human tendency to ascribe exceptional competence to those of higher rank. Highly visible status differences aggravate this tendency.

In the process the learned tendency of the individual toward obedience is evoked. As Chester Barnard maintains: "Men are eager to be 'bossed' by superior ability, but they resent being bossed by men of no greater ability than they themselves have. So strong is this need of assigning superior status to those in positions of command that, unless the obvious facts preclude it, men will impute abilities they cannot recognize or judge. They want to believe that those of higher authority 'know what they are doing'. . . . This desire for the justification of subordination leads often to profuse rationalization about status and even to mythological and mystical explanations of it." [8] It is only fair to note that Barnard's greatest emphasis is upon the rational aspects of status; he believes that the system effectively validates objective differences in ability and in the difficulty and importance of work. The problem of course is to distinguish between the rational and the charismatic bases of status. Unfortunately, one of the latent functions of status is to blur this distinction.

---

dominance: "Manners . . . are symbolical and conventionalized survivals representing former acts of dominion or of personal service or of personal contact. In large part they are an expression of the relation of status—a symbolic pantomime of mastery on the one hand and of subservience on the other," *The Theory of the Leisure Class: An Economic Study of the Evolution of Institutions* (New York: The Viking Press; 1899), p. 47. Also, H. Speier: "Honor and the Social Structure," *Social Forces*, Vol. 12, pp. 74-97.

[8] Barnard: loc. cit., pp. 60-1.

Bureaucratic conditions of work aggravate status demands. They also create anxiety by changing the basis of status ascription from objective criteria such as the importance of the work itself to subjective ones such as charisma and hierarchical rank which may or may not be correlated with basic social needs.[9] Specialization, hierarchy, and impersonality encourage efforts to personalize jobs. The breakdown of work into simple tasks and machine processes fosters alienation which diverts attention away from work toward its by-products of status and prestige. Particularly in the middle ranges of big organizations a "status panic" occurs in which employees make sustained and pathetic efforts to differentiate themselves as individuals. Such efforts may arise as a counterpoise to the increasing rationalization of work. As C. Wright Mills says:

> In the white-collar hierarchies, individuals are often segregated by minute gradations of rank, and, at the same time, subject to a fragmentation of skill. This bureaucratization often breaks up the occupational basis of their prestige. Since the individual may seize upon minute distinctions as bases for status, these distinctions operate against any status solidarity among the mass of employees, often lead to status estrangement from work associates, and to increased status competition. . . . Above all, the hierarchy is often accompanied by a delirium for status merely because of its authoritarian shape: as Karl Mannheim has observed, people who are dependent for everything, including images of themselves, upon place in an authoritarian hierarchy, will all the more frantically cling to claims of status.[1]

The demand for status often expresses itself in sustained efforts to borrow prestige from whatever source possible.

[9] W. Cohn: "Social Status and the Ambivalence Hypothesis," *American Sociological Review*, Vol. 25, pp. 508-13.

[1] C. Wright Mills: *White Collar* (New York: Oxford University Press, Inc.; 1951), pp. 254-5.

Organizations of many kinds now "sell" prestige to their members, and employees borrow status from the company in which they work. "If white-collar relations with supervisors and higher-ups, with customers or clients, become so impersonal as seriously to limit borrowing prestige from them, prestige is often borrowed from the firm or the company itself. The fetishism of the enterprise, and identification with the firm, are often as relevant for the white-collar hirelings as for the managers. This identification may be implemented by the fact that the work itself . . . offers little chance for external prestige claims and internal self-esteem. So the work one does is buried in the firm." [2]

In his analysis of union intellectuals, Harold Wilensky notes the status-borrowing activities of a "careerist" type who is closely identified with the hierarchy of his union and is oriented toward a career within it. Having no ideological commitments, no nonorganizational goals, and "very little if any professional identification," his satisfactions center around the chance for social mobility through his job. "His union job means a chance to bask in the reflected glory of great men." [3] Dwaine Marvick found similarly that those in hierarchical roles in a federal bureaucracy were considerably more concerned with organizational prestige, influence, security, and career advancement than their specialist colleagues.[4] Such "institutionalists" were also more committed to the organization; theirs was "place orientation" as opposed to the "task orientation" of specialists. Those in hierarchical roles tend to be less concerned with the intrinsic character of their work than with its by-products of status, prestige, and security. This is partly because their roles stress subjective, promotional, and human-relations skills and activities.

Following Sullivan, we assume that status anxiety con-

[2] Ibid., p. 243.

[3] H. Wilensky: *Intellectuals in Trade Unions* (Glencoe, Illinois: The Free Press; 1956), p. 146.

[4] D. Marvick: *Career Perspectives in a Bureaucratic Setting* (Ann Arbor: University of Michigan Press; 1954), pp. 52-4.

tributes to the acceptance of organizational authority. Essentially, the status system reinforces authority by structuring interpersonal relations in terms of the relative prestige of the actors. Their roles are nicely defined. Subordination and superordination are prescribed. In this sense, the status system provides a form of "staging" that conditions behavior in organizationally relevant directions.[5] Interpersonal transactions are always held in the senior's office, which always contains patent indexes of his superior prestige. The subordinate asks for an appointment with the superior. It is clear whose time is at a premium. If the superior wishes, he can aggravate the resulting dependency by requiring that the subordinate wait. His secretary constitutes a fairly obvious prop, validating her boss's prestige claims by virtue of his preoccupation with important affairs.

Although some pathological results may follow, this milieu may also increase organizational effectiveness. By making authority relations highly visible, the status system prescribes the roles of all parties. Ambiguity and conflict are reduced. No time is wasted establishing dominance by informal gamesmanship. One can turn immediately to the business at hand. The limits of discussion and dissent are outlined. Since important decisions can rarely be reconciled by an objectively superior alternative, the capacity to decide on the basis of authority becomes all the more significant. Because conclusive proof is not forthcoming, debate might otherwise go on indefinitely. Decisions can, moreover, be conclusive since once superior authority has legitimated them, no further discussion of their merits is permitted, at least officially. Interpersonal relations can be smoothly negotiated if both parties play their roles skillfully, the senior by masking his dominance, the junior by discreet validation of the superior's prestige and wisdom. The interplay of staging and learned deference attitudes makes manipulation rather than command the common organizational currency. Such results are

[5] Erving Goffman: *The Presentation of Self in Everyday Life* (New York: Doubleday & Co., Inc.; 1959).

illustrated by the way that men brought into the Navy during World War II quickly accepted its "affirm-and-conform" rationale.[6] The organization's "structured field" molded behavior in desired ways. Tradition, authority, and status prescribed appropriate responses in practically every situation.

The status system enhances motivation and discipline by its promise of highly valued rewards. Although the displacement of value from work to its by-products has distorted the traditional relationship between status and achievement, status and prestige are highly valued in themselves. Parenthetically, such displacement is one of the pathological results of the status system, some aspects of which will be treated in Chapter 9. We saw earlier that status anxiety is common in the middle and upper ranges of big organizations. Men strive to validate their uniqueness by the acquisition of greater status and prestige. Those in hierarchical posts assign disproportionate weight to such values because their work offers less intrinsic satisfaction than that of specialists. The absence of objective criteria of performance in higher posts aggravates status anxiety. Status perquisites are highly reinforced because they reduce such tensions. Meanwhile, control of the status-distribution system gives elites a powerful sanction. In sum, the high reward potential of the organization provides compelling incentives for many of its members.

The distribution of such rewards, moreover, makes for sustained effort. Status expectations and potentials are perceived as virtually unlimited. The higher one ascends in the organization, the greater the relative amounts of status, prestige, and income he enjoys. There is a continuing incentive to strive. However, it must be noted that such striving

[6] A.K. Davis: "Bureaucratic Patterns in the Navy Officer Corps," in R.K. Merton, *et al.*, eds.: *Reader in Bureaucracy* (Glencoe, Illinois: The Free Press; 1952). On the general question of individual fusion with the group, see P.M. Blau: "A Theory of Social Integration," *American Journal of Sociology*, Vol. 45, pp. 545-56.

varies with age and class. As Hollingshead and Redlich report, the career aspirations of upper-middle-class men (class 2) in New Haven are quite different during their early and late career stages. "A young male looks forward to the time when he will . . . earn $15,000, $25,000, or as much as $50,000 a year and will help make decisions, not just carry out those made by others." But at fifty, men had begun to say: "My job is to hold on." [7] Moreover, this class, over seventy per cent of whom are members of national business organizations, was the most status conscious of the five class strata in the city. They "are extremely sensitive to how they must behave . . . in order to continue to move upward in the managerial hierarchy." [8]

We can now consider the psychology of small-group behavior. The organization is composed of many *small groups* which compete for its resources and rewards. Each has its own social structure and its means of controlling its members. Research on small groups can help us understand behavior in big organizations. It is necessary to emphasize that the organization is not equated with the individuals in it. We say that "the organization" does this or that, but only as a convenient way of saying that certain *individuals* in the organization are behaving in one way or another. Having said this, a qualification is necessary. Big organizations often become a psychological reality, reflecting our tendency to reify abstractions such as the "church," or the "nation," endowing them with personality. When the retiring clerk says, "The corporation has been good to me," we may suppose that he actually thinks of the "corporation" as an entity distinct from those who represent it. The significance of such myths, of course, is not that they are illogical but that they influence behavior.

The group character of organization may be clearer when considered from the perspective of the individual. He usually

[7] A.B. Hollingshead and F.C. Redlich: *Social Class and Mental Illness* (New York: John Wiley & Sons, Inc.; 1958), p. 86.

[8] Ibid.

performs a specific task in a group of specialists, organized with a hierarchy not unlike that of the whole organization. For the individual, this subunit often becomes *the organization,* since his work and his life chances are bound up with it. He may develop considerable loyalty to it, regarding other groups as competitors. He will probably form close personal ties with some of his fellow workers, and he will certainly evaluate them in terms of their technical skill and personal attributes. In this sense organization behavior is group behavior, and the generalizations of small-group theory apply.

It is well known that most individuals need recognition and a sense of belonging; the strength of this need is shown by the fact that exclusion is among the most painful of group sanctions. Indeed, some individuals develop such strong identification with their subgroups that intergroup rivalry is the rule in big organizations. Roethlisberger and Dickson, for example, found a highly protective attitude among a bank-wiring group; also, the very knowledge that they were being investigated (read "recognized") increased the output of the group.[9] In comparing two departments in a big organization, Argyris found similarly that department X, which gave free rein to its members' needs for security, recognition, and variety, in turn developed warm personal relationships and high morale. The need for informal organization was hardly felt. On the other hand, in department Y, where such needs were unmet, members expressed a desire for recognition and for closer personal ties and sought them in informal ways.[1] Other evidence shows that workers try to ease feelings of anonymity and impersonality by informal personal relations, and that a permissive atmosphere often increases job satisfaction and even productivity.[2]

[9] F.J. Roethlisberger and W.J. Dickson: *Management and the Worker* (Cambridge: Harvard University Press; 1941).

[1] C. Argyris: "Fusion of the Individual with the Organization," *American Sociological Review,* Vol. 19, pp. 267-72.

[2] Among others, D. Katz, N. Jacoby, N. Morse: *Productivity, Supervision and Morale* (Ann Arbor: Survey Research Center; 1950).

However, some limitations of group research must be mentioned. One problem is that its frequent use of experimental designs creates artificial situations. For example, one well-known study of decision making established a statusless group. Yet in human behavior one of the firm generalizations is that whenever people meet, age, experience, expertise, and power create status differences. Research from which status factors have been excluded has important limitations. Much of the research also requires that participants be informed of the objectives and procedures of study, with the result that spontaneity is lost and behavior may be affected in unknown and perhaps unknowable ways. This disadvantage of social research is aggravated by the difficulty of securing accurate diagnoses when man himself is the observer.

Despite this, the findings of group research are very useful. Individuals behave differently in groups than when alone, and such differences have organizational consequences. An obvious example is seen in mob psychology where anonymity provokes behaviors that individuals qua individuals would not consider. Although crowd behavior undoubtedly reflects personal needs to release aggression, we know that group situations also encourage conformity. The hierarchical character of groups strengthens this tendency. If groups are to act, some structuring must exist. Even in antiauthoritarian associations, such as religious sects, the need "to achieve the imperative goals" of the organization insures bureaucratization and gradations of power and authority. While authority and power in such contexts lean more heavily upon charismatic legitimations, operational claims override equalitarian values.[3] In any informal group situation, once a goal is set, certain individuals gradually assume leadership, by virtue of skill, intelligence, the wish to dominate, or perhaps mere ignorance of their own limitations. The resulting pattern may become crystallized through group acceptance, apathy,

[3] P.M. Harrison: "Weber's Categories of Authority and Voluntary Associations," *American Sociological Review*, Vol. 25, pp. 232-7.

and oligarchy, all of which place a monopoly of information and patronage in a few hands. In such situations there is a tendency for the individual to seek "consensual validation" of his views by comparing them with the "official line," which is assumed to reflect "inside" information, an institution-wide view, etc. That is, he will look *elsewhere,* to the group and to its authority figures, for cues that define approved opinions.[4]

Group influence on the individual is thus partly the result of imitation. Much of learning and other social behavior is imitative. Examples include the child copying his parents' speech, the adolescent aping the dress and mannerisms of his peers, and the adult incorporating as his own the opinions of status figures on issues about which he has no first-hand information. The motivation is probably a desire for psychological security and a feeling of belonging. We imitate those we admire. The weight of such majority demands (which are often rationally determined and necessary, although on the other hand they may persist long after the conditions that inspired them have disappeared) is suggested by the finding that men on conservative university faculties are more likely to become increasingly conservative with age than are members of less conservative faculties.[5]

Rashevsky has explained the principle of imitation as follows: "Apparently the sight of another individual who exhibits R_1 (response) acts upon the first individual as an external stimulus S_1, which adds a *variable amount* E_1 (excitation) to the constant amount E_1 which is produced by inner psychological states and which determines the natural inner drive toward R_1." Again, "it is natural to assume that the sight of X individuals exhibiting R_1 will be X times as effec-

[4] Among others, J. Thibaut and H. Kelly: *The Social Psychology of Groups* (New York: John Wiley and Sons, Inc.; 1959), pp. 239-55.

[5] P. Lazarsfeld and W. Theilens: *The Academic Mind* (Glencoe, Illinois: The Free Press; 1958), pp. 248-9.

tive as the sight of one individual."[6] While we now have no way of precisely weighting X, and although a "law of diminishing returns" probably reduces the impact of repeated stimuli, it *is* "natural" that attitudes held by a majority of the group, including its leaders whose opinions carry exceptional weight, will induce compliance among its members.[7]

The individual's deference to group norms has been established by many experimental studies, including a celebrated one by Sherif.[8] Using a common perceptual illusion that a fixed light in a dark room is actually moving about, he found that different individuals gave consistently different judgments as to the alleged movements. He next placed three such individuals together and found that *under group influence each abandoned his earlier judgment in favor of a common evaluation.* (Everyone, by the way, still maintained that the light moved.)

Another experiment, involving a situation where a correct answer was possible, is equally suggestive.[9] Asch placed a small group (7-9) in a classroom, explaining that they would be shown lines of different lengths and that their task was to match those of equal length. The lines were placed vertically on a large card, with an index line on another card placed alongside. Each student called out the number of the line he believed identical with the index line. Three trials were given. During the first two the experiment proceeded smoothly because the distinctions between the lines

[6] N. Rashevsky: "Two Models: Imitative Behavior and Distribution of Status," in P. Lazarsfeld, ed.: *Mathematical Thinking in the Social Sciences* (Glencoe, Illinois: The Free Press; 1954), p. 80. (Italics in original.)

[7] E. Stotland: "Peer Groups and Reactions to Power Figures," in D. Cartwright, ed.: *Studies in Social Power* (Ann Arbor: Survey Research Center; 1959), pp. 53-68.

[8] M. Sherif and C. Sherif: *An Outline of Social Psychology* (New York: Harper & Brothers; 1952).

[9] S.E. Asch: *Social Psychology* (New York: Prentice-Hall, Inc.; 1952).

were obvious. But on the third trial one member began to call out numbers that were different from the others. Without his knowledge all other members of the group had been instructed to give unanimously a *wrong* answer.

Following the matching, this individual was questioned by the group. Was it likely that he could have been right and everyone else wrong? What were the reasons for his judgments, etc.? Finally he was told about the arrangement and its objectives. For our purposes the important thing is that despite the obvious length differences and the ease of matching them, after a series of tests one third of the dissenting individuals accepted the judgment of the group. Asch divided these "yielders" into three categories, those who actually thought they saw what the majority saw; those who immediately decided: "I am wrong, they are right"; and those who were not much concerned with accuracy but suppressed their own judgment because of a need to conform.

A study by Coch and French dealing with resistance to change in a factory is also useful.[1] Following a slight change in her job, a machine operator produced at a reduced rate of fifty units per hour. Some ten days later, however, she reached normal production (about sixty-five units), and soon began to exceed the rates of her group. She then became the target of considerable abuse as a "rate-buster," whereupon her productivity decreased to the group's level. Three weeks after the change, the other operators were transferred, leaving this girl alone. Within four days she was turning out eighty-three units per hour and produced steadily at that rate thereafter. A classic example of group influence was found by Roethlisberger and Dickson.[2] Their bank-wiring group set a standard for a fair day's work consisting of a certain number of completed units. Men who exceeded this rate were called "speed kings" and criticized severely by the group. On the other hand, those who failed

[1] L. Coch and J.R.P. French, Jr.: "Overcoming Resistance to Change," *Human Relations*, Vol. I, pp. 512-32.

[2] F.J. Roethlisberger and W.J. Dickson: op. cit.

to maintain the rate were called "chiselers" and were censored for violating the group's expectations.

Compliance in organizations is thus encouraged by small group sanctions, most of which invoke the anxiety-conformity-approval syndrome but vary considerably according to the situation. We know that middle-class child training fosters a high degree of discipline, whereas a lower-class background is considerably more tolerant of aggression. In the industrial situations mentioned above, ridicule, censure, and even blows were used to punish nonconformists. On the other hand, in organizations engaged in highly technical work requiring considerable education and training (correlated in turn with middle-class drives for success), sanctions are rather more Machiavellian, and rewards meet status needs more often than economic ones. Big organizations encourage the use of subtle deprivations. Decisions affecting an individual are sometimes made anonymously for reasons that remain unknown even to the subleaders of the group in which the individual works. Often the elite feels no compulsion to explain its actions, particularly if subjective or "political" reasons are involved. In such cases "the good of the organization" provides a sufficient rationalization. As a result the individual may not know for some time that he has been disciplined, while the actual reasons for it may elude him permanently. Here again, hierarchy, size, and the diffused responsibility of the organization are decisive.

Deprivation of response is a common reinforcement whereby the group disciplines the individual (and achieves discipline) by isolating him. This is at best a painful experience, since socialization insures that our emotional and physical needs are bound up with an accepted position in the group. An extreme case was reported in England recently when a crane operator who had refused to join his union in a walkout was given the "silent treatment" for several months. In our society where personal "maturity" is usually equated with conformity and group acceptance, deprivations of this kind are probably exceptionally painful. The need to be liked, which Europeans find one of our most noteworthy characteristics, is a powerful incentive to conformity.

Deprivation of response is most effective in highly self-conscious organizations, where desired behavior is induced by systematic conditioning. The uncanny ability of the Marine Corps' "boot-camp" program to instill loyalty and morale in recruits comes to mind, but this program differs only in degree from the indoctrination used by many big organizations. Organizational loyalty will always be strained by the disparity between individual expectations and satisfactions, and by such training, organizations are in effect anticipating the future. When high morale persists despite the disenchantment that experience must bring, we can assume that a high proportion of members have internalized the organization's values and accepted its means. In so doing each becomes a positive stimulus, increasing the authority of group values, making defection less likely and deprivations more painful.

In this chapter the bureaucratic model has been conceptualized as a "structured field." In such a field, highly differentiated systems of authority, status, and small groups provide patent and compelling stimuli that evoke the individual's learned deference to authority. They provide a psychological climate that encourages compliance. Such responses are rewarding because they reduce anxiety and increase mobility chances by securing the approval of authority figures who control the organization's distribution system. Small groups play a similar socializing role. They use various rewards and sanctions to inculcate desired values in their members. Although their norms may be either functional or dysfunctional in terms of organizational goals, the significant result is that small groups provide stimuli that condition individual behavior in large, bureaucratic organizations.

CHAPTER 6

PATTERNS OF ACCOMMODATION: UPWARD-MOBILES

WE NOW turn to the discrete types of personal accommodation that seem to occur in organizations. Following interpersonal theory, we assume that men behave according to the perceived expectations of a given social situation. Over a period of time such responses become relatively consistent; they are continually reinforced because they meet compelling individual needs for security, recognition, and group acceptance. While such accommodations are always the result of *interaction* between the bureaucratic situation and personality, social and organizational values mainly determine the character of functional (anxiety-reducing) and dysfunctional (anxiety-producing) behavior in a given culture. Personality is worked out in a social and interpersonal context. As Sullivan observes, man gradually develops through his relations with significant others a self-system, a personal style of behavior that rejects anxiety-producing responses in favor of those that insure approval. The bureaucratic situation seems to evoke three kinds of personal accommodation, each associated with one of our three personality types, the upward-mobiles, the indifferents, and the ambivalents. In this chapter we shall consider the most significant of these, the *upward-mobiles.*

Writing early in this century, Max Weber could speak of the contempt with which Americans regarded bureaucracy. This observation seems less germane today. Not only has respect for big organizations increased, since they meet our pragmatic test of success, but demands for conformity have muted criticism based upon less tangible criteria. In many sectors, personal and ideological conventionality have become prerequisite for jobs that once required only technical skill and adequate performance. The trend many be associated with decreasing mobility, or at least with more structured conditions of participation resulting from greater specialization, the increasing size of many work places, and an emerging career pattern of long service in a single organization.

Such changes brought the obsolescence of certain skill groups and their replacement by those who could meet the new conditions. Just as the guild artisan's craftsmanship yielded to mass production, the owner-entrepreneur was displaced by the corporation manager. An essentially "political" economy brought the need for new talents such as "human relations" that could placate employees and clientele disenchanted by the size and impersonality of modern organizations. Someone was also required to interpret the rhetoric of "service" which now eased the traditional profit theme. Hence the "public-relations" expert. Significantly, the new skills were often concerned with subjective matters, as if the dominant technical passion required some modification. These skills were often characteristic of upward-mobiles, who gradually assumed great influence through their monopolization of hierarchical roles and of the distribution of the organization's rewards.

This theory of adaptation rests upon the findings of cultural psychology, which replaced earlier conceptions of a static human nature with the idea of a "marketing personality" who could nicely adjust to changing social and organizational expectations. In this context we can think of a "bureaucratic personality" as an adaptive type. However, since the members of any organization will always react somewhat differently, some qualifications are necessary. While three discrete patterns of accommodation seem to exist, the "upward-mobiles," the "indifferents," and the "ambivalents," each is an ideal type. The bureaucratic situation evokes various degrees of motivation. One "upward-mobile" may have compulsive success drives that are quite unrealistic, while another may retain a rational estimate of his own ability and of the rewards he may reasonably expect. With the "indifferents" and "ambivalents" a similar range of behavior exists. Our types must, therefore, be viewed as *modal* patterns of adjustment to the bureaucratic situation.

The existence of such types underscores an important theoretical assumption in this study of the organizational society, namely, that not everything that is significant about an individual can be explained by the group or occupation in which he lives and works. While sociological theory provides a central basis for understanding behavior, it neglects to some extent the influence of individual personality. Man is not only a social animal; he is also a Hobbesian egoist whose unique personality and life experience influence his perception of interpersonal situations. To this extent every definition of a social phenomenon is individual, and we can assume that responses will vary somewhat accordingly. Social structure and socialization are undoubtedly dominant in shaping personality, but the individual is more than a passive cultural phenomenon.[1]

[1] The conception that human behavior occurs in the context of certain objective conditions and that a given individual's *perception* of these conditions is a vital factor in resultant behavior is often credited to W.I. Thomas. In his view, subjective experience is the intervening variable between objective conditions and individual behavior. For a summary and evaluation of his "situational approach," see E.H. Volkart: *Social Behavior and Personality: Contributions of W.I. Thomas to Theory and Social Research* (New York: Social Science Research Council; 1951). Note the similarity between this conception of behavior and

If social structure alone were responsible for personality and behavior, our discrete types of accommodation would presumably not exist. The organization would evoke very similar accommodations in all of its members. But as we have seen, not only do different patterns of class socialization and consequent differences in perception and reaction to interpersonal situations characterize individuals, but the same pattern of socialization may evoke different responses among those subject to it. This combining of social and psychological theory is validated by the experience of Durkheim who began his classic study of *Suicide* with the intention of isolating the social roots of self-destruction, but who ended with an essentially psychological and individual cause, *anomie*.

With these qualifications in mind, we now turn to an analysis of the values and behavior of the typical "upward-mobile." Although his behavior may at times appear unappealing, we are concerned with it only as a form of accommodation to the bureaucratic environment. Our interest is analytic rather than clinical.

The upward-mobiles are typically distinguished by high morale; their level of job satisfaction is high. Indeed, the process and criteria by which they are selected insures that they will have an unfailing optimism. The reasons for this are clear. They identify strongly with the organization and derive strength from their involvement. Their dividends also include disproportionate shares of the organization's rewards in power, income, and ego reinforcement. As we have seen, subjective inequality is a built-in feature of big organiza-

---

that of H.S. Sullivan whose personality theory rests essentially upon individual definitions of "*complex, peculiarly characterized situations,*" D.R. Blitsten: *The Social Theories of Harry Stack Sullivan* (New York: William-Frederick Press; 1953), p. 21. (Italics added.) For an early attempt to apply psychology to the analysis of political behavior, see Harold D. Lasswell: *Psychopathology and Politics* (Chicago: University of Chicago Press; 1930); his *Power and Personality* (New York: W.W. Norton & Co., Inc.; 1948), is also useful in this context.

tions and is rationalized on the basis of equality of opportunity. Power is easily justified by those who have it, since it confirms daily their right (achieved in fair competition) to possess it. The upward-mobiles will not, therefore, seriously question a system that has proved its rationality. The system remains an internalized article of faith until, as in the case of Arthur Miller's hero in *Death of A Salesman*, the disparity between rhetoric and reality becomes irrepressible. But even then, self-punitive mechanisms may be invoked to preserve the myth: *personal failure* rather than the failure of the system provides a rationalization.

This ability to identify strongly with the system is highly productive in personal terms since it qualifies the upward-mobile for the organization's major rewards. (As we saw earlier, group influence and rank are a function of acceptance of the group's values.) The organization qua organization has meaning for him, evoking loyalty, affirmation, and a constant point of reference. Having accepted its legitimacy and rationality, he can act on the basis of its value premises. The capacity for identification has great strategic value today because social power is rather evenly divided among competing groups. This condition sharpens the organization's conflicts with competitors and puts a premium on loyalty and certainty among its members. The organization tends to resemble a church, which needs champions to endorse its values and to increase its survival power. No dissenters need apply. The demand is for conformity. A rational and sustained attention to business is required; and the heterodoxy possible in a less organized, more secure society becomes a luxury, because it impairs unity.

Since he accepts the larger purposes of the organization, the upward-mobile finds involvement easy. His personality enables him to deal in oversimplification and idealization. He can act without an immaculate cause. He can overlook the contradictions in the routine operations of the organization, as distinct from its official myths. He is able to find certainty and consistency in an organization that is imperfect because it is real. In a sense, he must avoid reality by cultivating the illusion that its actions eventuate in perfect justice. This characteristic of perception calls to mind W. I. Thomas' observation: "If men define situations as real, they are real in their consequences."[2] The organization's values are internalized by the upward-mobile, and thus become premises of action. This psychic act provides him with an operational skill: *the capacity for action despite conflicting alternatives and contradictory aims.*

Here a distinction must be made between the upward-mobile's values and his behavior. His low toleration for ambiguity and his deference toward authority might seem to disqualify him for the versatile role playing that big organizations require. In a democratic society, for example, the upward-mobile must pay homage to democratic expectations of equality and impartiality, even though he knows that some are born to lead and others to follow. However, he can usually assume the appropriate roles whether or not he identifies with the underlying ideals. He manipulates the democratic consensus favoring permissive authority relations and recognizes that "getting along with people" has career utility. Such role playing emphasizes the need for mock behavior in which polite fictions, irony, and banter are used to "get a message across" without disrupting the status relations of those concerned.

Ritualistic behavior is often used to conceal resentment or hostility that, indulged in, would paralyze interpersonal relations:

> One afternoon, a conversation with the manager led to his talking about the effects of promotion on different men in the factory, and eventually, to something of a diatribe against one particular person who had moved up into an executive position the year before. He had tried to get support for the promotion from everybody,

[2] W.I. Thomas: *The Child in America: Behavior Problems and Programs* (New York: Alfred A. Knopf, Inc.; 1932), p. 572.

had blackened the man who was leaving and whose position he hoped to fill, had gone into local politics on the same side as the divisional manager, had displayed unpleasant anxiety when the time came for the decision. Now, despite his fulsome affability, he was unpopular with his colleagues, was looked on by those lower down as a tale-bearer, and so on. All this was delivered with gestures and emphasis distinctly more lively than earlier in the conversation, which ended with this episode, both of us returning to separate desks.

Later in the afternoon, he telephoned the man of whom he had been speaking; there was question of the allocation of a morning's time put in by a shiftworker in one or the other of their departments. The whole matter of dispute was handled with the greatest mateyness and ease; first names were used, there was no sense of effort in maintaining the demonstration of friendliness; there was no overemphasis, nor, on the other hand, any discrepancy between facial expression and words or tone of voice; each other's account of the facts was fully accepted and agreement quickly reached.

Inside the space of one hour, my companion had displayed quite marked enmity and equally well marked friendship toward the same person. There was, as far as I judge, no suspicion of awareness that there was any incompatibility between the two episodes—both were acted through natural expression of two distinct roles.[3]

Such displays of the "marketing orientation" are among the conditions of bureaucratic participation. One point of view suggests that the rigidity of the typical authoritarian sharply limits his ability to play such conflicting roles and thus disqualifies him for success in bureaucratic occupations. Although the upward-mobile type is often authoritarian and

[3] Tom Burns: "Friends, Enemies and the Polite Fiction," *American Sociological Review*, Vol. 18, pp. 659-60. Reprinted by permission of the author.

seems to fit well into authoritarian occupations such as business, medicine, the military, police work, and religion,[4] his manipulative, "other-directed" ethic enables him to play the roles required for success. There is therefore no real conflict between our perception of the upward-mobile as potentially authoritarian, yet at the same time as being able to adapt to several roles. No doubt he will occasionally experience considerable strain in adapting himself, but this problem is surely eased by the fact that most of the time he will occupy a superior position which meets his needs for dominance in interpersonal relations.

In the main, his "self-system" enables him to accept manipulation both of himself and of others as part of the vocaional bargain. Although he may lack spontaneity, he strives to master the "human-relations" approach. He masters the art of the calculated response, in which deference, warmth, enthusiasm, and disapproval are nicely weighted. Like the Navy's gentleman, the upward-mobile is never unintentionally rude. This is a luxury he cannot afford, since like firmly held views, such self-indulgence is of limited career utility.

His efforts to master interpersonal relations are often eased by his associates, who will also play the roles prescribed by their respective positions. Their self-images, their needs, their degree of sophistication, and their level in the hierarchy will guide their behavior. Meanwhile, feedback insures that everyone's behavior will be affected by the perceived reactions of those with whom he communicates. Facial expressions, verbal responses, subtle unspoken expectations, provide the cues. Just as a good lecturer senses when he is "reaching" his audience, the upward-mobile reads the signals his behavior evokes in others. Although this skill will vary among individuals, the distinguishing mark of the upward-mobile is that he *thinks* in such strategic terms

[4] D. Stewart and T. Hoult: "A Social-Psychological Theory of the Authoritarian Personality," *American Journal of Sociology*, Vol. 45, pp. 274-9.

and is able to modify his behavior accordingly. Such behavior is essentially rational and requires an ability to avoid passionate value attachments that might inhibit one's versatility.

We have seen that the power-oriented individual is likely to find the order and security of a bureaucratic career appealing, as opposed, say, to the uncertainty of writing or politics. It seems undeniable that our typical upward-mobile has an exceptional drive for power. This impulse is often symptomatic of a basic insecurity. Since we know that a fear of failure is common among successful executives, we may suppose that this anxiety provokes an exceptional need for control over the environment. Attempts to dominate others and to monopolize any discussion are common manifestations of this need. Whatever its source, anxiety explains some of the upward-mobile's discipline and energy. Certainly the relationship between compulsive striving and personal maladjustment is well known. In a test profile of 243 "best," "average," and "poorest" salespeople, Crafts found that the "best" group scored lower on "stability" and "self-sufficiency." He concluded that "too much" of these qualities was detrimental, "very probably because superiors must be relied on, catered to, and pleased, if the individual is to be successful." [5]

In the United States one finds that high bureaucratic positions are often held by men who are physically large or exceptionally forceful. Hollywood's idealization of the virile male, who solves most problems by a punch in the jaw, both reflects and molds American conceptions of the qualities required for success. Historically, political and economic power have often been grounded in sheer physical strength.[6]

[5] I.W. Crafts, *et al.: Recent Experiments in Psychology* (New York: McGraw-Hill Book Co.; 1938), p. 241.

[6] For an example of such single-mindedness coupled with great physical strength, see A. Gottfried: "The Use of Psychosomatic Categories in a Study of Political Personality," *Western Political Quarterly*, Vol. 8, p. 239, *passim;* an authority on executive recruitment reports that "industry generally won't hire sales trainees unless they are at least

Allied with this physical component is a subjective ability to assume what Weber called a "charismatic" (magical) role. Commanding presence, effective staging, long-range views, an air of infallibility, the ability to dignify commonplace observations—these are typical upward-mobile postures. Their object is to inspire confidence, to appeal to the father-needs of those who find life uncertain. In this context, if the upward-mobile appears a fraud because he promises more than anyone can deliver, it must be admitted that there is a vast market for his fraudulence. Popular naïveté and insecurity provide a sympathetic background for his magical role. The rewards for the ability to inspire confidence are therefore great. The peculiar talent of the upward-mobile is that he recognizes and manipulates this latent human need.

Clinical research supports our hypothesis about the power orientations of successful organization men.[7] The Kaiser Foundation's experience with over 2,000 psychiatric patients and some 1,000 psychosomatic and normal subjects revealed that the "managerial personality," who achieves interpersonal adjustment through dominance, was the most common type among 3,000 cases. Over 600 such individuals supply the basis for the following generalizations. Their behavior is most suggestive. They often assume what has been called a "doctor's-helper" role, that is, they cannot admit that they really need help, but instead they consistently deny their own symptoms and attempt to convince the therapist and others of their normality and excellence. Although they are the largest single group diagnosed, they do not tend to present themselves for therapy; and when they do, they rank lowest among all patients in the number of times they appear for treatment.

---

five feet ten inches tall." He attributes this practice to the belief that tall men possess overpowering personalities which help them close sales. *Nation's Business,* Vol. 49, p. 19.

[7] Timothy Leary: *Interpersonal Diagnosis of Personality* (New York: The Ronald Press Co.; 1956), p. 329 and Ch. 20.

Significantly, and in accordance with the authoritarianism findings, these men tend to misjudge their interpersonal relations. They consistently attribute too much weakness to those with whom they interact. They tend to look down on others. Parenthetically, three times as many military officers exhibit such power-oriented accommodations as do the general run of patients who appear for treatment. The "managerial personality" also tends to be closely identified with his parents, a common quality among those ranking high on the Adorno F scale.

This type is also identified by characteristic illnesses. A high proportion have psychosomatic ailments such as ulcers and hypertension. Anxiety attacks are another typical symptom, apparently because the compulsive, energetic façade used to defend their self-image of control and power breaks down. The admission of anxiety or any form of weakness is the most painful experience possible for this type, and the refusal to recognize it is in part responsible for the common "doctor's-helper" posture. As might be expected, such compulsive individuals tend to present themselves as right and strong; the neurotic person on the other hand presents himself as passive, guilty, and uncertain. In the American and German cultures, according to Timothy Leary, "successful, well-adjusted compulsives are generally respected by others for their diligence and organization. The notion of efficiency is heavily loaded with power connotations." [8]

In interpersonal terms, the managerial type accommodates by security operations that emphasize strength, efficiency, self-control, dominance, and compulsion. "Adjustment through power" provides him with security against anxiety by virtue of the control he achieves over situations and other people. "He gains a feeling of certitude and organization." [9] "He wins awe, admiration, and obedience from others." [1] His own needs and the power position to which

[8] Ibid., p. 328.
[9] Ibid., p. 325.
[1] Ibid.

they have driven him affect his interpersonal relations in predictable ways. "In general it will be found that rigid, autocratic individuals seek out docile, admiring followers. They are most comfortable when they are paired with those who symbiotically match their interpersonal reflexes—who flatter, obey, and respect them."[2] On the other hand, when such types must interact with those of similar character, a real power struggle may ensue.

The way in which individuals who work together become "locked" into mutually satisfying relationships suggests the utility of interpersonal theory in organizational analysis. Here again, evidence from the Kaiser research provides the example. As Leary says, a "most common setting for rigid interpersonal relationships is the occupational."[3] He then traces his experience with a management group comprising four executives responsible for a manufacturing and distributing plant of a national corporation. Although the analysis began at the request of the firm's general manager, who was worried about the drinking of one of the executives, it soon became apparent that the drinking was merely a symptom of rigid and destructive reactions among individuals in the group.

Each executive was given several tests, including a self-evaluation profile that enabled each to rate himself. All four men rated themselves as strong, hypernormal, and responsible. They were also asked to rate each of their colleagues. After these ratings had been charted (see page 177) and combined with the psychologists' evaluation of each individual's personality, a "self-deception" index was established. In each case there was considerable self-delusion about the character of each executive's interpersonal relations with other members of the group. While the production manager, for example, claimed to be strong and somewhat friendly, his associates saw him "as an extremely cold, hard, unfriendly, selfish person." The general manager, whom

[2] Ibid.

[3] Ibid., p. 403 and Ch. 25.

the psychologists regarded as the most effective member of the group, had the smallest perceptual disparity. While he was less sympathetic and friendly than he claimed, both his colleagues and the psychologists saw him as a "strong, forceful, nonhostile person." "They clearly admire and respect him."

In terms of interpersonal theory, such misconceptions of self and others must result in strained, unproductive relations. Moreover, these relations tend to be reinforced by the dynamics of the situation. For example, the general manager is locked into a close and "mutually self-deceptive" relation with the personnel manager. "Although they both try to believe that they have a collaborative, friendly union of equals, actually an intense leader-follower association exists." This relationship, moreover, meets the personal needs of each. Although neither is aware of its real character, the other members of the group are, and their perception of the situation further distorts the group's relationship. The production manager despises the personnel man for his dependence upon the general manager, while the sales manager is jealous of the general manager's approval of the personnel man. The latter, in turn, is terrified by the production and sales managers, who perceive him as weak and self-effacing.

The upward-mobile accommodation is worked out in similar interpersonal terms. Since upward-mobiles often get to the top of the organization and must deal with members at every level, the significance of their own values and behavior is clear. If these are marked by a need to ward off anxiety or to dominate others, organizational relations will be complicated. Since such compelling needs and the security operations they encourage are almost impossible to change, they may prove disastrous for the organization.

This probability suggests one of the built-in dysfunctions of big organizations, namely, the fact that the very qualities required for success, including great energy, dominance, status consciousness, and adaptive role playing, can very

SELF-DECEPTION INDEX*

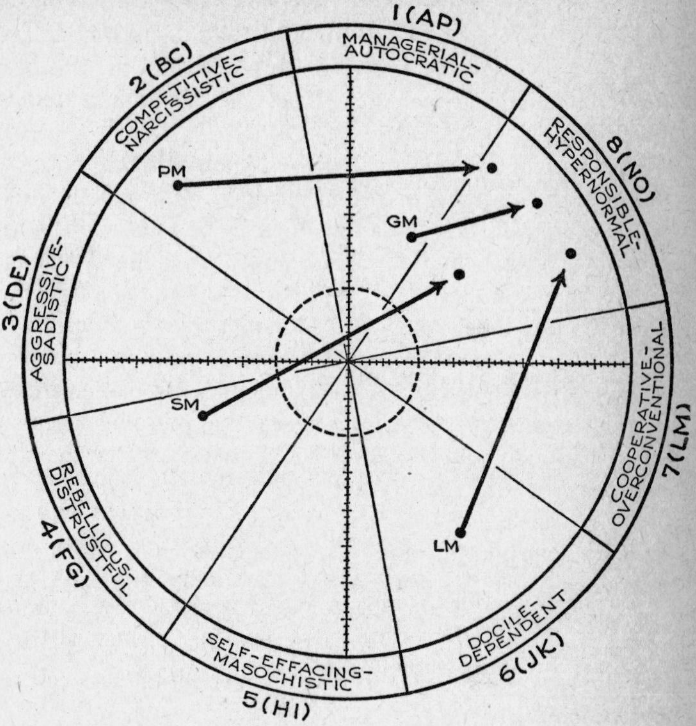

Social Stimulus Value of Four Executives; Plotted Indices of Self-Deception. *Key:* The labeled points (e.g., PM) represent the pooled Level I-S behavior of the subject as rated by others. The arrows link the Level I-S score to the subject's self-perception. The length of the arrow indicates how much self-deception exists. The direction of the arrow indicates what the subject misperceives.

* From Timothy Leary: *Interpersonal Diagnosis of Personality: A Functional Theory and Methodology for Personality Evaluation,* Fig. 47, p. 407. Copyright 1957 The Ronald Press Company.

easily distort interpersonal relations within the organization. However, organizations can take a great deal of punishment, and inertia itself often provides a substitute for leadership.

Bound up with the upward-mobile's capacity for action in ambiguous situations is an ability to view individuals in essentially detached terms. To some extent the successful organizer must view men as instruments, as pawns to be manipulated in some master plan. The intensity of this impulse varies from relatively innocuous forms, on the one hand, to the rigidity of a military leader who will make any sacrifice to take a strategic position. But the difference is merely one of degree; the mentality is often similar. Following a study of 473 executives from various fields, Gardner says of their relations with others:

> In general, the mobile and successful executive looks to his superiors with a feeling of personal attachment and tends to identify himself with them. His superiors represent for him a symbol of his own achievement and activity desires, and the successful junior tends to identify himself with these traits in those who have achieved more. . . . On the other hand, he looks to his subordinates in an essentially impersonal way, seeing them as "doers of work" rather than as people. This does not mean that he is cold and treats them casually. In fact, he tends to be rather sympathetic to their problems. But he still treats them impersonally, with no real or deep interest in them as persons. It is almost as if he viewed his subordinates as representatives of things he has left behind, both factually and emotionally. The only direction of his emotional energy that is real to him is upward and toward the symbols of that upward interest, his superiors.[4]

[4] B. Gardner: "What Makes Successful and Unsuccessful Executives," *Advanced Management*, Vol. 13, p. 118; similar attitudes are traced in W. Henry: "The Business Executive: The Psychodynamics of a Social Role," *American Journal of Sociology*, Vol. 54, pp. 286-91.

This suggests that the capacity to rationalize organizational claims is part of the value equipment of the upward-mobile. He may respect individual dissent and error, but the question is one of *priority,* and in the last analysis he will accept the organization's values. His ability to appraise situations objectively and to act appropriately is bound up with his loyalty to collective values and abstractions. Since he identifies himself with the organization, in a measure ranging from casual opportunism to compulsive surrender, he becomes an instrument of such values. He becomes *the organization* and can thus accept its logical imperatives without much regard for competing individual values. The wrongs inflicted in defense of institutionalized ideals are well known. To some extent they can be explained in terms of the total loyalty that organizations demand and some individuals seek.

In the context of Merton's distinction, the upward-mobile is typically a "local." [5] Unlike the "cosmopolitan" who has a broad disciplinary or national perspective, his interests and aspirations are tied to his own organization. Always loyal, he regards its rules and actions as "the one best way" to handle large numbers of people. If the organization's claims occasionally result in injustice, this is inevitable in an imperfect world. Never doubting the supremacy of collective values, the upward-mobile enthrones administrative, keeping-the-organization-going skills and values. This accounts in part for his ambivalence toward the specialist whose professional norms compete with his loyalty to the organization. In all this, he personifies the "routinization of charisma" whereby organizations have tended historically to become ever more rational and monistic. A man without a "calling," he brings little passion to his work. Rather, he is a "quill-

[5] Robert K. Merton: *Social Theory and Social Structure,* rev. ed. (Glencoe, Illinois: The Free Press; 1957), pp. 393-5 and Ch. 10; also, A.W. Gouldner: "Cosmopolitans and Locals: Toward an Analysis of Latent Social Roles," *Administrative Science Quarterly,* Vols. 2, 3, pp. 281-306; 444-80.

bearing mammal," a dealer in means for whom the paraphernalia of organization outweigh claims of "mission," creed, and party. These tend instead to become instrumental, honorific abstractions used to evoke affirmation and loyalty in the rank and file.

Acceptance of the organization's goals commits the upward-mobile to conformity and to impatience with those who qualify and dissent. As a result, he tends to personalize opposition, finding it difficult to accept as a matter of principle or honest divergence, and attributing it instead to a querulous wish on the dissenter's part to be different for difference's sake. His temperamental affinity for clear-cut causes and decisive action is relevant here. He will not understand those who fail to see what to him is so clearly evident. The fact that his personal values are not always shared will escape or puzzle him. His hostility toward heterodoxy may be sharpened by a natural resentment that others should escape the discipline and sacrifice that ambition has required of him.

The upward-mobile's dislike for controversial causes is functional because organizational claims now cover such matters. Political opinions, patterns of consumption, off-work activity, etc., tend to fall into the bureaucratic net. By honoring conventional values the upward-mobile not only reinforces the standards by which he himself is measured, he also increases the probability that conformity will occur throughout the organization. This phenomenon is clearly apparent in countries such as England where a remarkable social control is achieved through each class's imitation of the one above it. In big organizations a similar mechanism is apparent in the elite's personification of majority values and in the internalization of those values by subordinates. The efficiency and discipline insured by the resulting "upward-looking posture" is incalculable.

The upward-mobile defines such necessities as virtues and accommodates himself accordingly with a minimum of strain. In part this is because manipulation of self is perceived as a necessary instrument to preferred ends. On the other hand, he may not even think in these terms but may instead accept such behaviors as rational prescriptions that follow naturally from his career orientation. He may feel no sense of deprivation at being required to accommodate, because he feels no sense of conflict. As a result, he will not understand those "ambivalents" who object to the acquisitive demands of the organization. This distinction between bureaucratic types is the result of basic differences in their perception of situations. Their modes of accommodation differ accordingly.

The upward-mobile idealizes action and knows that it requires oversimplification. Here his capacity for impersonal thinking is helpful since it enables him to separate out the parts of a problem and to handle each in turn without regard for their complexity or for their broader implications. Any self-deception involved here may or may not be consciously experienced. The ability to set aside the personal or idealistic factors of a problem permits "universalistic" decisions that meet organization demands. As Goethe said, the "acting man" is often without conscience. But more than the mere recognition of the required measures is involved. There are many individuals, one suspects, who know what behavior is required in certain situations, but cannot fill the prescription. In such cases personality is involved, rather than strategy or information. The difference is that between diagnosis and cure. It is the difference between the friend who tells one to "stop worrying" and the psychiatrist who sets about removing the conditions that inspire worry.

In all this we have undoubtedly exaggerated the upward-mobile's rationality and oversimplified the behavioral mechanisms involved. In suggesting that his accommodation is mainly a matter of pragmatic choice, we have barely avoided saying that anyone could become an upward-mobile if he wished. However, desire must always be reinforced by an awareness of the conditions of successful participation, and the personality and the skills required to manipulate them. Our upward-mobiles include not only those who want power, but also those who have the self-discipline and the temperament necessary to achieve it.

Another characteristic of the upward-mobile is his status anxiety, often manifested in a compulsive concern with rank and the symbols of prestige. The term "anxiety" is deliberate since his concern with status and with its derivatives of power and prestige goes beyond mere sensitivity to define a general orientation. Like the search for power, status enchantment is a constant element in the upward-mobile equation. The authoritarian-personality research found, significantly, that such an orientation is common among individuals who seem to find the bureaucratic environment congenial. As we have seen, status differentiation plays a critical role in big organizations. It provides a psychological environment that is conducive to efficiency in operational terms, reinforcing authority, minimizing overt conflict, and structuring interpersonal relations.

Status will be defined here as the prestige or deference attached to the role or position one holds in an organizational hierarchy.[6] Although status is not always conferred according to formal hierarchical role, since some members (such as our "ambivalents") will not accept line or hierarchial definitions of relative status, in the main status and prestige are assigned and rewarded by elites in terms of formal organizational values. In contemporary society high status is usually articulated with high office in some large-scale organization. The other major basis for status ascription is occupational role, which may in the case of such high-status occupations as physician or Supreme Court justice be played independently or in a small group.

It seems equally clear that status has obligations as well as

[6] Sociologists define "status" as the *position* an individual occupies in the social hierarchy, but I use it here in its popular connotation. R. LaPiere: *A Theory of Social Control* (New York: McGraw-Hill Book Co.; 1954); K. Davis: "A Conceptual Analysis of Stratification," *American Sociological Review*, Vol. 7, pp. 309-21.

rights and privileges. Those possessing large amounts of it enjoy preferential amounts of income, authority, and security; but in return they must behave in ways approved by the status conferring group or organization. Such obligations, of course, discourage many (including our "indifferents") from seeking higher status, since the rewards do not seem worth the effort. At the same time, a parasitic alternative may be used, the borrowing of status through association with prestigeful figures who do meet their obligations. This is not easy, however, since the latter are naturally reluctant to risk depreciation of their own status currency by sharing it with those who have smaller amounts. In any case, status aspirations play an important part in behavior. By granting or withdrawing status and prestige, organizations control our actions. The effectiveness of status manipulation is based on the fact that status is the index for such highly prized values as security, recognition, income, and authority. In this sense, status is a function of the anxiety-adjustment-approval syndrome. We can assume that the intensity of status anxiety varies with individual needs for approval and self-esteem.

The status incentive is among the most powerful psychological weapons of big organizations. In business, status acquisition and reinforcement have become the subject of rational calculation.[7] Standard Oil of California, for example, classifies executives from type 1, who merit drapes, wall-to-wall carpeting, private offices, walnut desks, etc., to type 4, with no private office or oak desks. Although, as one president put it, "you'd expect executives to be more mature," corporations have found that if morale is to be maintained, office equipment for executives of identical ranks must be identical.[8] Some executives, it seems, have developed to a fine art the skill of being the first to acquire new status indexes, thus acquiring for themselves a sense of distinction. Such honor

[7] *Time,* Vol. 65, p. 80.

[8] Ibid.

is only temporary, however, since their colleagues will quickly acquire the new index for themselves, even if this requires spending their own money.

Status preoccupation is useful in two ways. It meets the organization's demand for bench marks of authority that ease routine operations; and it also meets the individual's demand for recognition. As Veblen saw, with characteristic prescience, the change from an economy of scarcity to one of consumption is involved. Life styles in an abundant yet anonymous society no longer differentiate individuals, resulting in a search for indexes that can set one apart in socially approved ways. When frustrated in meaningful areas, such needs may find expression in inconsequential, nonanxiety-producing activities. Veblen shows how the ownership of dogs and horses falls into this category, because they perform no useful service and are valued mainly for sporting or honorific purposes: "The dog commends himself to our favor by affording play to our propensity for mastery, and as he is also an item of expense, and commonly serves no industrial purpose, he holds an assured place in man's regard as a thing of good repute. The dog is at the same time associated in our imagination with the chase—a meritorious employment and an expression of the honorable predatory impulse." [9] Similarly, "the horse, displaced almost entirely from utility, has acquired a new rarity value as an emblem of class dignity." [1]

The theme of unlimited opportunity for those who have what it takes also aggravates status anxiety, because there are never enough rewards to satisfy expectations. Bureaucratic conditions, moreover, reduce the opportunity for achieving status at the same time that they stimulate the desire for it. The separation of the worker from his tools and his impotence in a big organization tend to reduce the opportunity for individual independence and self-realization.

[9] Thorstein Veblen: *The Theory of the Leisure Class: An Economic Study of the Evolution of Institutions* (New York: The Viking Press; 1899), p. 141.

[1] Ibid., p. 142.

At the same time, the minute gradations in bureaucratic income, skill, and seniority intensify the desire to assert one's uniqueness.

In many cases the upward-mobile's status anxiety is probably forced upon him by organizational demands. But here again his personality encourages acceptance since status symbols provide the reference points of power. Because status is an effective means of validating his claim to better things, status sensitivity becomes part of the skill equipment of the upward-mobile. He had learned a great truth, namely, that most of us are influenced by pretense and often confuse form with substance. He knows that a little sorcery is necessary in human affairs, and that if he does not take himself seriously, no one else will. The rigid upward-mobile often lacks such detachment, however, and plays the status game with deadly seriousness. Indeed, an upward-mobile may be roughly defined as one who can take seriously the status systems of big organizations. As we have seen, he tends to adore power and is somewhat humorless in his dedication to majority values. Status sensitivity thus becomes merely a part of the whole organizational ethic, to which he pays an attention similar to that paid its other prescriptions.

The upward-mobile's upward-looking mien and his conventionality reinforce this preoccupation. He will note that his seniors play the status game, and here as elsewhere they become models for his conduct. If he is to play an expansive role, which he must, the necessary props must be enlisted to show that he too has status. Like the military officer, he will gear his social activities to those of equal or, if possible, higher rank. Since those above him will be playing the same game, his association with them will probably be limited to a few formal occasions which, it will be quite clear, are in the line of duty. Since co-optation by one's seniors is the main avenue to success, the disadvantaged accept such conditions gracefully, confident that their turn will come in time. A common example of such behavior is the use of the surname by the senior when addressing his juniors. (However, on certain social occasions eased perhaps by liquor or bonhomie, given names may be used.) Such practices validate status and promote deference. In a democratic society they may entail some strain, but the upward-mobile's remarkable self-discipline and his affinity for authority usually outweigh any conflicting values.

Personal status and organizational discipline are also reinforced by structured patterns of communication. Seniors communicate through a secretary who becomes her master's alter ego and who often exaggerates the status factors inherent in the relationship. The senior rarely visits the subordinate, since this would put him at a psychological disadvantage and reduce his control of the interpersonal situation. Normally the subordinate will come to the senior, and the latter will set the tone of the meeting. Displeasure can be nicely weighted. The tone of voice, the form of address, the length of the meeting, the amount of time the subordinate is required to wait, whether interruptions for phone calls will be permitted—all tend to define the relative status of the participants, and all can be manipulated to obtain desired consequences. The upward-mobile must become extremely sensitive in measuring out and receiving such dispensations. Versatile role-playing is therefore a vital career skill.

The upward-mobile's preoccupation with status is functional because he is anxious to rise, and because a disciplined self-promotion is required to impress those above him with his suitability for bigger things. As the objective relationship between status and achievement becomes more difficult to establish, the collection of unearned status increments is encouraged. Here again the displacement of goals mentioned earlier is to be seen. *The acquisition of status and prestige becomes an end in itself rather than a derivative of some significant achievement.* A common manifestation is the discreet cultivation of prestigeful elders by young upward-mobiles in need of a patron. Such behavior is directly related to the co-optative mechanism which now governs bureaucratic succession. Significantly, it is also similar to the individual's early dependence upon authority-figures, e.g., his mother, his father, his teacher, etc. Perhaps big organizations often speak of themselves as a "family" in order to evoke loyalties and responses deeply anchored in the individual's past.

Vigorous self-promotion may occur, often characterized by assiduous name dropping and by monopolizing those who can provide access to publicity, awards, honorific offices, and other instruments of personal advantage. "Getting one's name known" is thus a bureaucratic skill, sometimes practiced without much reference to productive work. The manipulation of both self and others becomes common as upward-mobiles analyze the prevailing means to success and set about achieving it. Some psychologists emphasize the fact that negative results ensue, e.g., self-alienation. In speaking of such effects, C. Wright Mills concludes that the "personality market"

> underlies the all-pervasive distrust and self-alienation so characteristic of metropolitan people. Without common values and mutual trust, the cash nexus that links one man to another in transient contact has been made subtle in a dozen ways and made to bite deeper into all areas of life and relations. People are required by the salesman ethic and convention to pretend interest in others in order to manipulate them. In the course of time, and as this ethic spreads, it is got on to. Still, it is conformed to as part of one's job and one's style of life, but now with a winking eye, for one knows that manipulation is inherent in every human contact. Men are estranged from one another as each secretly tries to make an instrument of the other, and in time a full circle is made: one makes an instrument of himself, and is estranged from It also.[2]

[2] C. Wright Mills: *White Collar* (New York: Oxford University Press, Inc.; 1951), pp. 187-8. About 1887, on the basis of empirical research and observation, F. Tönnies made the following similar observation of

A related upward-mobile skill is the careful avoidance of anything controversial. A major objective is to avoid prejudicing any future career opportunity, since even undesired opportunities can pay status dividends within one's own organization by judicious and casual mention. To avoid controversial matters, to create an aura of unlimited friendship, and to borrow status by discreet name dropping may appear rather negative, but these are significant criteria in the bureaucratic situation where "personality" and "working with the team" are vital. William H. Whyte, Jr., reports a survey of 150 personnel directors of large companies who were asked to choose between an "adaptable administrator" and a man with "strong personal convictions who could make decisions." The directors voted three to one for the administrator.[3] By taking a firm stand on practically anything, the individual may alienate someone and thus jeopardize a career potential. The costs of the resulting conformity may be high. "We are raising a lot of thoroughly drilled 'yes ma'ams' in the big corporations, who have no minds of their own; no opinions. As soon as the old individualists die, and there are not so many of them left, I think the corporations will have a lot of trouble getting good executives. After a man has served twenty to thirty years in one of those monstrous

---

the effect of German industrialization on interpersonal relations: "In the conception of Gesellschaft [an ideal type of modern, rational capitalistic society] the original or natural relations of human beings to each other must be excluded. The possibility of a relation in the Gesellschaft assumes no more than a multitude of mere persons who are capable of delivering something and consequently of promising something. . . . In Gesellschaft every person strives for that which is to his own advantage and affirms the actions of others only in so far as and as long as they can further his interest. Before and outside of convention and also before and outside of each special contract, the relation of all to all may therefore be conceived as potential hostility or latent war," *Community and Association,* trans. by C.P. Loomis (London: Routledge, Kegan Paul, Ltd.; 1955), p. 88.

[3] William H. Whyte, Jr.: *The Organization Man* (New York: Simon and Schuster, Inc.; 1956), p. 160.

corporations, he is not liable to have much mind of his own." [4]

Another skill of the upward-mobile is the monopolization of status-rewarding activity and individuals. This is most clearly seen in the organizational practice of crediting all ideas and achievements to those at the top. The highly personalized, if not fictionalized, communication releases by General MacArthur in the Pacific theatre during World War II are only an extreme example of this practice.[5] Self-promotion also reveals itself in the cultivation of prestigeful figures by the elite, preventing access by the rank and file and preserving an image of distance and distinction that reinforces their own prestige. Like the Navy captain who is never seen, upward-mobiles know that isolation encourages myth making and deference.

The status ethic means that all participants will demand that each contribute status increments of equal value, thus insuring mutual benefits. Hierarchical principles of distribution insure that the elite controls the total status reservoir. Around every elite therefore may be seen a circle of aspirants awaiting the co-optative nod and seeking in various ways (including hard work) to enter the sanctuary. In our abundant society high reward potentials in status and income encourage such accommodations, as does also an increasing career commitment to a single organization. Such conditions emphasize middle-class skills and values such as discipline, the repression of aggression, and a long-run view.

The upward-mobile tends to analyze and to employ the status system rationally. Exceptionally sensitive to its implications, he evaluates social situations in status terms and manipulates interpersonal relationships accordingly. In practically every field achievement is evaluated in terms of derived power and status. The intrinsic aspects of work tend to

[4] Quoted in M. Newcomer: *The Big Business Executive* (New York: Columbia University Press; 1955), p. 99.

[5] R. Rovere and A.M. Schlesinger: *The President and the General* (New York: Farrar, Straus, and Cudahy, Inc.; 1952).

become secondary, while more tangible derivatives of prestige and income are decisive. When the divorce between work accomplishment and contrived status becomes widely acknowledged, a certain disenchantment follows for those who retain the puritan value that rewards "ought" to reflect objectively differentiable achievement. But this puritan ideal rests upon the premise that a set of shared values exists by which achievement can in fact be evaluated. Such agreement is precarious in the age of the publicist, of commercialized art and entertainment, and of the common-denominator sophistry of the mass media.

The upward-mobile's orientation is thus fundamentally "procedural," as distinguished from the "substantive" attitude toward work often regarded as decisive in career success. While he may possess the talent and inspiration to do creative work, this genial ethic encourages him to choose alternatives that promise greater reward in less time. Upward-mobiles are not necessarily those who lack talent and discipline; but it appears that they often consciously elect alternatives that lead more quickly to the ends they prefer.

Perhaps it should be emphasized that such a choice is not open to everyone. As noted earlier, temperamental affinity and self-discipline are always required. To sit through endless meetings; to consider gravely the opinions and suggestions of subordinates who neither know nor can they be told that higher policy imperatives have so narrowed the range of alternatives that discussion is really beside the point; to endure the often pointless discussions into which committees often degenerate; to give way gracefully on small things; to suppress dislike and irritation; to treat unequals equally; to seriously propose expansive plans and programs, most of which are sure to be still-born; to waste ruthlessly the time of others in an effort to legitimate one's role of co-ordination; to discuss every issue at the level of principle, meanwhile keeping an eye on its implications for one's power and perquisites; to weigh proposals both in terms of their substantive rationality and in terms of the influence of those who propose them; to see progress and hope where neither exist—all require great staying power, the ability to bend reality into desired shapes, and an impregnable optimism. As Veblen said of the business executive and the university administrator: they have a "business-like facility in the management of affairs, an engaging address, a fluent command of language before a popular audience and what is called 'optimism'—a serene and voluble loyalty to the current conventionalities and a conspicuously profound conviction that all things are working out for good." [6]

The conditions of upward-mobility are also seen in the fusion of vocational and off-the-job energies. As the following comments suggest, business and professional success are correlated with philanthropic activities.[7]

> *Public relations head of large retail firm:* If you study the lists of campaign workers, you will find an amazing parallel between the level a man holds in his place of business and the level he holds in the campaign. Thus, if you are working at the bottom part of some business organization, you will be ringing doorbells. You can't possibly head a campaign and deal with people who are the heads of large corporations. As you go up in the business world, you go up in philanthropy. If you are at the top in a business or financial corporation, you will appear at the top of the campaign.
>
> *President of firm:* You will find that when a man first gets into this game he will be given some sort of minor campaign position depending on his business position. My own men have taken these positions; but as they have progressed with the firm, so they have taken on more responsibility in these campaigns. Furthermore

[6] Thorstein Veblen: *The Higher Learning in America* (New York: The Viking Press; 1918), p. 245.

[7] A.E. Ross: "Philanthropic Activity and the Business Career," *Social Forces,* Vol. 32, pp. 275-8. Copyright by The Williams & Wilkins Company. Reprinted by permission of the publisher.

they are helping themselves since I am watching them to see how they get along. They are ambitious, which is all to the good. They realize that we want them to do this work, and they will do a good job when we set them to it.

Lawyer: The top leaders have participated from year to year in the campaigns. They become part of it, and each year they become more and more experienced. They are just moved up to the vacancy above. Of course there is a sort of screening process which takes into account the respectability of the person and the type of occupation that will permit him to hold the position. The whole organization of philanthropic activity is arranged like a ladder. Once you start in the system, you slowly climb up—and if you have real and vital interest, you reach the top rungs.

General Manager, Trust Company: You don't just volunteer for these positions—it isn't done; you wait until you are asked. In fact, I don't know what would happen if you *did* volunteer! When asked, you are expected to say 'Yes,' but it is considered bad to show any eagerness. I am sure that if someone volunteered to be chairman of the next campaign he would be turned down.

General Manager, Bank Y: Training for philanthropy is a very important part of the training in our bank. It's our policy to drill into our men from the very beginning that they *must* take an interest in the community they're working in. Even if they're just a manager in a small town they *must* take an interest in the new hospital, or school, or whatever it is. We get reports each year on every clerk in every branch, and this shows whether they have taken an interest in their community affairs or not. They're reprimanded if they don't show this community interest. Stress right through is on this. And it's all for public relations. We *have* to do it—the competition between banks is so great. So we are all trained to take community responsibility. We expect to see the result of it somewhere in our balance sheet!

Professional Organizer A: Even the ordinary volunteer canvassers get to know people whom they would not ordinarily meet. I can give you an example of this. There was a cocktail party at a particular home here in Wellsville a few days ago for the various team captains and vice-chairmen. Many of these men would never have gone to that house for a cocktail party, and they probably never will again. But the campaign gave them chance to see the inside of the house and meet other people whom they would not usually meet. That sort of thing goes on a lot. People know they will rub elbows with a lot of important people. They will make friends and contacts. A man makes acquaintances in his work and maybe at his club, but these campaigns are an opportunity for him to meet a lot of other people, and make a lot of friends. That's the way it works. You can see the friendships being made all around you.

Professional Organizer E: He is the center of all publicity. The spotlight is on him for a long time, and he is placed before people's eyes. It certainly helps him in his business or profession.

Social and philanthropic activities thus become subject to bureaucratic rationality. They may become manipulative, since they are frankly directed toward acquiring status values that have direct career benefits.

Consumption styles are also a means of validating and indexing career achievement. In exceptional cases they may become a subtle way of communicating to the elite any obvious disparity between social position and career position. The implication is that an individual's style of life and social skill "should" warrant greater recognition in terms of prestige and income. Since social status follows vocational role, there is something paradoxical about one who is a member of the elite in a social context but not in the other. Since they deny their own values, such deviations may produce anxiety among conventional upward-mobiles. Aspiring upward-mobiles are perceptive enough and skillful enough to rig such expectations. This proposition assumes considerable rationality, but it follows logically from the upward-mobile's status orientation and from his social insight, coupled of course with the temperament necessary to bridge the gap between perception and action. As David Riesman observes, "The vagueness and fluidity of the system favor the radar-sensitive types who are tuned to subtle and unspoken expectations." [8]

The upward-mobile, then, becomes a "joiner," a carrier of many institutionalized values, some of which are inevitably opposing. But not being seriously involved, he accommodates himself without strain. His lack of involvement is symbolized by frequent use of a vague, essentially "liberal" (eighteenth-century style) rhetoric of consensus. Social issues can be manipulated to whatever advantage is sought at the moment. He can be a rugged enterpriser or a believer in big government. He can inject whatever meaning he wishes into words because, like Humpty Dumpty, he knows that words mean whatever one chooses them to mean. He can express "democratic" values when necessary for rank-and-file appeal; he can admit the need for social progress and deplore the barriers of tradition. But he can also damn Washington and the muddled liberals. Given America's conservative social values, he leans toward social values that are conservative. "Progressive conservatism" in his hallmark. He plays the tunes the audience demands, and when asked for his favorite, replies that he loves them all.

Here the upward-mobile may seem to diverge from the the authoritarian who holds rigidly to conventional power-oriented values. Insofar as reality is distinguished from rhet-

[8] David Riesman: *The Lonely Crowd* (New Haven: Yale University Press; 1950), p. 135.

oric, however, he remains faithful to convention and power. His "liberalism" is merely part of the personal discipline that enables him to avoid unprofitable causes, anger, and resentment. But his essential skill is the ability to use an objective social reality, namely, a semantic confusion and the decline of traditional values, in a manipulative and rational way. His conclusion that sophistry is often preferred and preferable to sincerity ensures a high probability of functional behavior. Possessing what Fromm calls a "marketing orientation," he knows that the status game meets the common need for pretense. He knows too that a pervasive optimism nourishes the human desire to find answers and certainty where neither exists. In sum, the upward-mobile has an exceptionally clear perception of personal needs and social values.

His insight informs him that individualism languishes in a bureaucratic situation where quantitative standards and group efforts are common. *By changing the conditions of work, bureaucratic structure has tended to change the character of work.* This differentiated, group-work milieu diffuses individual contributions, making evaluation difficult. There is on the one hand less inducement for individual work, and at the same time more opportunity to secure unwarranted rewards from a joint product. Reward is found not in the intrinsic value of work, but in hierarchical roles of co-ordination which become valued as organizations become larger. Moreover, since those in such roles often control valued by-products of work such as income, recognition, and so on, the upward-mobile assumes disproportionate influence.

Here a variation of the displacement of goals may be seen. For the upward-mobile, the manifest goals of the organization may become instrumental, because a positive identification with organizational goals nourishes his own career. The ability to identify strongly with such goals and to assume a role of selfless service is functional in the organizational society. Personal rewards and power may appear as mere by-products which one reluctantly accepts because they are necessary to dignify the position and the organization. The inequality of organizations is rationalized in operational terms. Quite simply, unequal rewards are necessary to inspire and to validate unequal contributions. Here again the whole trend toward subjective evaluations of individual performance is apparent, e.g., loyalty by itself is highly valued in bureaucratic systems. As the official in charge of the State Department's security program put it, "An ounce of loyalty is worth a pound of brains."

The most significant item in the upward-mobile personality is his respect for authority. Since the organization is essentially a system of authority relations, individual perceptions of authority are critically related to adjustment. An easy acceptance of authority eases interpersonal relations. In a study of 2,179 first-year recruits at West Point, psychiatrists found that respect for authority and idealization of one's father were critical factors differentiating successful from unsuccessful cadets.[9] Concerned because a portion ranging from twenty to twenty-five per cent of their carefully selected men failed to complete the first year of training, the Academy gave detailed personal-history questionnaires to three first-year classes. These were supplemented by four-hour interviews with each cadet. The study found that successful cadets had "a closer, more gratifying relationship with the father . . . an admiration and respect for the father, and acceptance of him as an authority figure." Such cadets were able to "identify with the male role," and as a result, they adjusted well to classmates and to the stern officers

[9] United States Military Academy: *Adaptation to West Point: A Study of Some Psychological Factors Associated with Adjustment at the United States Military Academy* (West Point: 1959), pp. 31-9; J. Biere and R. Lobeck: "Acceptance of Authority and Parental Identification," *Journal of Personality*, Vol. 27, pp. 74-86; I. Hart: "Maternal Child-rearing Practices and Authoritarian Ideology," *Journal of Abnormal and Social Psychology*, Vol. 55, pp. 232-7.

who direct the Academy. On the other hand, unsuccessful cadets were seldom close to their fathers and did not admire them. They were often anxious, unsure of their masculinity, and unable to sustain the authority-laden relationships of the military system.

Such values were characteristic of the "pragmatic" and "idealistic" types discussed earlier. They suggest again the critical relationship between bureaucratic accommodations and attitudes toward authority. The "authoritarian personality," who may be equated with the upward-mobile, divides people into those who are weak and those who are strong. He needs certainty and admires strength. Successful executives regard their superiors as friendly models, while at the same time they view their subordinates with detachment. The upward-mobile's ability to make "universalistic" decisions, i.e., those that give priority to organizational over personal goals, is also related to respect for authority.[1]

This affinity for authority is therefore functional in both personal and organizational terms. We have seen that individuals have a strong need to impute superior ability to those who exercise authority over them. This "security operation" validates both the authority relationship and the act of submission. The latter may produce tension because of democratic values and the fear of authority that socialization instills in some individuals; but the upward-mobile finds it easy to legitimate such relationships. They justify his perception of the organization as a rational system in which authority, status, and income *must* be unequally distributed. The achievement of the organization's goals and the recognition of individual differences in ability require it. He easily accepts authority from those above while exercising it over those below himself. Individuals who score high on the F scale are more likely to choose strong, dominant leaders; whereas those who score low on the F scale prefer leaders

[1] E. Mishler: "Personality Characteristics and the Resolution of Role Conflicts," *Public Opinion Quarterly*, Vol. 17, pp. 115-35.

who diagnose situations, ask for expressions of opinion, and interpret their own actions to the group.[2]

The bureaucratic situation nicely accommodates authoritarian needs. Hierarchy is so constructed that a chain of command runs throughout the organization. Ideally, the "pecking order" insures an unbroken line of control from the highest office to the lowest. Individuals must play a dual role of super- and subordination. They must be able to move facilely from one role to the other. Although some conflict may result, the high submission and dominance needs of the typical upward-mobile probably ease this accommodation. In effect, personality and role are mutually reinforcing.

Big organizations probably attract those who have such perceptions of authority. As a system of interlocking subhierarchies, they permit the indulgence of many degrees of authority at many levels. This psychic income is not limited to elites but percolates down to the lower levels. Only the private of the organizational army is virtually powerless. Moreover, the indulgence permitted by such a structure is increased by informal power centers with similar hierarchies and similar satisfactions. If status is to be satisfying, there must be hierarchy and someone to validate it. The bureaucratic situation provides both. Thus it seems to attract those who need certainty and authority.

His respect for authority also helps the upward-mobile reconcile any moral conflict arising from the injustice that organizations must at times commit. If the good of the organization is assigned the highest value, individual values must be subordinated to it. As the federal loyalty program shows, when individual and organizational interests collide, it is the individual who must submit. The upward-mobile's orientation enables him to submerge, diffuse, or rationalize any attending moral issue. The organization is what counts. Both his mobility claims and his personal values ease the problem of making such "tough-minded" decisions. We find,

[2] W. Haythorn, *et al.*: "The Behavior of Authoritarian and Equalitarian Personalities in Groups," *Human Relations*, Vol. 9, pp. 67-9.

significantly, a correlation between ambition and lack of faith in people. As one study found, whereas only thirty-eight per cent of those who thought it important to get ahead had high faith in people, sixty-two per cent of those who felt that "getting ahead" was "not very important" had high faith.[3]

Obviously, the capacity for rationalizing injustice varies among individuals. Idealization of power, personal ambition, psychological insecurity, attitudes toward authority, value patterns of introversion and extroversion—all in various combinations play a part. But we may assume that the upward-mobile possesses an exceptional ability to accept the inequities that unequal collective and individual power bring. Like that of most men, his attachment to individualism is an abstraction that rarely survives translation into concrete, personal terms. The limited utility of this principle in a pragmatic society contributes further to the tendency to look the other way when injustice occurs.

Despite his facile role playing, the upward-mobile is apparently unwavering in his devotion to power. This item is also part of the authoritarian cluster that seems useful in defining him. Among the changing requirements of success and personality that confront him, this value remains constant. Here again there is a danger in exaggerating his rationality, but he seems to have an exceptional capacity for realistic appraisals and action. He thinks in terms of power and is sensitive to the long-range consequences of his actions. He knows what he wants and how to get it. Few reflections about what "might have been" disturb his preoccupation with the main chance. As a result, his job and the organization will often be viewed *instrumentally*, as a means of personal ascendancy.

In part, this ethic is forced upon him by the changing structure of participation in many fields. Such changes are

[3] M. Rosenberg: "Faith in People and Success-Orientation," in P. Lazarsfeld, ed.: *The Language of Social Research* (Glencoe, Illinois: The Free Press; 1955), p. 159.

nicely illustrated by the big foundations, such as Ford and Carnegie, which now have great influence over the intellectual market place. Their activities in financing research and other university programs have restructured academic work and opportunity. By supporting group research on a grand scale, they are modifying the structure, the premises of recruitment and rewards, and the self-image of the university. They are providing new avenues for upward-mobiles whose forte is to understand the implications of such changes and to bend them to their advantage. By giving most of their funds to the prestige universities which already have the most money and research facilities, they are solidifying the intellectual status quo. As William H. Whyte, Jr., concludes, "They are not countering the bureaucratization of research, they are intensifying it." [4]

These conditions have bred a new academic role, the research entrepreneur (often called the vice-president for research), whose function is to get money from those who have it. To do so he must develop an extraordinary sensitivity to the desires of foundation executives and trustees. As these desires become the framework for shaping the interests and skills of the university in its search for financial support, the familiar displacement of goals follows. Does the director of the relevant foundation division prefer quantitative or qualitative, rigorously defined or cosmic projects? The entrepreneur knows, or he will soon find out. Even faculty recruitment is now influenced by the research-grant-producing potential of the candidates. And major rewards tend to go to those who get grants, actively seek them, or at least endorse the system of grant getting. The academic upward-mobile's energies are devoted to designing projects that meet the foundations' major interests and values, which are "wide ranging; but characteristically they are critical examinations of prevailing orthodoxy." [5]

[4] William H. Whyte: "Where the Foundations Fall Down," *Fortune*, Vol. 52 (November, 1955), p. 141.

[5] Ibid., p. 140.

Similar observations can be made concerning the federal government's vast university research programs, which are almost exclusively devoted to physical science except for a very small amount of militarily relevant social research. Among the disquieting implications here is the impact upon the university's ability to maintain some balance between the claims of physical science and of social science, and between teaching and research, and to preserve a rough equality in working conditions and rewards between physical-science faculties and those whose skills and interests are technologically irrelevant. Also challenged is the university's autonomy in matters of program development, in recruitment, and in the definition of its essential purpose. For example, the by-products of federally sponsored research include a requirement that faculty members in physical-science departments be able to meet the security requirements of the government, whose grants are usually contingent upon security clearances for everyone involved. Thus the university is obliged to share with outsiders, whose knowledge of university traditions and the conditions of productive research is likely to be limited, its right and obligation to determine the qualifications of its members. When, as today, something like fifty per cent of the total budget of the better private universities comes from federal research funds, the implications for the autonomy of higher education become apparent.

The work, work place, interests, and skills of intellectuals are thus shaped. Grants mean personal and institutional prestige, freedom from boresome and professionally unrewarding teaching, leverage vis-à-vis the administration, and often, fresh opportunities to do meaningful work. But the suggestive point here is the impact of social change upon academic work, including new frontiers for the upward-mobile type.

At the same time, some of the frontiers are constricting. Like other men, upward-mobiles are faced by the sobering fact that the advantages of education, economic security, and social skill are often retained within the families who have achieved them. Social and economic differences rather than intellectual ones often differentiate university from non-university youth. And even twenty years ago the "equal-opportunity" theme was losing ground in view of the fact that more often than not corporation executives were the sons of corporation executives.[6] While higher education increasingly challenges wealth and family as the main avenue of mobility, it too is correlated with income and class expectations. In 1955 top executives in business had twelve times the amount of education of their age group in the entire male population,[7] and a disproportionate number were from families of "medium" and "wealthy" incomes.[8]

Meanwhile, the pattern of career mobility is changing. Independent business experience has been replaced by long service in a single organization as the common path to success. Whereas two thirds of the major business executives in 1900 had had independent experience, by 1950 only eleven per cent could claim so.[9] And, as Newcomer concludes, "The proportion whose entire business career had been limited to the company they head had increased from seven per cent for the 1900 executives to twenty-two per cent for the 1950 executives."[1] Such developments place a premium on bureaucratic qualities of discipline, loyalty, and the long-run view. Above all, they dramatize the need for interpersonal skills that can weather the strains of extended association with the same superiors and subordinates.

Such demands may prove extremely trying. The upward-mobile must reconcile many conflicting roles and interests. Permissive authority relations require a discipline that cannot always survive the tensions of a competitive, power-oriented milieu. What may result is a mock egalitarianism

[6] M. Newcomer: op. cit.
[7] Ibid., p. 146.
[8] Ibid., p. 63.
[9] Ibid., p. 148.
[1] Ibid.

and "false personalization" that are widely recognized as a façade. When tension and conflict occur, the upward-mobile's preference for dominance may demand expression. However, if our analysis is accurate, he will usually muster the required discipline. As Burleigh Gardner says, successful executives "know what they are and what they want." [2] They also know "techniques for getting what they want within the framework of their desires and within the often narrow possibilities of their own organization." [3] His determination to make the most of such "narrow possibilities" explains much about the upward-mobile's behavior. His rationality encourages him to make the most of what he has, both for immediate personal satisfactions and for the enhancement of his own image of being qualified for further mobility.

Despite any conflict between his personality and his role, the upward-mobile is characterized by an ability to overcome doubt and ambivalence. He does not need perfect causes, and his devotion to prestige and power characteristically enable him to reach a satisfactory personal accommodation. However, this is putting the matter too negatively. It is clear that he finds the bureaucratic situation congenial, and that he can often adapt with relatively little strain.

This chapter has analyzed the upward-mobile as a bureaucratic type. His values and behavior include the capacity to identify strongly with the organization, permitting a nice synthesis of personal rewards and organizational goals. A typical form of accommodation is adjustment through power and special efforts to control situations and people. His "security operations" stress efficiency, strength, self-control, and dominance. His most functional value is a deep respect for authority. Not only are his interpersonal relations characterized by considerable sensitivity to authority and to status differences, but his superiors are viewed as non-threatening models for his own conduct. Meanwhile, his subordinates are regarded with a considerable detachment

[2] B. Gardner: op. cit., p. 118.

[3] Ibid.

which permits "universalistic" decisions that meet organizational as opposed to individual needs. Finally, we saw that changing social conditions and values have increased the utility of upward-mobile skills and values, as illustrated by the impact of the big foundations upon academic work and changing patterns of mobility in business and industry.

CHAPTER 7

PATTERNS OF ACCOMMODATION: INDIFFERENTS

Our second ideal type of accommodation in big organizations is one of indifference or withdrawal. Security, prestige, and power are the values that mediate accommodation, and men act in ways that seem to secure them. Such values have been endorsed by society's authority figures, and since we all hope to gain some measure of security and prestige, the behavior of such figures becomes a model for our own. Although anxiety reduction is probably the main impetus for such emulation, the ways of reducing it vary with the individual and with the situation. The same situation impels different reactions from different people. Status anxiety may push some of us into compulsive success striving, while others displace this need upon other values. The upward-mobile regards organizations as excellent instruments for satisfying his claims, but the indifferent defines them as calculated systems of frustration. He refuses to compete for the rewards they promise.

Indifference is the typical pattern of accommodation for the majority of organization men. The indifferents are found among the great mass of waged and salaried employees who work in the bureaucratic situation. In 1960 such employees comprised almost ninety per cent of the labor force, divided almost equally into blue- and white-collar workers. By a very rough estimate, we can say that some twenty-five million of them, just about half the wage-earning labor force, now work in big organizations. Moreover, this vast reservoir of potential indifferents is steadily increasing. From 1950 to 1960, for example, while the number of managers, proprietors, and officials remained almost unchanged, professional and technical workers increased by over sixty per cent, and the number of clerks by about twenty per cent.

It is not to be inferred that all of these employees are indifferents, nor can anyone determine the number who are. Both logic and empirical research, however, suggest that a considerable proportion of them have been alienated by the structural conditions of big organization. Since these conditions have been covered in detail, let us merely outline them here as a framework for the following analysis:

1. The bureaucratic worker's role as a waged or salaried employee who is not directly sharing in either the ownership or the profits of the organization. In the past 20 years, for example, (U.S. Statistical Abstracts) the number of "self-employed workers" (nonagricultural) declined from 9,758,000 to 6,268,000. During the same period, the number of "private wage and salary workers" increased from 30 million to almost 60 million. Government workers more than doubled, rising from 3,560,000 in 1940 to 8,000,000.

2. Centralized power and decision making within big organizations have shut the employee out from real participation and influence over the decisions that affect him. As Edwin G. Nourse, former head of the Council of Economic Advisers, says, "responsibility for determining the direction of the nation's economic life today and of furnishing both opportunity and incentives to

the masses centers upon some one or two per cent of the gainfully employed." [1]

3. The size and impersonality of big organizations and the standardized, *process-determined* nature of their work encourages alienation by reducing the education and skill demands, and consequently the prestige, of both white- and blue-collar jobs. "Skilled" work is rather hard to define. But if "craftsmen, foremen, and kindred workers" can be called "skilled," we find that their relative proportion in an expanding labor force has decreased from 14.6 per cent in 1948 to 13 per cent in 1960. Meanwhile, the chances of entry and survival in a business of one's own have been reduced by the difficulty of securing capital, and the growth of huge national enterprises whose resources make them virtually impregnable to competition and economic cycles.

4. Opportunities for higher education, now the major instrument of social mobility, are unequal. As C. Wright Mills says, "the son of an unskilled laborer has 6 chances out of 100 of ever getting into a college; the son of a professional man has better than a 50-50 chance." [2] Warner concludes, "of the 580 boys and girls in a thousand who reach the third year of high school, about half are taking a course which leads to college. One hundred and fifty enter college, and 70 graduate. These are average figures for the country as a whole." [3]

5. Finally, the general shift of attention and energy from work to recreation and leisure. The decline of the Protestant Ethic, which deified work and accumulation, brings with it a re-evaluation of the whole vocational bargain, subtlely reinforced by the suspicion that one's

[1] Cited in C. Wright Mills: *White Collar* (New York: Oxford University Press, Inc.; 1951), p. 81.

[2] Ibid., p. 276.

[3] Cited in ibid., p. 268.

life chances have been exaggerated in any case. Thus work becomes an instrument for buying off-work satisfactions.

Do these conditions really inspire indifference and alienation? After a word about the typical indifferent and the ideal of mobility, we shall turn to the evidence.

The indifferents are those who have come to terms with their *work environment* by withdrawal and by a redirection of their interests toward off-the-job satisfactions. They have also been alienated by the *work itself*, which has often been downgraded by machine processing and by assembly-line methods. This dual basis for alienation must be recognized. In industrial psychology the main effort has been to compensate for the deadening effect of the work itself by providing a happy work place. Less attention has been given to alienation from the job itself.

We are not speaking here of pathological kinds of alienation, but of modes of accommodation that often seem basically healthy. The typical indifferent has rejected majority values of success and power. While the upward-mobile strives for such values, obtainable today mainly through big organizations, the indifferent seeks that security which the organization can also provide for those who merely "go along." Such security seeking varies in accord with the demands of personality. One individual may have been taught to expect more than life can reasonably offer, and anxiety and frustration follow as his unrealistic claims are discounted. Another may have learned to expect less; he may refuse to accept success values or to compete for them. This role is encouraged by such bureaucratic conditions as hierarchy, oligarchy, and specialization.

The indifferent reaction, then, is the product of both social and organizational influences. But organizational factors seem to outweigh class-induced mobility expectations. However strong such expectations, they rarely survive in an unsympathetic institutional environment. Today, many a potential entrepreneur languishes in some cul-de-sac because the organizational context no longer sustains his aspirations. The resulting accommodation may also reflect personal failures of nerve and energy, bad luck, and so on. But, essentially, indifference is manifested in a psychic withdrawal from the work arena and a transfer of interest to off-work activities. The employee "goes through the motions," paying lip-service to organizational values, but he no longer retains any real interest in the organization or in work for its own sake.

This accommodation may occur in two stages: alienation and indifference. The alienated are those who come into the organization with great expectations. They are determined to climb. But when bureaucratic and personal limitations blunt their hopes, they become alienated. Over a period of time, it seems, this reaction works itself into indifference. On another level, we are dealing with indifference as an *initial* orientation. Such individuals, usually of working or lower-middle-class origin, have been taught not to expect very much. Both socialization and work experience reinforce this perception of their life chances. And both alienation and indifference counter the organization's claims for loyalty, predictability, and hard work.

We know that such prebureaucratic values are decisive within the organization. For example, social influences condition the attitudes of members toward their mobility chances in the organization. Both indifference and upward-mobility are functions of class and education. Attitudes toward mobility, however, are complex and contradictory.[4]

[4] For a survey of mobility studies which concludes that mobility rates are about the same in the United States and Western Europe, see S.M. Lipset and R. Bendix: *Social Mobility in Industrial Society* (Berkeley: University of California Press; 1959). Whether the different cultural contexts and methods of such studies make them *incomparable* remains moot.

At the popular level one finds an uncritical acceptance of the American dream of unlimited mobility for those who have what it takes. In social science, however, some observers accept this belief while others insist that mobility is considerably more limited. Since research supporting either view can be found, both interpretations have apparently been influenced by the historical context in which they occurred. During the depression years the pessimistic view dominated; today, after twenty years of prosperity, some observers regard mobility more happily.[5]

The problem is defined somewhat by discrete class attitudes toward mobility. Roughly speaking, white-collar people retain faith in the "high-mobility" idea. On the other hand, blue-collar workers often pay lip-service to mobility, but their expectations are usually transferred to their children. Among the white-collar class there is no doubt that science and technology have created a new lower-middle class of office and sales people who have moved up from "manual" families. Mass production and liberal credit have helped validate their middle-class image by making widely available the material goods that partly define class status.

Moreover, class is a psychic phenomenon. Most Americans, it seems, are not class conscious in the way that Europeans, with their feudal legacy, continue to be. A *Fortune* survey (1940) found that almost eighty per cent of an American sample defined themselves as being of the "middle class." Although this finding has been challenged by later research, Americans tend to see existing disparities in power and income as *individual* rather than as *class* differences.[6] While Centers found that fifty-one per cent of his sample called themselves "working class," which seems to indicate some

[5] Among others, see Robert and Helen Lynd, Lloyd Warner, C. Wright Mills, A.B. Hollingshead, all of whom either wrote during, or experienced, the depression of the 1930's; N. Rogoff: *Recent Trends in Occupational Mobility* (Glencoe, Illinois: The Free Press; 1953).

[6] Robin M. Williams, Jr.: *American Society* (New York: Alfred A. Knopf; 1951), p. 121.

class sensitivity,[7] this response might also be interpreted to mean the absence of any Marxian connotation of "working class." Pragmatic Americans might very well reason: "Yes, I work for a living, therefore I am obviously a member of the 'working class.'"

But our concern is less with class than with mobility, and here the evidence has been carefully summarized.[8] Once again, however, one encounters the problem of determining what the data really mean, since the same evidence can be interpreted in different ways. For example, Warner and Abegglen's survey (1952) of the origins of big business leaders found that thirty-one per cent were descended from fathers who were also big business leaders.[9] Only five per cent had fathers in skilled and semiskilled occupations. These leaders, in effect, were drawn from existing elites some eight times oftener than would have been expected had succession been random. This suggests that mobility at the top of our social structure is highly restricted, but Joseph Kahl, who has made a painstaking analysis of mobility research, cautions, as follows: "These figures can be interpreted to indicate that American society is either relatively closed or relatively open, depending upon one's expectations. The statement that sixty-nine per cent of the business elite were recruited from other levels suggests considerable openness. On the other hand, the statement that the business elite was recruited from its own ranks 7.75 times oftener than randomly suggests that American society is relatively closed."[1]

[7] R. Centers: "The American Class Structure: A Psychological Analysis," in G.E. Swanson, T.M. Newcomb, and E.L. Hartley, *et al.*, eds.: *Readings in Social Psychology* (New York: Holt, Rinehart & Winston; 1952).

[8] J.A. Kahl: *The American Class Structure* (New York: Rinehart and Co.; 1957).

[9] W.L. Warner and J.C. Abegglen: *Occupational Mobility in American Business and Industry* (Minneapolis: University of Minnesota Press; 1955).

[1] J. A. Kahl: op. cit., p. 269.

Kahl has a generally optimistic view of mobility, for he concludes that "between one half and three quarters of the men who are in professional, clerical, or skilled jobs, have climbed relative to their fathers." [2] From 1920 to 1950, moreover, "total mobility" (the combined effects of technological change, individual effort, reproduction, and step-by-step progress) was enjoyed by full sixty-seven per cent of the entire labor force.[3] Even in the proprietorship category where the proportion of self-employed in the entire labor force has been sharply reduced (mainly by the urbanization of farm owners), he estimates that only four per cent have been downwardly mobile.[4] This estimate is based upon a National Opinion Research Center study of 1947, in which 1334 sons were asked to indicate their fathers' occupations.

But other research is less optimistic. Rogoff, for example, shows that mobility among her sample of Indianapolis men was no greater in 1940 than it had been in 1910.[5] She concludes, moreover, that no more men crossed the critical blue-collar-white-collar line in the later period. Her findings refer only to "individual effort," however, and to "step by step" mobility. Technological advances during the period would presumably have increased mobility by opening up large numbers of semiskilled, skilled, and administrative jobs. Census figures show that the number of professional jobs has increased by some three and one-half times since 1900.

A comparison of the Warner-Abegglen study (1952) and a similar one by Taussig and Joslyn (1928) shows that recruitment to top business positions from businessmen decreased from 9.67 to 4.73. Yet recruitment from professional groups, clerks and salesmen, farmers and laborers increased either not at all, or very little. Kahl concludes from this that "entry

[2] Ibid., p. 272.

[3] Ibid., pp. 260-1.

[4] Ibid., p. 262.

[5] N. Rogoff: *Recent Trends in Occupational Mobility* (Glencoe, Illinois: The Free Press; 1953).

into the top levels of business management is becoming slightly more open through time."[6]

Such conflicting evidence indicates the difficulty of comparing data from studies that differ in point of time, method, and definition. For our purposes, however, quantitative rates of mobility are less significant than *qualitative* changes brought about by the conditions of work in bureaucratic organizations. The essential change has been from a rather competitive system in which mobility hinged upon the impartial dictates of the market to a highly structured, rule-and-certificated system in which mobility often rests upon the ability to please one's superiors. When aligned with concentration and consequent disparities in power, this condition fosters anxiety, dependency, and alienation. In this context, one may move upward objectively, but the subjective consequences in terms of autonomy, self-realization, and influence upon the organization's policies remain much the same. The grinding reality persists; regardless of an individual's functional skill and achievement, control of the organization, its objectives, and its rewards remain largely in the hands of its hierarchical elite.

Many qualitative issues arise. Did the occupational categories mean in 1900, 1928, and even 1940 what they mean today? What kinds of changes have occurred in the relative status and prestige of jobs during the past half century? Are the payoffs in income, satisfaction, and independence of a contemporary "professional" or a "skilled worker" really comparable with those of his counterparts in 1900? What about the vast number of farm proprietors who have turned to unskilled and skilled work in industry? While their income may be higher, what is their relative condition with regard to independence and morale? It is impressive that students of mobility tend to undervalue *farm* proprietorship, while accepting movement from unskilled or skilled work into *business* proprietorship as a valid index of upward mobility.

[6] J.A. Kahl: op. cit., p. 271.

We saw earlier, too, that a great deal of mock mobility has been achieved through verbal magic by upgrading the titles of socially devalued jobs. Janitors become custodians; reporters become journalists; clerks become administrators; secretaries become executive assistants; salesmen become sales executives; the large banks create innumerable vice-presidencies. Do these psychic emoluments skew the statistics on mobility compiled by the Census Bureau and the National Opinion Research Center? When American success values mean that the very admission of nonmobility is a self-indictment, how much confidence can be placed in the answers of individuals about their own or their father's occupational status? We know that respondents commonly exaggerate their education, knowledge, and income. When higher education has become the critical factor in mobility, we must certainly ask how equal educational chances are in our society. Although great strides have been taken since World War II, the answer is not entirely reassuring, as will be shown in a moment.

Not only can it be shown that educational opportunity is unequal, but difficulties of entry and survival in the entrepreneurial field provide less opportunity for economic independence and for real gains in personal autonomy as contrasted with the built-in dependency of bureaucratic work. We have seen that huge capital requirements restrict entry in industry, while high failure rates (combined with a chronic capital shortage) make small business a precarious venture. Meanwhile, the manual worker who rises may find that white-collar status has been downgraded as mechanization reduces the skill demands of his job, and as the unionized blue-collar worker equals and often surpasses him in pay and fringe benefits. Nor have the professions remained immune to organizational demands. Increasingly, the conditions of professional work are bureaucratically determined. In sum, the structural characteristics of big organization have so modified the conditions of work and the work place that we cannot assume comparability between occupations and mobility in the past with that of today.

Turning to the indifferent's accommodation to the bureaucratic situation, we find that he is typically of working-class or lower-middle-class origin. This implies a distinctive style of socialization. Not only will he rarely have been inculcated with the desire to excel, but class status and limited education have not usually prepared him for the graceful acceptance of authority which has become the critical factor in organizational mobility. While middle-class child training has emphasized self-discipline, respect for authority, and the muffling of aggression, lower-class socialization has been rather more tolerant of fighting, truancy, haphazard toilet training, etc. It must be noted that such differences are narrowing, at least in selected areas. Since World War II middle-class parents have become more permissive about aggression, thumb sucking, toilet mistakes, and sex play. However, a summary of research on child-training practices since 1932 concludes: "By and large, the middle-class mother expects more of her child than her working-class counterpart." The techniques used by middle-class parents, moreover, are more likely to encourage "the development of internalized values and control." Physical punishment, for example, is used much more by working-class parents.[7] This tends to increase aggressiveness in the child. Middle-class parents, on the other hand, use psychological deprivations. The middle-class father is likely to have more authority and status in the family. While there is apparently a shift toward more equalitarian relations in such families, the "middle-class youngster is ex-

[7] U. Bronfenbrenner: "Socialization and Social Class Through Time and Space," in Eleanor E. Maccoby, *et al.*: *Readings in Social Psychology* (New York: Holt, Rinehart & Winston; 1958), pp. 400-5. Also, A. Davis and R.J. Havighurst: "Social Class and Color Differences in Child Rearing," *American Sociological Review*, Vol. 11, pp. 698-710; K.B. Mazur: *Class and Society* (New York: Random House; 1955); H.W. Pfautz: "The Current Literature on Social Stratification," *American Journal of Sociology*, Vol. 48, pp. 397-418.

pected to take care of himself earlier, to accept more responsibilities about the home, and—above all—to progress further in school." [8]

Such findings are directly related to accommodations in the bureaucratic situation, with its authority-structured context and attending behavioral demands. The indifferent type seems especially disadvantaged. The facile assumption of a "professional mask;" the stifling of anxiety, resentment, and irritation; the personal discipline required when seniority and dependence upon the man above are common criteria for mobility; the ability to play a variety of roles—such qualities are not characteristic of the typical lower-class indifferent. His self-image and career expectations are often of a different order.

Upward-mobility, moreover, is often bought at great cost.

[8] Bronfenbrenner, loc. cit., p. 424. Similarly, A.E. Cohen points out that, "middle class socialization, in comparison with working-class socialization, is conscious, rational, deliberate and demanding. Relatively little is left to chance and 'just-growing.' Middle-class parents are likely to be concerned and anxious about their children's achievement of age-graded 'norms,' and this anxiety is likely to be communicated to the child. They are more geared to a timetable, to the future as well as the present. The child is constantly aware of what his parents want him to *be* and to *become*. He learns early to take the long view and becomes habituated to the self-discipline and effort necessary to meeting parental expectations." *Delinquent Boys* (Glencoe, Illinois: The Free Press; 1955), p. 98. In a study of New Haven, A.B. Hollingshead and F.C. Redlich found significant class differences, including different expectations as to educational achievement and, among his Class 11 (upper-middle class) families, an expressed need "for a 'good education' for their children . . . by parents who attribute their success to education or who believe their mobility strivings are limited by the wrong kind or amount of education; . . . many of these parents project their strivings for higher status upon their children." A.B. Hollingshead and F.C. Redlich: *Social Class and Mental Illness* (New York: John Wiley & Sons, Inc.; 1958), p. 89. Again, as reported in a survey of top-level automobile executives, a clergyman-counselor says of their sons and daughters, "they are disciplined, serious children, extremely anxious to get ahead," S. Freedgood: "Life in Bloomfield Hills," *Fortune*, Vol. 64 (July, 1961), p. 236.

As W.N. Christensen and L.E. Hickle, Jr., of Cornell University Medical School, found, executives of working-class origin experience a great deal more psychosomatic illness than their middle-class colleagues.[9] One hundred and thirty-nine executives on the lower rungs of big corporations, who differed with respect to education (fifty-five were college graduates, eighty-four high-school only), were studied over a three year period. The high-school graduates had twice the number of illnesses and ten times the risk of death. Many more of them showed signs of premature cardiovascular disease. Neither heredity nor personal habits were significant. Both groups were of white, northern-European stock. The crucial factor was *stress,* which was related in turn to the different class backgrounds of the men. University graduates were from "substantial middle-class families" and assumed their executive roles easily. On the other hand, the high-school graduates were sons and daughters of immigrant families with lower incomes. They married earlier, had more domestic problems, and did more "do-it-yourself" jobs at home. The researchers concluded: "Their relative ill health might well be regarded as the price they pay for getting ahead in the world."

The discrete socialization patterns of middle and lower-class families have different utilities in the bureaucratic situation. Miller and Swanson found that middle- and working-class youth from bureaucratic families differed significantly in their use of defenses against conflict. Working class boys *denied* their failures, whereas middle class boys typically used repression and self-criticism as defenses. Repression is more functional because "this mechanism facilitates socially adjustive behavior."[1] Denial tends to be dysfunctional because it permits the individual to distort experience to the extent where failure may even be turned into success. The working-class youth's tendency toward denial thus inhibits

[9] *Time,* Vol. 75 (May 16, 1960), p. 45.

[1] D.R. Miller and G.E. Swanson: *Inner Conflict and Defense* (New York: Holt, Rinehart & Winston; 1960), p. 232.

his ability to make the kinds of *realistic self-appraisals* required to meet bureaucratic claims for discipline, rationality, and adaptability. By the time he becomes aware of such handicaps, it is often too late to change deep-seated security operations.

On the other hand, the upward-mobile will usually be of middle- or upper-class origin. He may be neurotically ambitious, because children of these strata are subject to intense pressure to succeed. More amenable to group norms, he accepts prevailing values of success and prestige. He wants to rise, and his mobility expectations are high. Studies of mobility show, moreover, that such expectations have a firm basis in reality. *The American Soldier* research, for example, found that both expectations and achievement (defined as promotion) depended on education,[2] which in turn reflects social class. It is perhaps fortunate that the size and diversity of big organizations can accommodate several levels of expectation.

The indifferent's rejection of status and prestige values often insures a felicitous accommodation. Since job satisfaction is a product of the relation between aspirations and achievement, he is often the most satisfied of organization men. His aspirations are based on a realistic appraisal of existing opportunities. He rejects the status anxiety, the success striving, the self-discipline, and the conformity demanded of self and family that confront the upward-mobile. In this sense, the indifferent is the most "normal" of individuals. Emancipated from the puritan heritage that honors work, he is somewhat out of step with majority values. Escaping the commitments of the "true believer" and the anxiety of the neurotic striver, he receives big dividends in privacy, tranquillity, and self-realization through his *extravocational* orientation.

To some extent, then, the indifferent deflects bureaucratic

[2] *Adjustment During Army Life,* Vol. 1, pp. 246-50.

claims by limiting his aspirations and transferring them elsewhere. His off-the-job activities rarely reinforce his occupational role. Unlike the upward-mobile, for whom work is all important, he separates his work experience from a more meaningful personal area. Work becomes a tool with which he buys satisfactions totally unrelated to work. Like the Hormel employee, he regards his paid vacation as the most satisfying thing about his job. Whereas forty-five per cent of nonmanual employees (professionals, business executives, and upper-white-collar individuals report an "unqualified preference for work," only twenty-seven per cent of active union members share this preference. While fifty-four per cent of the latter have "an unqualified preference for leisure," only twenty-seven per cent of the nonmanuals do.[3]

Even at professional and managerial levels, technological change has made work more like factory production. Thus indifference is becoming a more likely pattern of accommodation for white- as well as for blue-collar workers. Alienation from work that has become routinized, yet demands manipulation in the "personality market," is visible in both groups. This condition has important qualitative implications for mobility as white-collar people who have risen from "manual" families do not find their rise paying off in the expected independence and occupational challenge (and certainly not in pay). Even in such highly skilled work as university teaching, the feeling of being "just a number" may exist, particularly in the big state universities. As C. Wright Mills says: "If white-collar people are not free to control their working actions, they, in time, habitually submit to the order of others and, insofar as they try to act freely, do so in other spheres. . . . If there is a split between their work and play, and their work and culture, they admit that split as a commonsense fact of existence. If their way of earning a living does

[3] S.M. Lipset and J. Gordon: "Mobility and Trade Union Membership," in Bendix and Lipset, eds.: *Class, Status and Power* (Glencoe, Illinois: The Free Press; 1953), pp. 495-6.

not infuse their mode of living, they try to build their real life outside their work." [4]

This separation of work from "personal" life underlies the indifferent's perception of the bureaucratic situation. Aware of his essentially commercial nexus with the organization, he resists the image of himself as a commodity. Although he must accept the economic bargain, selling his skill and energy for forty hours a week, the remaining time is jealously guarded as his own. Since he is immune to the organization's values, loyalty is not included in the bargain. In some cases, indifference approaches hostility as noninvolvement becomes a form of retaliation for his instrumental role. In mass-production industries, retaliation may take such forms as deprecating the product ("If people only knew how these things were made, they would never buy them"). The product may be regarded as a symbol of "profits," which appear immoral when the "real producers" work for wages.

Attitudes toward authority also affect involvement. Those who fear or hate authority find identification difficult; the sharp differentiation of authority in organizations aggravates this condition. As we have seen, such feelings reflect one's experiences with authority from infancy onward. Here again, selective perception is at work, compelling some individuals to "see" superiors as threatening, and thereby reinforcing the fear of authority. However, this kind of anxiety is rarely characteristic of the upward-mobile or of the indifferent. The former regards his superiors as friendly models; his particular brand of anxiety is fear of failure. The latter, who neither expects nor wants anything from the organization, is immune to its discipline. The tragic figure in this context is the "ambivalent" type, who can neither resist the claims of status and power nor play the roles required to achieve them on the organization's terms. He sees authority figures as remote and threatening. As a result, his interpersonal relations are often strained.

[4] C.W. Mills: op. cit., pp. 227-8.

This conception of indifference conflicts with the "human-relations" view which defines organizations as "co-operative systems" composed of many intimate work groups which meet individual needs for identification. While small groups undoubtedly meet such needs, however, it seems clear that their members do not necessarily identify with the *whole* organization. With rare exceptions, the influence of any given individual on this level is inconsequential, and he knows it. As the Hawthorne studies found, the small group often plays a *protective* role, shielding its members from real or imaginary threats of management.[5] Small group relations are often compensatory and negative; they may even underscore the employee's alienation from the larger organization. A study of the automobile industry concludes: "When the worker discussed his relations with other workers and reported social interaction, such as joking, gossiping, or general conversation, he mentioned them chiefly as a fortunate *counterbalance and compensation* for the disliked features" of his job.[6] Certainly, identifying with immediate work companions and identifying with a big organization are different things.

The indifferent recaptures his identity by withdrawing; by the very act of withholding part of himself, he experiences a certain autonomy. Like the consumer who refuses to patronize chain stores because of small-business values, he takes a stand, however quixotic. Alienation is encouraged by the instrumental role of the worker, whose assignment, level of output, status, and income are largely determined by technical demand, by the *work process*. Supervisory jobs, on the other hand, tend to encourage identification because the work is more responsible and less stereotyped, permitting greater freedom of action. Nevertheless, even the attitudes of those who do identify with the organization are as often competitive as they are co-operative. The upward-mobile's desire for

[5] F.J. Roethlisberger and W.J. Dickson: *Management and the Worker* (Cambridge: Harvard University Press; 1941).

[6] C.R. Walker and R.H. Guest: *The Man on the Assembly Line* (Cambridge: Harvard University Press; 1952), p. 142. (Italics added.)

personal advancement sometimes outweighs the claims of group acceptance.

Indifference and withdrawal are also encouraged by the corrosion of friendship in bureaucratic society. As we have seen, organizational roles require the manufacture of affection, the ready smile, the "human-relations" approach—often animated by a manipulative ethic. Yet, when everyone suspects that everyone is insincere much of the time, disenchantment encourages alienation and the separation of work from one's "personal" life. One's "real" self is revealed only to his family and intimate friends. Emotional commitments at work that may expose one to frustration or to exploitation are avoided. This accommodation is also encouraged by the tendency to carry both status and business interests into off-the-job social relations. In the upward-mobile's one-track world, this mode is unquestioned; but the indifferent's eight-to-five orientation inhibits the blending of on- and off-the-job interests.

Speaking very generally, the ubiquity of indifference seems to be associated with the routinization of work and with the limits on economic independence in an employee society. Over a period of time, smaller opportunities probably make for smaller expectations. If size breeds oligarchy and co-optation, which then outline the conditions of personal mobility, the very existence of big organizations encourages indifference. Blocked in traditional avenues requiring traditional skills, the individual seeks other channels of self-expression. Oligarchic leadership patterns, the restructuring of competition, and the bewildering complexity of decision making in big organizations reduce the motivation and the chance for involvement, deflecting mens' energies into off-work channels.

Reduced opportunities for real participation, as distinguished from the mock participation seen, for example, in stock-holders' meetings, underlie the indifferent reaction. As Clarence B. Randall said: "We entice him [the stock-holder] to the annual meeting with every blandishment at our command . . . but when it comes to the exercise of the prerogative of ownership, we do not vouchsafe him the opportunity of making even one little cross on a piece of paper once a year in token recognition of the fact that we work for him." [7]

In view of mass education and the efficiency of the mass media, one might have assumed that participation would have increased, but the facts suggest otherwise. Voting participation, for example, ranges from about twenty-five per cent in local contests to something over sixty per cent in presidential elections. As V.O. Key has shown, throughout the South a constellation of factors including tradition, class, caste, race, and poverty makes politics a highly minoritarian craft. From 1920 to 1946, only in North Carolina and Louisiana did the average percentages of all citizens over twenty-one voting in primaries to nominate senators and governors exceed thirty per cent.[8]

It seems clear that America is less a nation of "joiners" than is generally assumed, and, indeed, that alienation from political and community affairs is common.[9] Studies of group membership in New York City show that sixty per cent of working-class and fifty-three per cent of white-collar workers do not belong to even a *single* organization;[1] in Erie County, Ohio, less than fifty per cent of the population belong to voluntary groups;[2] and in their study of a small New England town of 17,000, Warner and Lunt found that only forty-one per cent belonged.[3] Moreover, as suggested above, membership does not necessarily mean participation.

[7] "The Myths of Communications," *Dun's Review*, Vol. 75, p. 39.

[8] *Southern Politics* (New York: Alfred A. Knopf; 1949), pp. 504-5.

[9] B. Barber: "Participation and Mass Apathy in Associations," in Alvin W. Gouldner: *Studies in Leadership* (New York: Harper & Brothers; 1950); J. Foskett: "Social Structure and Social Participation," *American Sociological Review*, Vol. 20, pp. 431-8.

[1] M. Komarovsky: "Voluntary Associations of Urban Dwellers," *American Sociological Review*, Vol. 11, pp. 686-98.

[2] P. Lazarsfeld, B. Berelson, and H. Gaudet: *The People's Choice* (New York: Columbia University Press; 1944), p. 145.

[3] W.L. Warner and P.S. Lunt: *The Social Life of a Modern Community* (New Haven: Yale University Press; 1941).

Indifference may reflect a deeper value change in which traditional success aspirations collide with the demand for economic security and a maturer view of work. For example, the preference of university graduates for careers in big, risk-free corporations rather than entrepreneurship may signal a tacit redirection of values based in part upon an awareness of economic realities.[4] Such changes are apparent in the emerging themes of the mass media. As C. Wright Mills observes, a "literature of resignation . . . fits in with all those institutional changes involving the goal of security."[5] As the periphery of individual choice contracts, traditional success models of wealth and power are challenged by themes of spiritual and emotional maturity. As Sloan Wilson's hero concluded, the rewards of upward-mobility no longer seem so appealing.[6] Dale Carnegie is superseded by Norman Vincent Peale and the Overstreets. The new emphasis is suggested by the competition over employee-benefit programs in which private enterprise has now overcome government's historic advantage. The worker's preoccupation with the security and the fringe benefits suggests a realistic appraisal of bureaucratic conditions of work. The results are similar: the acceptance of an employee society and the weakening of traditional success images.[7]

Noninvolvement as a typical pattern of accommodation is encouraged by size itself. A survey of some 100,000 workers in the Sears Roebuck empire found that "mere size is unquestionably one of the most important factors in determining the quality of employee relationships; the smaller the unit the higher the morale and vice versa."[8] In big organizations both the character of the work and the process-determined inter-

[4] William H. Whyte, Jr.: *The Organization Man* (New York: Simon and Schuster, Inc.; 1956).

[5] C.W. Mills: op. cit., p. 285.

[6] Sloan Wilson: *The Man in the Grey Flannel Suit* (New York: Simon and Schuster, Inc.; 1955).

[7] W.H. Whyte, Jr.: op. cit.

[8] J.C. Worthy: "Organizational Structure and Employee Morale," *American Sociological Review*, Vol. 15, p. 173.

personal relations are often unsatisfying. "As a result of over-specialization a very large number of employees in American industry today have been deprived of the sense of performing interesting, significant work." [9] Similarly: "Where jobs are broken down too finely we are more likely to have both low output and low morale." [1] Other studies show a similar relation between size and output,[2] absenteeism (morale),[3] and motivation.[4] In each case the result is negative: absenteeism increases while output and incentive decline.

The indifferent thus tends to find his real satisfactions in extravocational activities. While the upward-mobile "carries his job home with him," the indifferent separates his work from his "personal" experiences, and work is often repressed as something unpleasant. The pay check is what counts. "Studies agree beyond doubt that persons at the lower end of the socio-economic scale are more likely . . . to emphasize the *economic* aspects of work, whereas those at the upper end more typically stress the *satisfaction* they find in work itself." [5] Indifferents, then, are among the large number of employees who reject advancement because of the added responsibility it entails. They prefer instead to be left alone; instead of advancement they expect security.

The indifferent's interpersonal relations are generally satisfactory. Since there is little danger that he will become either a "speed king" or a "chiseler," he is not perceived as threatening by his colleagues. Since neither the organization's rewards nor its sanctions are very compelling, his attitudes toward authority are generally uncomplicated. His lack of ambition

[9] Ibid., p. 175.

[1] Ibid., p. 174.

[2] R. Marriott: "Size of Working Group and Output," *Occupational Psychology*, Vol. 23, pp. 47-57.

[3] D. Hewitt and J. Parfit: "A Note on Working Morale and Size of Group," *Occupational Psychology*, Vol. 27, pp. 38-42.

[4] H. Campbell: "Group Incentive Pay Schemes," *Occupational Psychology*, Vol. 26, pp. 15-21.

[5] E.L. Lyman: "Occupational Differences in the Value Attached to Work," *American Journal of Sociology*, Vol. 41, p. 138.

insures a large measure of psychic independence. Unlike the upward-mobile who strains to be "on top" in every situation, or the "ambivalent" who suffers from unrealistic claims and comparisons of himself and his job with idealized alternatives, the indifferent concludes that people, jobs, and organizations are not much different. He adjusts himself accordingly.

While the personal qualities that permit the indifferent to accommodate without undue strain vary individually, we can assume that some constant values are at work. Clearly, he is not driven by exceptional needs for power and success, since these would require intense involvement if they were to be achieved through the organization. Feeling no compulsion to control his work environment, he does not see the work situation as an instrument for manipulation. Since he is quite literally not going anywhere, he escapes the status pressure and the manipulation of self and others often required for organizational success. The bureaucratic struggle is observed with detachment. The capacity to be aware of majority values, to understand their fascination for others, yet to escape becoming personally involved is a major item in his personality.

But we must not give him too much credit for maturity since his accommodation may rest upon a naïve unawareness of the ways and rewards of power. It may simply reflect class and family backgrounds that failed to include great expectations among their motivating claims. Insofar as mobility now occurs in time spans of generations, his initial expectations may have been quite moderate, again reflecting humble social origins. If so, another rationalization becomes available. In our society where the mobility claims of parents are commonly transferred to children, the indifferent can similarly displace his ambitions. This alternative undoubtedly provides a necessary cathartic because idealized career hopes necessarily result in a great deal of personal anxiety and frustration.

We can expect, as a result, that the indifferent's career expectations are realistic. Surveys of experienced workers suggest that success claims are generally revised downward in recognition of bureaucratic and personal limitations. A confluence of class and structural factors encourages indifference. In mass production industries technology and organization have constricted both income range and promotional opportunities. Walker and Guest, for example, found that: "The introduction of conveyors and machine hand tools have narrowed the wage distance between the day laborer's job and that of the skilled craftsman . . . the individual work operations have either been so mechanized or so fractionalized . . . that craft skills have been virtually eliminated. One result of this technological development has been wage standardization." [6]

Moreover, promotional opportunities are limited. In an automobile plant with 6,000 workers Chinoy found "only ten or twelve openings" occurring each year.[7] Guest found only one foreman's job opening each year for 120 automobile workers.[8] They conclude that such conditions result in a wholesale lowering of aspirations. Other studies suggest that despite their expressed hopes of owning their own business, eighty per cent of manual workers have limited their expectations to manual jobs. When asked about their chances of getting just the job they want, less than thirty per cent of union members believe they have a "good chance." [9] Even within his big union, organized to offset the loss of power and of skill pride attending automation, the ordinary worker becomes part of a mass constituency providing numerical support for decisions made by others.

While supervisory jobs have increased in big organizations, the mobility expectations of industrial employees have probably been reduced during the recent past. Fifteen years ago

[6] C.R. Walker and R.H. Guest: op. cit.

[7] E. Chinoy: *Automobile Workers and the American Dream* (New York: Random House; 1955), p. 44.

[8] R.H. Guest: "Work Careers and Aspirations of Automobile Workers," *American Sociological Review*, Vol. 19, p. 157.

[9] Lipset and Gordon: loc. cit., p. 494.

Warner and Low concluded pessimistically that "social mobility is no longer present and the American worker realizes it." [1] Blum found similarly that although most workers were content with Hormel's as a place to work, "the limited possibilities of advancement do not permit widespread feelings of satisfaction." [2] Guest says with regard to mobility in the automobile industry:

> Workers do not look for nor do they expect jobs which will give them a higher economic and social status within the existing organization. Instead they hope for the break that will relieve them of the anonymity and impersonality of the line. They want jobs which they can handle as they grow older and which will give them more individual control over work pace. Their inability to achieve even these short-run and immediate gains was found to be a source of frustration.[3]

In mass industry, then, mobility and the worker's influence over his work have been reduced by the increasing size of industrial organizations and by the replacement of individual judgment by bureaucratic rules. Just as trade associations govern the individual businessman in matters of price and production, so big unions collectivize decisions affecting entry and work in their sphere. The total effect is to structure the conditions of participation. As Clark Kerr concludes: "The institutionalization of labor markets is one aspect of the general trend from the atomistic to the pluralistic, and from the largely open to the partially closed society" [4] This is not to

[1] W.L. Warner and J.C. Low: *The Social System of the Modern Factory* (New Haven: Yale University Press; 1947), p. 183.

[2] *Toward a Democratic Work Process* (New York: Harper & Brothers; 1953), p. 73.

[3] R.H. Guest, loc. cit., p. 158.

[4] Clark Kerr: "The Balkanization of Labor Markets," in Social Science Research Council Committee on Labor Market Research, *Labor Mobility and Economic Opportunity* (New York: John Wiley and Sons, Inc.; 1954), p. 96.

suggest of course that labor's bargaining power and its real income have not risen as a result of union activities, but only that organizational conditions often limit the chances of mobility and participation for the great mass of workers who cannot afford an education, now the most common avenue of mobility. Both in blue- and white-collar jobs, machine operations in office work, the rationalization of repetitive tasks, and the aggrandizement of administration have reduced the individual's influence.

Meanwhile, the sharp rise in school attendance is indicative of an American tendency to exaggerate the extent to which increased mobility follows increased education. For not only is it true that as educational levels have risen, the educational requirements for many jobs have also risen; but it is not realized (especially by those who have "worked their way through" and thus assume that anyone can do the same) that *social barriers* as well as economic ones prevent many talented youngsters from developing their abilities. The President's Committee on Education Beyond High School found that in 1956 only half of the most intelligent high school graduates entered college. We know too that the primary factor differentiating college from noncollege youth is often class, not intelligence.[5] Lower-middle- and working-class children who aspire to university training often have neither the support nor the background of family expectation that insure the necessary encouragement. Indeed, as Hollingshead shows, both their parents and their social peers may actively oppose what they regard as presumptuous aspirations.[6]

Although the number of college graduates in the U.S. rose from 15,000 in 1890 to 340,000 in 1957, and although federal educational grants for veterans after World War II were a

[5] B.S. Hollingshead: *Who Should Go to College* (New York: Oxford University Press; 1952), pp. 171-81; also see, A.B. Hollingshead and F.C. Redlich: *Social Class and Mental Illness.*

[6] A.B. Hollingshead: *Elmstown's Youth* (John Wiley and Sons, Inc.; 1949).

great step forward, such gains do not necessarily result in a comparable degree of increased mobility. This is partly because graduates from families that already enjoy relatively high status are overrepresented. Whereas "relatively few" of the children of professionals or business executives leave school *before* college, "over forty-five per cent of the children of farmers and about a third of the children of semiskilled and unskilled workers never obtain more than a rudimentary grammar-school education." [7] *Moreover, only twenty-six per cent of the children of manual workers enter college, while sixty-seven per cent of the sons of nonmanual fathers do.*[8] Since social mobility today requires extended university training, it can be seen that unequal educational chances tend to crystallize social and occupational barriers.

This conclusion is reinforced by evidence that mobility now occurs mainly among individuals who move from an employee status to one of self-employment. "The greatest social mobility occurs in the form of shifts into 'own business,' and shifts into the white-collar occupation and sales rank next. These are the occupations of most of those who manage to pass from manual to nonmanual work." [9] Although it is clear from the shocking rate of business failures (over 1,200 per month in 1961) that such shifts are often temporary, they provide a basis for loyalty to the entrepreneurial idea. "To run a business of one's own is still a much-cherished ideal. But with the growth of large-scale organizations in all parts of American society it has lost some of its meaning, although its ideological appeal has not necessarily been weakened thereby. Many still cherish it, though their own careers show little evidence that 'private enterprise' has had much significance for them personally." [1]

The social framework for such conclusions is explicit in the

[7] Lipset and Gordon: loc. cit.

[8] D. Wolfe: *America's Resources of Specialized Talent* (New York: Harper & Brothers; 1954), p. 160.

[9] Lipset and Gordon: loc. cit., p. 457.

[1] Ibid., p. 458.

following summary from a study of worker attitudes in local unions.[2]

> The steady rise in the size of the business unit, the larger amount of capital required, and the high percentage of failures among small business enterprises have made it increasingly difficult and hazardous for a wage earner to attempt to enter many lines of business. Acceptance of relatively permanent wage-earning status is apt to be accompanied by a greater acceptance of the need for group action to protect and advance one's interests in the employment relationship. Workers tend to settle early in life for the security of a steady job, depending upon their mounting seniority to shield them against the hazards of the layoff. The aspirations of factory workers are scaled down to industrial realities; for everyone who dreams of a business of his own, there are many who hope to move up to a better-paying job at a somewhat higher level of skill or responsibility or at most a foreman's position. [Moreover,] most of those who dream of a business of their own know that it is but a dream and project their hopes for upward social mobility upon their children, hoping that an education superior to their own will open the doors to professional status, to managerial positions, or at least to white-collar employment.[3]

Although workers want to be independent and retain hopes of owning their own business, it is clear that they often accept the principle behind existing patterns of control in industrial society. Some indicate that if *they* were running *their* own business, they would not want workers telling them what to do. Apparently, workers can accept the logic of big organization but at the same time reject the instrumental position they play in it. Shut out from meaningful participa-

[2] Joe Seidman, *et al.*: *The Worker Views His Union* (Chicago: University of Chicago Press; 1958), p. 257. Copyright 1958 by the University of Chicago.

[3] Ibid.

tion, yet unable to break away, the indifferent becomes resigned, using his job as a means to security and off-work enjoyment where frustrated status claims can be bought in the wish-fulfilling world of entertainment and consumption. "For the great majority of automobile workers, the only meaning of the job is the pay check, not in anything connected with the work or the product." [4]

As C. Wright Mills has shown, the structural influences that strain blue-collar identification are also at work among white-collar workers. Their disenchantment is aggravated by higher mobility claims nourished by education and the precious white-collar self-image. Despite the equalization of white- and blue-collar status and income, this idealized image persists, preserved by youth and by the preferential status that our society gives to those who work with their heads instead of their hands.

Industrial sociologists have turned blue-collar man inside out, but we know less about white-collar attitudes toward work and self. Analysis has been made difficult by the number and diversity of groups included under the white-collar rubric.

This is a highly fluid and variable class ranging from dependent, salaried professionals to precarious sales and clerical people. As Mills says:

> The three largest groups of the white-collar spectrum are office workers (forty per cent), school teachers (twenty-five per cent), and salespeople (twenty-five per cent). The remaining ten per cent is made up of managers. . . . [These people range from] almost the top to almost the bottom of modern society. [They are not a horizontal layer within society, but] a new pyramid within the old pyramid [of society]. Their characteristic skills involve the handling of paper and money and people. They are expert in dealing with people transiently

[4] Walker and Guest: op. cit.

> and impersonally; they are masters of the commercial, professional, and technical relationships. . . . They live off the social machineries that organize and coordinate the people who make things. . . .
>
> The organizational reason for the expansion of the white-collar occupations is the rise of big business and big government, and the consequent trend of modern social structure, the steady growth of bureaucracy. In every branch of the economy, as firms merge and corporations become dominant, free entrepreneurs become employees, and the calculations of accountant, statistician, bookkeeper, and clerk . . . replace the free "movement of prices" as the coordinating agent of the economic system.[5]

This class works mainly in big organizations. And its members are in a sense exceptionally vulnerable to its structural conditions and to its claims because, as we have seen, their aspirations have been higher than those of blue-collar workers. Moreover, at the higher levels they have enjoyed considerable autonomy in their work place. The narrowing of job alternatives and the fusing of the differences in pay and status between themselves and unionized workers have brought a special disenchantment. Since it is statistically impossible for the vast majority of them to cash in their success claims, theirs is an indifference of frustration, rather than of resignation as in the blue-collar class.

As Mills concludes:

> The chance to rise has been affected by the shape-up of white-collar jobs. Their concentration into larger units and their specialization have made for many blind alleys, lessened the opportunity to learn about 'other departments,' or the business as a whole. The rationalization of white-collar work means that as the number of replaceable positions expands more than the number of higher

[5] C.W. Mills: op. cit., pp. 64-5, 68-9.

positions, the chances of climbing decrease. Also, as higher positions become more technical, they are often more likely to be filled by people from outside the hierarchy. So the ideology of promotion—the expectation of a step-by-step ascent—no longer seems a sure thing.[6]

At the same time it seems that most white-collar people continue to receive some psychic income from their favored prestige position as compared with industrial workers. Indeed, we may assume that as the indexes that set them off are reduced by unionization and decreased skill demands, prestige becomes more valued. We know that status needs can be met in many ways, including identification with a powerful organization. The very opportunity to wear a white collar is rewarding and provides an opportunity for borrowing the prestige and authority of superiors in the hierarchy. Equally important, white-collar individuals have had significantly more education than either businessmen or industrial workers. In 1940 they had an *average* school achievement of twelve years, compared with only eight years for the other two groups.[7] Bureaucratic work conditions are undermining this prestige advantage, however, suggesting that indifference and a turn toward off-work satisfactions will become more common among all levels of the white-collar class.

What does the evidence show about changing work attitudes in the white-collar world? So far, our problem has been easy, since research shows clearly that blue-collar workers are often alienated from their work and from their work place. As Dubin concludes: "Work is no longer the central interest of workers. . . . Only about ten per cent of the industrial workers perceive their important primary social relationships as taking place at work."[8] While some evidence suggests that about seventy-five per cent of all types of work-

[6] Ibid., pp. 274-5.
[7] Ibid., p. 246.
[8] R. Dubin: "Industrial Workers' World: Study of the Central Life Interests of Industrial Workers," *Social Problems,* Vol. 3, pp. 132, 140.

ers will answer "Yes" to the question, "Are you satisfied with your job?", this seems unconvincing. The question as stated is just too simple. Moreover, there are both psychological and social pressures against a negative answer. "There is a certain naïveté in expecting frank and simple answers to job-satisfaction questions in a society where work is so important a part of one's self that to demean one's job is to question one's very competence as a person."[9] Indeed, as we have seen, the whole trend in bureaucratic work is to *upgrade* ordinary jobs by verbal magic, to compensate for the erosion of skill demands and satisfaction in work itself with status benefits.

A more sophisticated index of job satisfaction is one which asked workers whether they would continue in the same kind of work if they inherited enough money to live comfortably. This interrogation produced the following results:[1]

OCCUPATIONAL GROUP	AFFIRMATIVE REPLIES
Professionals	68%
Sales	59%
Managers	55%
Skilled Manuals	40%
Service	33%
Semi-skilled Operatives	32%
Unskilled	16%

Such questions avoid the slanting which follows when one is asked, in effect, to grade both his job and himself; there is usually too much ego involvement to downgrade either. Also, by posing a hypothetical situation, they give the worker a "real" chance to make a choice.

[9] R. Blauner: "Work Satisfaction and Industrial Trends in Modern Society," in W. Galeson and S.M. Lipset, eds.: *Labor and Trade Unionism: An Interdisciplinary Reader* (New York: John Wiley and Sons, Inc.; 1960), p. 355. This selection is a survey of research on job satisfaction in both blue- and white-collar worlds.

[1] N.C. Morse and R.S. Weiss: "The Function and Meaning of Work and the Job," *American Sociological Review*, Vol. 20, p. 197, cited in R. Blauner: loc. cit., p. 342.

In white-collar jobs, of course, we know that satisfaction is encouraged by higher educational levels, by clean, pleasant working conditions, by the chance to borrow status from the organization ("I am with U.S. Steel"), superiors, customers, etc. A recent study of nurses found that "about two thirds select work as the preferred source of personal satisfaction." [2] Moreover, fifty-five per cent of the nurses found satisfying personal relations on the job, whereas in the Dubin study only ten per cent of the workers did. The nurses' attitudes also relate to their associations with doctors, who not only have great prestige with nurses but also tend to have a democratic working relationship with them, in which "banter and joking . . . cancel out status differences." [3] Nevertheless, one or two qualifications seem necessary. Nursing, of course, is primarily a female vocation, suggesting that dedication would be more common than in most "male" occupations. We know that girls who go into nursing are strongly motivated by service ideals; the Florence Nightingale tradition persists.

When one turns to professional work, such psychological factors become even more significant. Not only are professionals unusually sensitive to status symbols, but there is a public expectation that they will enjoy their work. In Chapter 4 we saw that individual behavior is largely the result of our perceptions of the expectations of others. A social role is usually defined as a series of *expected* behaviors. "The professional is expected to be dedicated to his profession and have an intense intrinsic interest in his area of specialized competence; the white-collar employee is expected to be "company" oriented and to like his work; but the loyalty of the blue-collar worker is never taken for granted." [4]

There is little doubt that white-collar work provides an

[2] L.H. Orzack: "Work as a 'Central Life Interest' of Professionals," *Social Problems*, Vol. 7, p. 132.

[3] R.L. Coser: "Authority and Decision-Making in a Hospital," *American Sociological Review*, Vol. 23, p. 61.

[4] Blauner: loc. cit., p. 343.

opportunity for satisfaction and the fulfillment of status claims. The school teacher likes her summer vacation and the opportunity to travel. She may even like teaching. The office worker enjoys his pleasant office, clean work, and steady pay. The intensity of the private secretary's identification with her boss, her delight in sharing and ramifying his authority, deserve extended inquiry. The receptionist borrows the prestige and quiet opulence of her well-appointed office in a big firm; the sales clerk on upper Fifth Avenue deals with the finest people, even though his salary is no better than his brethren on Thirty-Fourth Street. The salesman's expense account insures both psychic and economic dividends. The "dedicated professional" is a common stereotype, based upon rigorous training, self-government as to achievement and behavior, and considerable independence in deciding when and how his work will be done.

But although professionals and white-collar individuals identify closely with work and the organization, both logic and evidence suggest that they too are disenchanted by increasing bureaucratization.

Logically, one can argue that job satisfaction and prestige are bound up with the *degree of control* that one exercises over the work process. As Robert Blauner says: "The fact that work inherently involves a surrender of control is probably what makes the relative degree of control in work so important an aspect of job attitudes." Unskilled workers are found at the bottom of every job-satisfaction scale, for they tend to work on the assembly-line type of job in which they have virtually nothing to say about the work process. "The very evidence of his daily work life brings home to the manual worker the degree to which he is directed in his behavior with only limited free choice available. From the moment of starting work by punching a time clock, through work routines that are established at fixed times, until the day ends at the same mechanical time recorder, there is impressed upon the industrial worker his narrow niche in a complex and ordered system of interdependency." [5]

On the other hand, the professional, who appears at the top of every job satisfaction scale, has long enjoyed a maximum of control over the conditions of his work. Ideally, his time is his own to allocate. There is no hierarchy of authority over him. His is the authority of knowledge, reinforced in the case of law and medicine by powerful associations which determine the conditions of training and of practice, protect him, and preserve inviolate the "official secrets" upon which his power rests. His prestige and training mean that his competence is *assumed* until proven otherwise. In the independent professions such as medicine he works for himself. Theoretically, there is no limit to his income, which is derived from fees assigned on the basis of judgments which he again has some latitude in making. He tends to work by himself and for himself.

We can thus assume that the degree of control over one's work and the lack of direct supervision are primary factors in job satisfaction. But the essence of bureaucratic work is the replacement of individual control by the control of *the work process*. Even in highly skilled fields work is evaluated by supervisors; "work measurement" is a hallmark of bureaucracy. This is so whether the product is turned out by men or by machines. As we have seen, big organizations are systems of graded authority that insure supervision, uniformity, and predictability. Everything follows rational prescriptions. The penetration of such logic into most work areas has enthroned collective judgments. On every hand, organizations fix the conditions of participation, limiting individual discretion by rules, certifications, and tacit expectations of many kinds.

Such demands tend to undercut traditional self-images in professional as well as in blue-collar fields. "The contemporary professional is increasingly an 'organization man,' sub-

[5] R. Dubin: "Constructive Aspects of Industrial Conflict" in A. Kornhauser, *et al.*, eds.: *Industrial Conflict* (New York: McGraw-Hill Book Co.; 1954) cited in Blauner: op. cit., p. 345.

ject to job standardization, procedures, personal policies, and other structural coercions."[6] The effects are to level work roles, to lump men together as employees, and to standardize their incentives, rewards, and evaluations. Scientists and university professors, for example, seem especially susceptible to alienation and indifference because their expectations of autonomy in their work and work place are higher than those of many groups. Yet they often work in bureaucratic work places. As the following analysis suggests, such conditions as the substitution of hierarchical authority for skill authority prove especially disenchanting.

In discussing academic work, it is important to differentiate as follows. While there are over 1,800 universities and colleges in the United States, only a very small proportion, certainly not over three per cent, can be called first-rate. Among this group there is an inner core of some twenty distinguished schools, including mainly the prestige schools in the Northeast and a handful of small, private colleges scattered around the country. Moreover, while these schools include two or three state universities, the latter suffer from certain inherent problems that encourage indifference among their faculties. Such problems include their great size and their respect for size. More important is their ultimate subordination to the common denominator of understanding of their regents and state legislatures. Neither group is likely to know much about academic traditions and values, nor do they come to know personally faculty members who might help overcome the gap in understanding. Although both public and private universities report that legislatures and politicians are the greatest single source of pressure upon their administrations, such pressures, as might be expected, increase with size and are relatively more frequent in the public universities.[7]

As a result, such institutions are constrained in social and

[6] Orzack: loc. cit., p. 132.

[7] P. Lazarsfeld and W. Theilens: *The Academic Mind* (Glencoe, Illinois: The Free Press; 1958), pp. 180-3.

political fields; they tend to build up physical science and the professional schools, which are either innately conservative or whose subject matter is rarely controversial. A dramatic example of the resulting differences in climate between the best state and private universities occurred during the mid-1950's when the House Un-American Activities Committee was flourishing. Whereas Harvard in the Furry case and Cornell in the Singer case could refuse to surrender to the Committee their right and obligation to determine the qualifications of their faculty, the University of Michigan felt obliged to welcome the Committee, and subsequently fired two instructors whose political views were suspect. Similarly, the University of California was subjected to a loyalty conflict which disrupted its internal affairs for several years.

These tragic events symbolize the conflict between bureaucratic demands for control and orthodoxy and the demands of research and teaching for freedom. Organizational logic is insensitive to subtle matters of spirit, which is precisely the major area of difference between the best private and the best public schools. Their libraries, faculties, and physical plants are not substantially different (indeed, the state universities usually have superior physical plants); but they are distinct in terms of academic traditions, bureaucratic rules, faculty influence, and the priorities they assign to quality, controversy, and freedom as over against public opinion, "service," and conformity.

While the universities remain our major centers of creativity and disinterest, and while the best ones nourish the freedom required to continue this role, organizational logic has made deep inroads. Here again, organizational values and methods have been applied to an inappropriate area. Not only is the American university president an innovation that the great European universities have never found any need for, but as scientist Robert A. Millikan says: "There has developed . . . a semimilitary form of organization with lines of authority and responsibility clearly marked. Let me call it the Pentagon philosophy of organization, and let me recognize the fact that wherever *action* is more important than *wisdom,* as in military operations and to a lesser extent in American business, it represents at any rate a natural, if not a necessary, mode of organization." [8]

The resulting subordination of highly skilled and learned men has been responsible for a considerable amount of alienation among faculty members. As one said in the *New York Times Magazine* (October 12, 1958): "The truth of the matter is that the teachers in our large universities are the low men on the totem pole. The administrators look down their noses at the faculty. . . ." In their study of 375 academic men in nine first-rate institutions, Caplow and McGee similarly found an "extraordinarily high incidence of conflict reported . . . and [a] widespread dissatisfaction of professors with the workings of academic government." [9] If this is so in prestige schools, one can imagine the situation in the others where administrative control tends to be more pervasive.

This alienation is aggravated when both status and economic rewards tend to go to a rapidly expanding administrative group which despite its remoteness from the essential purpose of the university somehow manages to symbolize it before the public. Let me say again that this passion for administration and vice-presidencies for all is less characteristic of the very best schools. But the latter, unfortunately, are extremely limited in number. In the vast majority of larger institutions, bureaucratic patterns dominate. Hierarchy again places control of the distribution of authority, prestige, and income in administrative hands. Speaking of the effects of the distribution of power in universities, Logan Wilson says: "Those who dispense largesse are certain to make dependents,

[8] *The Autobiography of Robert A. Millikan* (New York: Prentice-Hall, Inc.; 1950), p. 225.

[9] T. Caplow and R.J. McGee: *The Academic Marketplace* (New York: Basic Books, Inc.; 1958), pp. 42, 181.

if not create disciples; for much of the academician's immediate welfare, irrespective of his technical competence, depends on administrative policy and how he fits into the scheme of things." [1]

While it is customary for faculty members to deplore administration, recent world events raise grave questions about the efficacy of the present system of administrative control. Oskar Morgenstern, coauthor of the classic, *Theory of Games and Economic Behavior*, says:

> The universities must provide a new leadership and take the initiative. No one else can. There will have to be much soul searching and a pushing back of mushrooming administrations. The scholars and the scientists themselves will have to run the universities where they do not do it already—and there are precious few where they do even to a limited extent. Teaching will have to be raised to higher levels. . . . It is not enough to provide money. *The milieu in which the sciences and arts will flourish is infinitely more important.* . . . But it is difficult to create the right milieu. I believe that in the extensive discussions about science and education in America which have taken place since Sputnik I this point has been neglected. The fact is that the universities, which should provide the ideal milieu, do not do so, and no one else can. *They have not evolved an organization conducive to the unfettered growth of intellectual life. This is the really serious matter.*[2]

[1] Logan Wilson: *The Academic Man* (New York: Oxford University Press; 1942), p. 90. Here again, Veblen was the first to analyze the implications of administrative-business control of universities, *The Higher Learning in America* (New York: The Viking Press; 1918).

[2] Oskar Morgenstern: *The Question of National Defense* (New York: Random House; 1959), pp. 182-6. Reprinted by permission of the author. For another commentary on academic organization and policy making, see "A.B. Academic Bureaucracy," *The New York Times Magazine* (October 12, 1958), p. 95. Walter Gellhorn notes that "academic institutions in increasing numbers have manifested an interest in se-

Considerable evidence of faculty alienation and indifference exists. We can assume that the following statistics are related to bureaucratic conditions of size, equal pay for unequal performance, blocked career avenues, and the use of quantitative rather than qualitative criteria for evaluating productivity. One result is that a smaller proportion of qualified candidates enter university work. In 1930, for example, only eighteen per cent of Ph.D.'s took nonacademic jobs, but by 1956 fully thirty-five per cent entered fields other than teaching.[3] Of the 9,000 Ph.D.'s now awarded each year, only three out of five become teachers. This trend is especially strong in mathematics, chemistry, and the physical sciences, which not only attract the brightest candidates but also provide the greatest number of career alternatives. This condition suggests that graduates are becoming more aware of the career limitations of university teaching.

The implications for the quality of college instruction are clear enough. As one philanthropoid put it: "We are destroying our seed corn." Of all new full-time university teachers hired in 1953-54, thirty-one per cent had Ph.D.'s; only three years later this proportion had fallen to twenty-three per cent. Meanwhile, the National Education Association reported in 1959 that eighty-three per cent of some 900 reporting colleges "were experiencing a shortage of candidates in a wide variety of fields." Worse, the NEA added; "Almost all types of institutions are showing an increased willingness to employ members of the preceding *bachelor's*

---

curity clearance before making an appointment of teaching or research staffs. This self-created limitation upon institutional freedom has seemingly been induced chiefly by a desire to obtain research funds from federal agencies," *Security, Loyalty, and Science* (Ithaca, New York: Cornell University Press; 1950), p. 115; on the geometric rate of expansion of administration in education, see F. Terrien and D.L. Mills: "The Effect of Changing Size Upon the Internal Structure of Organizations," *American Sociological Review*, Vol. 20, pp. 11-13.

[3] *Teaching Salaries Then and Now* (New York: Fund for the Advancement of Education; 1955), p. 54.

degree class for full-time classroom service." [4] The number of such teachers doubled between 1955 and 1959. Of these half-trained recruits one can properly say with Wellington: "I don't know if they will frighten the enemy, but by God they frighten me!"

While administrators worked hard for more buildings, most observers agreed that low salaries were a basic factor in the shortage. Beardsley Ruml dramatized the professor's plight by putting salaries in terms of purchasing power.[4] By this measure they were worse off than they had been in 1904, his base year. Then, the full professor had an average salary of $2,000, which provided him the same amount in "real purchasing power." By 1940 his salary of $4,245 gave him only $2,575 worth of real income; and by 1953, his $7,000 was worth only $1,956. In 1958 (NEA figures) median salaries for professors were $8,072; for associate professors, $6,563; for assistant professors, $5,595; while instructors received $4,562.

The disparity between administrative and faculty salaries, between the two styles of life, and between the two levels of status income in such terms as office and secretarial facilities nourishes alienation. It is quite common to find world-famous scholars stuck off in some garretlike office, while the lowest man on the administrative totem pole enjoys the accoutrements of a junior executive in the business world, upon which administrative pay and perquisites are patterned. In 1959, the average salary of university presidents was over $16,000, higher than the median income reported for medical doctors. Moreover, a smaller share of the educational dollar now tends to go to the faculty. As Harris concludes: "What is expecially striking is the large proportion of the increased costs to be charged to nonacademic salaries: though nonacademic employees were only two-thirds as numerous as faculty members, their pay rose so much more that they contributed one-third more to the inflation of out-

[4] National Education Association: *Salaries in Colleges and Universities* (Washington, D.C.: Government Printing Office; 1957-1958).

lays for institutions of higher learning than did faculty salaries." [5] In sum, universities have two salary scales: one for administrators, another for faculty. Few universities can afford this practice which stands in the way of equitable pay for professors. It seems that higher faculty salaries have a low priority among most administrators. The latter pay lip service to the current vogue for improvement; and the Ford Foundation's subsidy has pushed some into action since, happily, the grants are based upon what the institutions themselves have done. But the typical administrator's essential concern is with new buildings, prestige, and physical growth. He prefers the existing system in which handsome salaries are paid to a few "name" professors without affecting the general salary structure.

In the lower school systems, the pecuniary advantages of an administrative career are equally clear. In 1958-59 (NEA figures), in school districts of 100,000 population and over, high school superintendents averaged $17,204 per year; co-ordinators, $9,300; principals, about $9,000; supervisors, $8,700. Teachers received about $5,200.

Some observers insist that men would not become professors had they not been scared in the first place; but evidence suggests that size, conformity demands, and bureaucratic conditions of work encourage anxiety and alienation. Here again, our concern is mainly with the larger universities, some seventy of which in 1959 had over 10,000 students each, and eight per cent of which contained fifty per cent of all professors. These institutions meet the size criterion for "big organizations," and they include the quality universities and the productive scholars who set the standard for the rest. What is the nexus between size and faculty-administrative relations? In their recent survey of 2,451 social scientists in 165 institutions, Lazarsfeld and Theilens found that fifty-one per cent of faculty members in "very small" colleges reported "unusually good relations be-

[5] S.E. Harris: "Faculty Salaries," *Bulletin of the American Association of University Professors,* Vol. 43. p. 587.

tween faculty and administration." *Only twenty-one per cent did in the "very large" group.*[6] A similar but less marked analogy appeared regarding "good relations among faculty members," which ranged from fifty per cent in small schools to thirty-three per cent in the large.[7]

Although size and anxiety concerning attacks from community groups and administrative support against them were less dramatically related, apprehension still increased with size. Fully fifty per cent of faculty members in "large" institutions were anxious, as compared with thirty-seven per cent in "small" schools. In large Catholic universities, thirty-eight per cent reported apprehension, while in small ones only fourteen per cent did.[8]

Interpersonal theory is helpful in explaining tensions between faculty and administration. An individual's perceptions of others, i.e., his evaluation of their motives, is largely a function of his own personality. Sullivan, it will be recalled, defined personality as a "self-system," a style of behavior that had proved successful in one's interpersonal relations. Lazarsfeld and Theilens found three major attitudes among professors that characterized their unhappy relations with administrators.[9] First was the assumption on the part of administrators that the teacher is in the wrong when outside complaints occur. Teachers who felt their administrations were distrustful also felt a sense of powerlessness in their dealings with the administration. Some felt that resignation was their only weapon. An economics professor at a large Midwestern university, who felt that his administration could hire and fire at will, says: "The administration of the university so arranges it that the faculty doesn't know the answers to these questions—we never know why a man isn't hired, never know why a man left."[1] Finally, faculty

[6] Op. cit., p. 25.
[7] Ibid.
[8] Ibid.
[9] Ibid., pp. 228-9.
[1] Ibid., p. 229.

members harbored guilt feelings over their compromises of principle in dealing with the administration. The objective validity of these perceptions is less significant than is the fact that they are *believed* to be true and are the basis for action.

There is a well-known relationship between our values and the kinds of work we undertake. Here again, there is a gap between the academic and the administrative mind. In a study of occupational choice and "faith in people," Rosenberg found that occupations such as teaching and science ranked at the top, whereas "self-interested" vocations such as business, finance, and public relations, ranked at the bottom.[2] The latter were chosen by people who had high mobility drives and low faith in people. The "aggressive personality type," who "respects only the powerful and the successful," was found to be more self-confident and manipulative. Significantly, he chose "organizing-administrative" occupations.[3] The "detached" type who was "deeply concerned with his independence . . . and fundamentally resistant to coercion or domination of any sort," chose art, architecture, and natural science as occupations.[4] Obviously, such characterizations refer only to general tendencies; they cannot be applied in individual cases.

These differing values complicate relations between professors, who are often "people-oriented," and administrators, who are usually (and perhaps necessarily) concerned with controls, techniques, and financial considerations. Each define situations and motivations differently. Each has a different "self-system," reflecting his discrete personal needs and values. They do not understand each other, or perhaps they understand each other too well.

The existing disparity in self-perceptions rests on other evidence. In their study of nine prestigeful universities out

[2] M. Rosenberg, *et al.*: *Occupations and Values* (Glencoe, Illinois: The Free Press; 1957), p. 27.

[3] Ibid., pp. 40, 46.

[4] Ibid., p. 42.

of some thirty-nine major ones in the United States, Caplow and McGee conclude:

> The vast majority of personal problems reported in the interviews have less to do with long-range career opportunities than with the immediate working situations. The typical professor, if such there be, suffers from his acceptance of an ideology which is incongruous with his situation. He tends to see himself as a free member of an autonomous company of scholars, subject to no evaluation but the judgment of his peers. But he is likely to find himself under the sway of a chairman or dean or president whose authority is personal and arbitrary. . . . Academic authority is exercised largely by means of the personal control which the administrator has over the salary, rank, and prerogatives of the working professor. This control is essentially illegitimate. It serves in default of a workable system of academic government. . . . The violent opposition between the academician's image of himself as a kind of oligarch, independent of lay authority, and the galling subjection which he actually experiences is presumably responsible for the combination of private resentment and public submissiveness that so often characterizes the faculty attitude toward administrators.[5]

Perhaps the embattled professor is an "inner-directed" anachronism, maintaining a perception of himself that has never been viable in American universities.

But a more impressive index of alienation is the number of academic men who leave university work for industry, private research groups, or the foundations. Unfortunately, little is known about this point. Universities are reluctant to reveal their turnover figures, salaries, and hiring practices since these may seem to reflect adversely upon their in-

[5] Caplow and McGee: op. cit., pp. 228-9.

ternal policies.[6] One knows colleagues who have left, often reluctantly, to enter government service and industry. While these are also citadels of bureaucracy, their pay is substantially above that of academia, which is critical given marginal university salaries. As economist Seymour E. Harris found in 1957, although the average salary of a full professor at Harvard in Arts and Sciences was almost $14,000, from 1930 to 1956 his *real income* had declined from 15 to 20 per cent. This in a period when the real income of the average member of the labor market rose by 80 per cent, and the real per capita income of the nation rose by 75 per cent. Thus even the full professor at the superior institution had suffered a 50 per cent deterioration in real income.[7] Those at lesser schools had been even more disadvantaged. As we saw a moment ago, the *national* median salary for full professors in 1958 was only $8,072.

Although careful studies of attrition are not available, some evidence exists. A survey of California state colleges provides some information. This system is run pretty much in line with state-government practices, with automatic promotions and pay raises, an emphasis on teaching, and with little encouragement for research. During 1959 the combined colleges lost 292 teachers, about eighteen per cent of the entire staff. While this is probably not an alarming proportion, note where these faculty members went; and think of the implications for the current teacher shortage, the loss in continuity

[6] Some evidence of this reluctance is offered by Caplow and McGee, who found in their survey of ten leading U.S. universities that the presidents of the state schools responded promptly to their requests for co-operation, but the five private schools proved more difficult. One of them, rated among the best in the world, never answered their letter requesting help. The president of this institution later refused to countenance any such research not done by alumni. A second private school president refused for technical reasons. And the three remaining prestige schools required detailed explanations and assurances before they consented to co-operate fully. At one of these, the researchers were requested not to discuss faculty salaries at the institution, op. cit., pp. 33-5.

[7] S.E. Harris: loc. cit., pp. 585-6.

and efficiency, and the cost of recruiting their replacements. On the basis of a survey of 160 of these men, twenty-one per cent went into industry; thirty-one per cent went into "other careers" or did not reveal their plans. Only forty-eight per cent remained in education. Although almost half of these gave low pay as their reason for leaving, the largest remaining group, thirty-four per cent, either did not specify or had "personal" reasons.

Michigan State University, one of the largest Midwestern institutions, provides another example of turnover among publicly supported institutions. There is no way of determining whether the following rates are representative of similar institutions around the country. One suspects that they reflect, at least during 1958-59, the state's financial crisis. From August, 1956, through June, 1959, according to official University figures, 524 members of a faculty which averaged about 1200 left the institution—a forty-four per cent turnover during the three-year period. While no standards exist for "low," "moderate," or "excessive" turnover, the figure is nevertheless impressive in view of the costs of replacing these men, in view of the dislocations in the departments they left, and in view of the impact upon the continuity of student programs, particularly at the graduate level. There is a widespread belief in university circles that turnover at MSU is excessive in certain fields. Indeed, in one social-science department, fully eighteen members of a full-time faculty averaging twenty-seven men (instructors through full professors) resigned during the same three-year period.

In their survey of academia, which leaves one between laughter and tears, Caplow and McGee describe turnover in prestige schools as excessive. They attribute it in part to the "internal dissension and low morale which follow the appointment of outsiders on unduly favorable terms." [8] This situation reflects the common policy of attracting new faculty members by substantial pay increases and related in-

[8] Caplow and McGee: op. cit., p. 228.

ducements such as limited teaching duties and liberal research time. "This practice provides a perpetual incentive for everyone on the academic ladder to circulate among institutions. The result is a vicious circle whereby the appointment of outsiders on unduly favorable terms causes dissatisfaction among the staff members in place, so that some of them seek their fortunes elsewhere, which requires more new appointments to be made by means of extra inducements, which has a further unsettling effect upon the remaining members of the staff." [9] The current market situation is also related since salaries have risen much faster at the lower ranks in order to meet the short supply of young Ph.D's.

Caplow and McGee also trace the displacement of values from teaching to publishing ("No one gives a damn if you can teach"), the mania for prestige, and persistent administrative inroads upon faculty autonomy. The domination of academic policy by trustees, who rarely know much about education, and by presidents who are selected by the trustees in their own image, also contributes to faculty alienation. Ironically, this exclusion of the faculty may actually increase their productivity by driving them into furious work as a compensation. The result, of course, is to further exclude them from questions of educational policy with which they are well qualified to deal.

The weakness of academic man at a time when his skills are so badly needed and highly valued, if often for the wrong reasons, is ironic. It rests upon several structural and personality factors. Certainly his debility is in direct proportion to his failure to think and act collectively in an organizational society. A professor has been well defined as a man who thinks otherwise. In part this posture stems from the nature of academic work, which has traditionally been highly individualistic. The scholar's is a lonely role. Criticism of majority values and conventional wisdom requires and rein-

[9] Ibid., p. 235.

forces his isolation and his independence, and disqualifies him for success on the organization's terms. Taking a public stand in lectures and writings may also require a certain individuality. Personality plays its role too, since we may assume that a self-selection process occurs whereby those who resist majority values are likely to find themselves in university teaching and research.

One result of such influence is an incapacity for the kind of group action which might enable the academic to play a more active role in the university and in the social and political arena. As in the evolution of the American university president, the political sterilization of the intellectual is another area where, unfortunately, we chose to deviate from European precedent. Not only is the American academic unable to see the need to meet organized power with organization; he often seems afraid to assume a larger role. This may reflect in turn an occupational infirmity, namely, the tendency for one's capacity for action to vary inversely with his knowledge. When combined with the guise of "objectivity," which is encouraged by knowing a great many facts, this posture guarantees immobilization.

But much of the academic's weakness rests upon his jejune status as an employee rather than an independent professional. His hired-hand role excludes him from significant university affairs, particularly those relating to community issues and major educational policy. The only effective counterpoise seems to be an accommodation in the form of a militant organization of university faculties. Such a solution would be about as controversial, of course, as the Ford Foundation in the post-Hoffman Hutchins era; but many professors would nevertheless regard it as the work of the devil.

The problem and a possible solution have been well put by A.M. Carr-Saunders:

> The status of the free-lance worker has long been envied; he calls no man master. It has long been customary

> to express regret for the relative decline in numbers of persons with this status, and at the same time to say that it is inevitable. Under large-scale organization this decline in one sense is inevitable, but it does not follow that the positions of the salaried and wage-earning workers must remain as they now are. At present there goes with the employed status a sense of dependence; that is so because organizations have been permitted to gain control. . . . [But] the man who belongs to a profession which has won for itself prestige and a position of dignity, may pass from the service of one organization to that of another. Though he remains salaried all his life, he takes his stand upon his proved competence and experience; he serves one client after another much as does a free-lance worker. He is attached primarily to his profession, whence he goes out, as occasion may offer, to render his services in some co-operative organization, and whither he returns. The difference between the position of such a man and that of an ordinary salaried worker is not to be found in their respective legal situations; the difference is subtle, but it is vital.[1]

The difference between the "ordinary salaried worker" and the professional has become subtle indeed. It is tempting to say that it has become nonexistent in the twenty-eight years since Carr-Saunders wrote. Unfortunately, as we have seen, the effect of bureaucratic work is to reduce such distinctions, to rationalize, and to level off both people and tasks. Status anxiety and the attempts to personalize work through "human relations" attest both the intensity of this claim and the attempts to blunt it. In the best universities such distinctions are recognized, but this is done in violation of organizational logic. In all but a few institutions the battle has been lost. Structure and control have overcome spirit and purpose. Not only are professors defined as

[1] A.M. Carr-Saunders and P.A. Wilson: *The Professions* (Oxford: Oxford University Press; 1933), pp. 503-4.

employees, but many of them accept this definition. Few have the prestige or the security to resist as individuals, and both academic work and temperament have so far discouraged the only practical alternative, collective action.

In this chapter, we have analyzed the behavior of the *indifferent* as a modal type of accommodation. Bureaucratic conditions of work have encouraged indifference in white-collar and professional areas as well as in the blue-collar world. The university environment has been used to document this trend because the writer knows it well, and more importantly because it has traditionally been among the least structured of work environments. Nevertheless, with the exception of a few prestige schools, the universities now have a significant proportion of indifferents in their faculties. This is explained in part by the high expectations of academic men for autonomy, as well as by the personal need for independent work which brought them to the university in the first instance. A major cause is bureaucratic conditions of work and evaluation that undercut professional standards and values.

The typical indifferent tends to reject the organizational bargain which promises authority, status, prestige, and income in exchange for loyalty, hard work, and identification with its values. Instead, he separates his work from the "meaningful" aspects of his life, which latter include recreation and leisure activities. Like the Hormel employee who spoke of "accomplishing something for the day," he is referring to what he plans to do *after* work. If the indifferent remains committed to his work, he will sometimes distinguish between it and the organization. If he is a college instructor, he may assume a "cosmopolitan" view in which his interests, loyalty, and future are seen as bound up with his *profession*, rather than with the particular school in which he happens to practice it.[2]

The indifferent posture also mediates preorganizational in-

[2] A.W. Gouldner: "Cosmopolitans and Locals: Toward an Analysis of Latent Social Roles," *Admin. Sci. Q.*, Vols. 2, 3, pp. 281-306; 444-80.

fluences of class and education that failed to honor success and the repression of unprofitable opinions. The tension between such values and the organization's claims encourages withdrawal, the rejection of majority values, and a refusal to compete for them. In so defining the work bargain the worker often reveals a realistic perception of himself and his life chances.

One result of this mode of accommodation seems to be alienation from political and community affairs. The indifferent tends to reject his company, his union, his political party, and other voluntary organizations. The mass character of society, the power and remoteness of its organizations, and one's resulting feelings of helplessness are among the psychological bases for alienation. The structural conditions of big organization often mean, too, that the organization rejects the indifferent. Oligarchy, for example, breeds alienation by excluding the vast majority of employees from real participation. The need for skilled leaders; the difficulty of getting the word to large numbers of people; the leaders' drive for power and continuity in office; the complexity of decisions; the need and the desire for secrecy in negotiations with other power groups—all restrict active participation.

Today, as C. Wright Mills concludes, most men do not shape the decisions that affect them; they are shaped by the decisions. In industry, the work process determines the worker's role. In education, remote boards of trustees and administrators set down the conditions of work. In the big unions, "pork choppers" deal with management and control union government. In national politics, by a most generous estimate of their influence some 3,000 "pros" (delegates to the two presidential nominating conventions) "decide" who will run for president,[3] while the number determining who runs for Congress is probably much smaller. In big govern-

[3] In 1960, there were 1,521 delegates to the Republican convention and 1,331 to the Democratic. Actually, of course, congressmen, governors, big city mayors, and presidential hopefuls and their organizational entourage usually control these delegates.

ment, the civil servant serves at least three masters: the politician-as-legislator, the administration in power, and the hierarchy of officialdom in which he works. Such conditions make indifference the most common pattern of bureaucratic accommodation.

CHAPTER 8

PATTERNS OF ACCOMMODATION: AMBIVALENTS

ONLY AMBIVALENCE remains to be discussed as a mode of accommodation. In this chapter the social context, personality, and behavior of the small disenchanted minority of whom this mode is characteristic will be set against organizational patterns of authority, status, and small groups. In both personal and organizational terms, the ambivalent's self-system is generally dysfunctional. Creative and anxious, his values conflict with bureaucratic claims for loyalty and adaptability. While the upward-mobile finds the organization congenial, and the indifferent refuses to become engaged, the ambivalent can neither reject its promise of success and power, nor can he play the roles required to compete for them. While upward-mobile anxiety is usually adaptive, ambivalent anxiety tends toward the neurotic.[1] In the bureaucratic situation, the ambivalent in-

[1] The distinction between adaptive anxiety and neurotic anxiety is widely accepted in psychology. Among others, see K. Horney: *Neurosis and Human Growth* (New York: W.W. Norton & Co., Inc.; 1950); *The Neurotic Personality of our Time* (New York: W.W. Norton & Co., Inc.; 1937); R. May: *The Meaning of Anxiety* (New York: The Ronald

dividual is a marginal man with limited career chances.

One important qualification is required. Despite his inability to meet bureaucratic demands, the ambivalent type plays a critical social role, namely, that of providing the insight, motivation, and the dialectic that inspire change. The upward-mobile honors the status quo and the indifferent accepts it, but the ambivalent is always sensitive to the need for change. His innovating role is often obscured because the authority, leadership, and money needed to institutionalize change remain in the hands of organizational elites. Nevertheless, few ideals or institutions escape his critical scrutiny. In his view custom is no guarantee of either rationality or legitimacy. This perception is sharpened by his inability to accept charismatic and traditional bases of authority; rationality alone provides a compelling standard. Certain personality traits underlie this critical posture.

The ambivalent personality is typically an introvert, with intense intellectual interests and limited interpersonal facility. Unlike the upward-mobiles, who stress action, objectivity, and easy interpersonal relations,[2] ambivalents are often subjective and withdrawn. Introversion has been found to be related to neurosis; anxiety and depression are common ailments.[3] Ambivalents have high aspirations, complicated by habitual under-rating of their own performance.

Press Co.; 1950); F. Fromm-Reichmann: *An Outline of Psychoanalysis* (New York: Random House; 1955); R. Grinker: *Psychosomatic Research* (New York: W.W. Norton & Co.; 1953); H.S. Sullivan: *Interpersonal Theory of Psychiatry* and *Conceptions of Modern Psychiatry;* Horney: *New Ways in Psychoanalysis* (New York: W.W. Norton & Co.; 1939); M.R. Stein, *et al.: Identity and Anxiety* (Glencoe, Illinois: The Free Press; 1960).

[2] H.J. Eysenck: *The Dimensions of Personality* (London: Routledge, Kegan Paul; 1947), p. 160.

[3] In a study of 3,083 factory workers, for example, R. Fraser found that about 30 per cent suffered from minor and disabling neuroses, and that this condition was commonly associated with a "decrease in social contacts," a characteristic behavior of introvert types, *The Incidence of Neuroses Among Factory Workers* (London: H.M.S.O. Report No. 90; 1947).

Compared with extroverts, their intellectual interests are narrow and deep, accuracy and persistence are highly developed, and verbal facility and intelligence are markedly superior.[4]

The ambivalent ordinarily plays a *specialist,* "cosmopolitan" role. He honors theory, knowledge, and skill. Socialization as an independent professional often blinds him to legitimate organizational needs for control and co-ordination. Believing explicitly that both motivation and expertise come from within, he resists bureaucratic rules and supervision. Attempts to impose standards from without are seen as presumptuous and denigrating. As a result, there is always a gap between his self-perception as an independent professional and the galling realization, punctuated daily by the organization's authority and status differentiations, that he is really an employee. His skill authority is not always recognized, even though it is perfectly clear that his technical judgments have been decisive. The managerial façade with which he is confronted confirms his belief that hierarchical authority is often specious. This tension between skill and hierarchical authority is aggravated by the organization's subjective criteria of seniority and obedience. In sum, the bureaucratic situation is inapposite to his personal and professional values.

The heart of the ambivalent reaction is a tenacious self-concern. Most events are perceived by the ambivalent in terms of himself; personal goals are usually primary. His own experiences and skills seem unique; and when his career expectations prove unrealistic, as they often do, he may invoke humanistic themes to buttress his claims for preference. In terms of an earlier distinction, we may regard the ambivalent as an idealistic, independent personality. Unable to achieve distinction on the organization's terms, he may adopt idiosyncratic alternatives, a reaction encouraged by the erosion of qualitative standards. If he aspires to artistic

[4] Eysenck: op. cit.

achievement, he may assume a bohemian role. If inadequate discipline or talent frustrate his intellectual claims, he may again enlist conventional substitutes. But since majority values usually prove irresistible, such behaviors are unsatisfactory to him. Sensitive, emotionally undisciplined, an individual in a mass society, he is perpetually out of step.

So much has been said about neurosis in contemporary society that it seems necessary here to review only its immediately relevant aspects. Some psychiatrists maintain that our society encourages neurotic behavior, manifested in personal anxiety and a pathetic reliance upon others to tell us what we are worth.[5] On the one hand, the demands of society for conformity without conviction provide for a built-in anxiety as the individual seeks approval by mimicking approved styles. On the other, his needs for self-expression impel deviant behavior that nourishes anxiety because he is unable to sustain the resulting censorship. As he resists majority values, yet cannot rise above them, an interminable conflict may ensue in which he oscillates between defiance and submission. Not only is such behavior inimical to bureaucratic claims for loyalty and consistency, but we may assume that it is aggravated by the organization's authority, status, and group systems which sharpen the disparity between organizational demands and the ambivalent's inability to honor them.

It follows that his perception of interpersonal relations will often be distorted. As Sullivan observes of the neurotic type who personifies extreme ambivalence:

> [his] delusion of unique individuality cuts off all communion. . . . We see quite a number of people in whom effectual development of personality was arrested at this stage; the later matured needs for intimacy . . . having then been tortured into strange channels of maladap-

[5] Horney: *The Neurotic Personality of our Time;* May: op. cit.; Erich Fromm: *The Sane Society* (New York: Rinehart & Co., Inc.; 1955) and *Man For Himself* (New York: Rinehart & Co., Inc.; 1947).

tive expression, and the artistic-magical interpersonal behavior evolved in delusions of reference, of persecution, and of grandeur, or along an uncertain course in which other people are treated as troublesome units more or less useful to a flaming ambition.[6]

Since anxiety is often functional because it helps individuals identify and accept authoritative stimuli, the ambivalent type might seem more adaptable because he is more anxious. But while a certain amount of anxiety eases learning and performance, particularly of simple tasks, a point of diminishing returns soon occurs. Anxiety then distorts perception and encourages dysfunctional reactions.[7] At the very least,

[6] H.S. Sullivan: "A Note on the Implications of Psychiatry for Investigations in the Social Sciences," *American Journal of Sociology*, Vol. 42, pp. 848-61; how neurotic tendencies are inculcated in middle-class children by the contradictory family requirement that the child be obedient and loving *within* the family, while exhibiting aggression and independence *outside* the home is analyzed in A.W. Green, "The Middle-Class Male Child and Neurosis," in A.M. Rose, ed.: *Mental Health and Mental Disorder* (New York: W.W. Norton & Co.; 1955), pp. 341-57; Fromm also finds the origin of neuroses in child-family relations in which the parents' imposition of "irrational authority" generates conflict usually ending in defeat for the child: "the scars left from this defeat . . . are to be found at the bottom of every neurosis," from "Individual and Social Origins of Neurosis," in Rose, ed.: op. cit., p. 287.

[7] Evidence on the effect of anxiety upon performance is not entirely consistent. In highly-routinized tasks, anxiety apparently improves performance, while in complex, difficult, and spontaneous kinds of activities, anxiety inhibits effectiveness. Grinker concludes, "if anxiety is mild, it is stimulating and facilitates increased and efficient action or thought. If it becomes too intense, disruptive effects ensue, calling forth emergency substitutive mechanisms of defense or, in greater degrees, differentiated regressive behavior." *Psychosomatic Research* (New York: W.W. Norton & Co.; 1953), p. 170. It seems that anxiety may also produce very high mobility drives, without providing the behavioral qualities required to satisfy them. Sullivan calls many of the security operations that individuals develop to ease anxiety "excess baggage" that hinders mature personality development, however useful it may be in allaying anxiety. For a summary of research on this subject, see R.S. Lazarus, *et al.*: "The Effects of Psychological Stress upon Performance,"

it undercuts the outward show of strength, control, and serenity required for bureaucratic success. Anxiety's effects are particularly apparent in the ambivalent's reaction to authority. We saw earlier, for example, that the remoteness of decision making in big organizations could result in distorted perceptions of elite power and expectations, followed by extreme and often pathetic efforts to anticipate its will. When anxiety approaches this level, it becomes dysfunctional by definition. Its effects are often aggravated by the bureaucratic situation.

We know that adaptive anxiety is largely an upper- and middle-class phenomenon. Hollingshead and Redlich, for example, show that neuroses are associated with class: "In classes I and II, some sixty-five per cent of the patients are diagnosed as neurotic; in class III the percentage drops to forty-five, in class IV to approximately twenty, and in class V to ten per cent." [8] While some research has suggested that anxiety does not vary from class to class,[9] it is significant that the *kinds* of anxiety experienced by each class may vary. Hollingshead and Redlich found that relatively milder and nonorganic neuroses were proportionally higher among the

---

Psychological Bulletin, Vol. 49, pp. 293-317; also, J.W. Thibaut and H.H. Kelley: *The Social Psychology of Groups,* pp. 56-8; and Sullivan: *Interpersonal Theory of Psychiatry,* pp. 168-71, 190-2, 373-5; Grinker and S. Spiegel: *Men Under Stress* (Philadelphia: Blakiston; 1945); R.B. Cattell and I.H. Scheier: *The Measurement and Meaning of Neuroticism and Anxiety* (New York: The Ronald Press Co.; 1961); J. Taylor: "The Relationship of Anxiety to the Conditioned Eyelid Response," *Journal of Experimental Psychology,* Vol. 41, pp. 81-92; K.W. Spence and J.A. Taylor: "The Relation of Conditioned Response Strength to Anxiety in Normal Neurotic and Psychiatric Subjects," op. cit., Vol. 45, pp. 265-72; G. Mandler and S.B. Sarason: "A Study of Anxiety and Learning," *Journal of Abnormal and Social Psychology,* Vol. 47, pp. 166-73.

[8] A.B. Hollingshead and F.C. Redlich: *Social Class and Mental Illness* (New York: John Wiley & Sons, Inc.; 1958), pp. 222, 223-9, Ch. 8.

[9] T.A.C. Rennie and L. Srole: "Social Class Prevalence and Distribution of Psychosomatic Conditions in an Urban Population," *Psychosomatic Medicine,* Vol. 18, pp. 449-556.

upper two classes, whereas incapacitating neuroses such as antisocial, hysterical, and phobic reactions, in which the individual "acts out" his destructive behavior, were substantially more common among classes IV and V. It is significant too that obsessive-compulsive neuroses, often characteristic of upward-mobile types, are concentrated in classes I and II. On the other hand, hysterical reactions, which paralyze work and self-discipline, occur six to twelve times as frequently in classes IV and V as in classes I, II, and III.[1] This suggests that the kinds of anxiety critical for organizational adjustment tend to occur disproportionally among upper- and middle-class individuals. At the same time, *within* these classes different kinds of anxiety have different organizational implications. For example, depression, which is characteristic of highly intelligent, anxious introverts, declines steadily from class I to class V. This form of neurosis is at the top of the rank order of personality disturbances among Cornell University students. As we have tried to show, the excessive doubt and guilt symptomatic of depression-prone individuals are dysfunctional in the bureaucratic situation.

In view of the compelling status needs, the intellectual orientation, and the marked educational achievement often characteristic of the introverted type, we may assume that our ambivalent is typically of middle-class origin. However, his socialization has apparently not included the respect for success which is crucial for bureaucratic success. "Success," probably the dominant value in our society, is usually defined in terms of competitive, personal achievement, with references that are mainly economic, but that also include almost any other value that can nourish self-esteem. As Kardiner observes, individual, competitive success is to modern man what salvation was to man during the Middle Ages.[2] This condition generates anxiety as men strive for the unrealistic heights set for them by well-meaning authority fig-

[1] Hollingshead and Redlich: op. cit., pp. 223-6.

[2] A. Kardiner: *The Psychological Frontiers of Society* (New York: Columbia University Press; 1945), p. 445.

ures. Meanwhile chance, change, lack of opportunity, and irrelevant or anachronistic personal skills frustrate many claims. Since youth itself is a substitute for achievement, and since extended education is often the instrument of success, the day of reckoning may be long postponed. But the very knowledge that new ways to power are available for those with skill and nerve encourages anxiety, lest opportunity pass one by.

As this idealized image of success flourishes, and many fail, self-punitive mechanisms are encouraged, ramifying inferiority feelings and in some cases providing a satisfying instrument of masochism. Generous self-assessments may be used to ease individual status needs, but such usually prove unsatisfying because the individual has been taught to rely on someone else's judgment to validate his own. Anxiety is increased as he turns elsewhere to find out what he is worth, and attempts to play the roles that will enhance his market value. Because a social theory of unlimited opportunity encourages neurotic claims and frustrations, and because uncertainty is related to not knowing just where one fits or how long he will be there, both the myth and the reality of high mobility evoke anxiety. The popularization of activities that once insured distinction, such as higher education, foreign travel, and class-laden recreations such as golf, may also sharpen the search for alternative indexes of superiority. Indeed, the declining status value of such instruments and the difficulty of inventing new ones may provoke a subtle demoralization. Conspicuous consumption, great expectations, and trading on the achievement of parents may provide temporary respite, but somewhere around the age of forty an accounting must be made. Status anxiety then becomes common, resulting in prestige claims whose ingenuity is matched only by their pathos.[3]

[3] Among others, consult William F. Whyte: *Human Relations in the Restaurant Industry* (New York: McGraw-Hill Book Co.; 1948); F. Oppenheimer: "Pamela: A Case Study in Status Symbols," *Journal of Abnormal and Social Psychology*, Vol. 40, pp. 187-94.

Having outlined the social basis of ambivalence, we can now turn to its organizational aspect. The ambivalent's reaction may be clearer if we think of the organization as a system of highly circumscribed roles. Such roles are partly the result of personal accommodations to the bureaucratic situation, worked out in the context of its systems of authority, status and small groups. Since satisfactory accommodations depend in part upon the number of behavioral alternatives available, this situation limits the probability that idiosyncratic individual needs will be met. While such needs will vary in terms of personality, individual growth often requires the opportunity for multiple choices and acceptance of the responsibility for their outcome. In the ambivalent's case, the bureaucratic situation evokes role strain because it tends severely to prescribe and to limit the range of accommodations.[4] Such conditions violate his permissive values and expectations, which resist the organization's claims for order and consistency. He is rarely able to bargain effectively in an arena which limits spontaneity by its concern with status, precedent, and authority.

As we have seen, authority is distributed disproportionately in organizations. It clusters around the top and decreases at an increasing rate as one descends the hierarchy. Its gradations are clearly marked. A specialist with idealistic value preferences, the typical ambivalent will find it difficult to accept the legitimacy of this system. He cannot believe that those who have great authority really merit it in terms of talent, wisdom, or morality. In this context, psychological tests and interviews of managerial employees in several companies found "no relationship between intelligence and aptitude and individual success as defined by their ranks or by their salaries." [5] Such evidence suggests that the ambivalent's judgments are not entirely imaginary.

[4] W.J. Goode: "A Theory of Role Strain," *American Sociological Review*, Vol. 25, pp. 483-96.

[5] F. Herzberg, *et al.*: *The Motivation to Work* (New York: John Wiley & Sons, Inc.; 1959), p. 129.

On a philosophical basis, he finds it hard to believe that objectively superior solutions to problems exist. He rejects the organization's "one-best-way" ethos.[6] He knows enough about risk and uncertainty to conclude that decision making at best is highly tentative. If solutions were known, there would be no need for decisions. He may thus find it pretentious that anyone should pretend to have very much knowledge, let alone superior knowledge. Furthermore, he does not need certainty, nor yet authoritative individuals to interpret reality for him. He does not believe that he or anyone else is master of his fate.[7] This tolerance for ambiguity permits him to live with a highly tentative view of men and events. Thus the very bases of the authority system are questioned; neither its legal nor its charismatic bases carry much weight. Perhaps, he agrees, it is necessary to have someone in command, but it seems naïve to impute superior qualities to him.

His most important dysfunction is a distorted, fearful perception of authority. The resulting anxiety is a constant handicap in dealing with his superiors. As we have seen, perhaps the most significant item in organizational adjustment and mobility is one's attitude toward authority. Is the authority system perceived as threatening, or as the natural result of size, specialization, and task-oriented relationships?

[6] For an analysis of such philosophical underpinnings of administrative theory, see D. Waldo: *The Administrative State* (New York: The Ronald Press Co.; 1948), p. 59.

[7] Contrast with this the following self-conception of a management group. "Beneath the surface and rarely verbalized as a formal code of belief, lies a basic faith in the American conception that a man can help shape his environment and, more specifically, that a man can to a considerable degree determine his own life chances . . . Nine out of ten give a categorical or qualified 'yes' to the question, 'Do you feel that fate is pretty much in your own hands?' A typical answer is, 'It's almost completely. What happens to me is the result of the way I conduct myself. I may get a little help along the way but it's up to me and nobody else.' " J. and R. Useem: 'Social Stresses Among Middle Management Men,' in E. G. Jaco, ed.: *Patients, Physicians, and Illness* (Glencoe, Illinois: The Free Press; 1958), p. 86.

Is authority regarded as a necessary evil or a positive good? Here again the ambivalent is disadvantaged. While the upward-mobile has a close bond with his father and accepts authority easily, the ambivalent tends to view authority figures as threatening, probably because of rejection or dominance by his father but also because authority figures personify conventional values which he resists.[8]

Empirical studies suggest that upward-mobiles and ambivalents have different perceptions of authority. Each has a distinctive cluster of attitudes. Stegner found, for example, that "persons accepting authority . . . show a conservative orientation, hostile to labor unions, endorsing war as a policy, nationalistic, intolerant of minority groups, and leaning to forceful solutions of social problems."[9] Moreover, there is "a trend for pro-authority subjects to have a conscious idealization of parents."[1] On the other hand, the ambivalent type tends to resist and to fear authority. Clearly, if one accepts authority, he must believe that there are *answers*, and that certain persons have them. Yet, as we have seen, the ambivalent regards truth as relative and changing. He believes, with Oliver Wendell Holmes, Jr., that absolute truth is for others to discover. Such skepticism is ill-suited to the organization's demands for loyalty and discipline.

Learning theory tells us that socialization results in *generalized* attitudes. This means that the authority system will evoke the anxiety residual from all of one's past conflicts with

[8] Adorno, *et al.*: *The Authoritarian Personality* (New York: Harper & Brothers; 1950); B.K. Ruebush: "Interfering and Facilitating Effects of Test Anxiety," *Journal of Abnormal and Social Psychology*, Vol. 60, pp. 205-12.

[9] R. Stegner: "Attitudes Toward Authority," *Journal of Social Psychology*, Vol. 40, p. 210; "One of the most striking features of work-role flexibility [of middle managers] is what we have termed 'tolerance of irrational authority.'" Management-oriented types can apparently justify wide deviations in the authority exercised by their superiors, including "an ability to relate oneself to a superior whose decisions may not appear sound . . . ," Useem: loc. cit., p. 87.

[1] Stegner: loc. cit.

authority. A legacy of antiauthority attitudes exists and is easily called into action. These same authority symbols impel positive reactions in the upward-mobiles and, indeed, in all those whose dependency needs have been amply gratified. Authority, in a word, has both anxiety-producing and anxiety-reducing functions; personality is the mediating factor. Here again the ambivalent is torn between the conflicting needs of self-realization and the security bought with dependency and submission. And once again, his reactions are often contrary to organizational needs.

As we have seen, the upward-mobile views those above him as friendly models, while the ambivalent regards them as threatening figures having the power to disadvantage him. His interpersonal relations become difficult both for himself and his superiors, who are much less interested in him than he thinks. They will be embarrassed by his rejection of the friendly patina that colors their relationship. Whether his reaction takes the form of passive resistance, resigned acceptance, or eager submission, the ambivalent is bound to disrupt the desired smoothness. If he assumes an air of submission, the senior may resent the fact that the relationship now rests on hierarchy rather than on commonsense, precedent, or his own wisdom. Submissiveness marks again the ambivalent's inability to accept the need for the kind of nimble role playing which insures that such relations *seem* permissive at the same time they nicely accommodate the authority structure of the situation. Although upward-mobiles learn to play such roles facilely, the ambivalent is often disqualified by self-consciousness and by awkward notions about equality, compounded at the same time by inconsistent needs within himself to reduce anxiety by submission.

The relationsip between personality and organizational roles has been studied among hospital aides.[2] Dividing their

[2] F. Pine and D.J. Levinson: "Two Patterns of Ideology, Role Conception and Personality among Mental Hospital Aides," in M. Greenblatt, D.J. Levinson, and R.H. Williams: *The Patient and the Mental*

subjects into "custodial" (authoritarian) and "humanistic" (equalitarian) types on the basis of thematic apperception tests, Pine and Levinson found the work orientation and behavior of each type discrete. While humanistic types had a permissive view of authority, custodials were authoritarian. "Whether the hospital authority is male or female, the custodial aide tends to conceive of him (her) as a traditional, autocratic, masculine leader." [3] Although some hostility may be expressed indirectly, he tends to "accept and idealize the authority of the doctor." He also idealizes his parents and may view the doctor as a father-figure. This suggests again that authoritarian values encourage dominance and dependency in interpersonal behavior.

Each type has a different conception of patients. Custodial aides regard them as aggressive trouble makers who could "snap out" of their illness if they really tried. Humanistic aides, on the other hand, are generally more permissive and feel personally involved with the doctors in the therapeutic process. They believe that their job enables them to understand themselves better. They accept the view that there is a "basic identity" between some personality aspects of those who are normal and those who are mentally ill. Both types, moreover, have discrete views about treatment: custodial-authoritarians believe in somatic methods such as shock therapy, while humanistic-equalitarians prefer psychological methods.

Significantly, in the context of organizational demands and modal interpersonal styles, it seems that the custodials severely repress their aggressions; they are more *disciplined* in their interactions with others. Humanists, on the other hand, often express such impulses directly and verbally. They are also more inclined to admit inadequacy or fears.

Hospital (Glencoe, Illinois: The Free Press; 1957), pp. 209-15; the phenomenon of adult personality change in an occupational context is seen in H.S. Becker and A.L. Strauss: "Careers, Personality, and Adult Socialization," *American Journal of Sociology*, Vol. 62, pp. 253-63.

[3] Pine and Levinson: loc. cit., p. 212.

Custodial types sharply differentiate right from wrong. They have conventional values, while humanistic types "have more individualized value systems." We have seen that discipline, strength, the honoring of majority norms, and respect for authority are functional values in bureaucratic work places. Such values enable one to repress the aggression within himself built up by elite monopolization of authority, prestige, and status. By definition, only a few individuals can secure large amounts of the latter. In this context, the organization inevitably fails to satisfy the claims of many of its members. The inner frustration and hostility which result make great self-discipline a necessity in those who hope to qualify for a larger share of rewards. Frustration and hostility also result in a great deal of ritualized behavior whose main function is to deny the existence of aggression.[4] Significantly, when social distance between individuals in the organizations is narrowed, such ritualized behavior tends to disappear. For example, during combat equalitarian relations between officer and man are at a peak. The combat situation permits the enlisted man to displace his hostility from the officer to the enemy. Characteristically, however, ritual behavior remains in effect, demanding considerable personal discipline and tact. The ambivalent personality does not typically possess such skills.

We cannot account for one exception in the hospital aide findings, namely, that humanistic-equalitarian aides apparently have easier authority relations with both doctors and nurses. "Doctors and [humanistic] aides are friendly. They both seem to be at ease."[5] This behavior is not characteristic of the ambivalent type, who seems to reject the authority system. Despite this, the humanistic aides criticize the doctors and the hospital more freely than the custodials, which indicates that even though their interpersonal relations with superiors may be less structured, they are less prone to

[4] Y.A. Cohen: "Some Aspects of Ritualized Behavior in Interpersonal Relations," *Human Relations*, Vol. 11, pp. 195-216.

[5] Pine and Levinson: loc. cit., p. 214.

accept authority. In general, however, the findings suggest again that personality affects organizational role, and that the bureaucratic situation provides opportunities to indulge authoritarian preferences. They also suggest that the tendency of our ambivalent-humanistic type to be freely aggressive, to criticize authority, to admit personal fears and inadequacy, and to stress personal value systems is dysfunctional. Specifically, his values make it difficult for him to accept bureaucratic norms as the basis for his actions.

He tends instead to substitute his own subjective, "tender-minded" preferences. It is well known that personality affects the resolution of role conflicts. In terms of issues involving organizational ("universalistic") norms and individual-family ("particularistic") values,[6] individuals high in conformity and "external" security values find it easier to make decisions that affect personal friends adversely.[7] Here is a suggestive distinction between those who rise in big organizations and those who do not. As we have seen, the ability to identify with the organization's manifest goals and to act accordingly is a typical upward-mobile value. On the other hand, "particularism" (the preference for individual values) is "associated with the rejection of authority, a permissive view of dissent, an acceptance of one's own impulses, and an objective appraisal of one's parents." [8] Such values are characteristic of our ambivalent type.

His inability to accept the organization's authority system compels him to reject its status system also. As we have seen, status is closely articulated with authority. Those at the top

[6] Talcott Parsons: *The Structure of Social Action* (Glencoe, Illinois: The Free Press; 1949), pp. 350-1. T. Parsons and E. Shils: *Toward a General Theory of Action* (Cambridge: Harvard University Press; 1951), pp. 80-2.

[7] E.G. Mishler: "Personality Characteristics and the Resolution of Role Conflicts," *Public Opinion Quarterly*, Vol. 17, pp. 115-35. S.A. Stouffer and J. Toby: "Role Conflict and Personality," in T. Parsons and E. Shils, eds.: op. cit.; Greenblatt, Levinson, and Williams: op. cit., pp. 197-208.

[8] Mishler: loc. cit., p. 124.

enjoy disproportionate amounts of status, and deflation sets in quickly as one descends the hierarchy. While the manifest function of status is to reward differences in ability and achievement, one of its latent functions is to validate authority. The system draws upon the common human need to legitimate dependency by imputing superiority to those upon whom one is dependent. Moreover, when status differentials are earned, i.e., when they represent objective differences in skill, achievement, and contributions to the organization, the system may enjoy widespread support. "The status system constitutes a form of currency with which members upon whom the group is highly dependent may be paid off. . . . When a consensus exists about status this currency has a dependable, common value, being regarded in very much the same way by each member and thus having high interpersonal comparability." [9] "Status congruency," the belief that individuals in a group are fairly and objectively ranked, is related to organizational morale. "As congruency increases, the [air force] crews show higher friendship ratings, greater mutual trust, greater intimacy, and (most remarkably) *less* perception of rank differences within the crew." [1]

Bureaucratic structure may thus reduce anxiety and conflict by objective definitions of authority and status. But the leveling effects of bureaucratic work also induce status anxiety as men try to find ways to recapture their individuality. The routinization of work evokes intense efforts to personalize one's job. Also relevant is the impulse to compensate for any loss of pride in skill attending the mechanization of many jobs.[2] Bureaucratic structure thus aggravates status anxiety by its specialization and anonymity, encouraging a preoccupation with indexes, however trivial, that can vali-

[9] J.W. Thibaut and H.H. Kelley: op. cit., p. 232.

[1] Ibid., p. 233.

[2] E.L. Trist and K.W. Bamforth: "Some Social Psychological Consequences of the Long-wall Method of Coal-getting," *Human Relations,* Vol. 4, pp. 3-38.

date minute differentiations in prestige and income. If the ambivalent could accept the status system and his position in it, his anxiety would indeed be eased, but both restrict his discretion in favor of organizational goals. Accommodation is viewed as a surrender of his individualistic values. Not only are the organization's rules and rewards the instruments of authority, but they symbolize an ordered system which challenges his preference for complexity and spontaneity.

In sum, the ambivalent cannot honor the status system. Although he recognizes that felicitous status relations are a bureaucratic necessity, he often rejects the compromise required to play the status game. Acutely aware of status differentials, he objects to the blurring of objective evaluations of men and work that the system brings. His professional values insist that status gradations "should" precisely differentiate skill and achievement, but it is clear that considerable displacement has occurred. Status rewards often mediate dependability, seniority, and interpersonal alliances. In the words of one professional: "After I saw the least competent man promoted because he was friendly with the chief, I was through. I wasn't up for promotion myself, but I didn't have the feeling I would get a fair shake when I would be. The first chance I had several months later I resigned and left for a new job." [3]

Placing the highest value upon creativity and individuality, normally specialist qualities, yet knowing that the big rewards go to those in hierarchical roles, the ambivalent rebels against the existing system. As Herzberg concludes in a study of 200 professional engineers and accountants in nine industrial companies, when dissatisfaction was reported, it was not associated with the work itself but with the *conditions,* i.e., the bureaucratic situation, in which the work was done. The effects of hierarchy upon work orientation are further documented by his conclusion that accountants, who

[3] Herzberg, *et al.:* op. cit., p. 88.

worked in a more structured situation, were significantly more concerned with status and personal advancement than engineers who valued work achievement more highly.[4]

The ambivalent's rebellion is based upon what seems an illegitimate ascription of authority and status to position rather than to knowledge. The status hierarchy inhibits his work by encouraging competitive relationships which make the job to be done almost secondary. In trying to work on an objective, task-oriented basis, the ambivalent often finds himself in conflict with hierarchical status barriers. A study of professionals in a hospital concluded: "There is the constant attempt in interpersonal relations to break through the logical administrative setup or the realistic hierarchies and to deal with one another as individual personalities." [5] The effort to penetrate such barriers requires "political" and interpersonal skills that the ambivalent does not always have. Rarely willing to admit that such complications are operationally necessary, he often attributes them to ritualistic demands for clearance and co-ordination that serve mainly to validate hierarchical status.

Such attitudes tend to paralyze his interpersonal relationships, which are often characterized by excessive candor and a devotion to "principle" when indirection would suffice. Others are embarrassed by his iconoclasm and his insistence upon analyzing every nuance of their relationship, stripping it of all spontaneity, warmth, and charisma. His egocentricity, which often masks a gnawing uncertainty, insures further distortion. His peers resent his inability to concede that they have problems too. This is ironic since he often has a real concern for others. Meanwhile, he cannot believe that they really like and respect him for himself. Karen Horney observes: "As long as we do not love ourselves, we cannot possibly believe that others can love us." [6] The am-

[4] Ibid., pp. 101-2.

[5] M.B. Loeb: "Role Definition in the Social World of a Psychiatric Hospital," in Greenblatt, *et al.:* op. cit., p. 18.

[6] Horney: *The Neurotic Personality of our Time*, p. 45.

bivalent concludes that if he is not respected for himself, other, less worthy motives must be involved. Thus his anxiety is fed and his interpersonal relations clouded by uncertainty about the motives of his work companions.

As we have seen, the ability to play contradictory roles gracefully is a critical bureaucratic skill. There is some evidence that the main reason for executive failure is rarely technical or professional incompetence, but the inability to "get along" with others.[7] One must be able to shift nicely from dominance to dependency. Although the organization's structured field usually defines appropriate behavior, considerable versatility may be required in situations where the relative status of actors is muted, tentative, or unknown. Transactions with equals may evoke tension among upward-mobiles, but dealing either up or down is relatively simple. (Such variations may account for the widely differing perceptions of an executive held by those at various levels in the hierarchy. In effect, each is interacting with a different person, or more precisely, with the same person in a different role.) The ambivalent, however, lacks such adaptability. Regardless of the role, he plays himself.

The small group in which he works similarly demands identifications and loyalties that he is unable to give. In organizations, many groups compete for resources that are inevitably scarce. Their competitive chances rest mainly upon the ability to close ranks and to present a united front against other factions. Group solidarity in turn is based upon value consensus among its members. Each must accept both the group's motivating values and its allocations of authority, prestige, and affection. In this context, the small group presents a structural and psychological frame quite like that of the larger organization. It socializes its members, using the tactics of learning, reward, and reinforcement. It disciplines those who dissent, denying them recognition and empathy. Like the larger system, its authority, status, and

[7] K. McFarland: "Why Men and Women Get Fired," *Personnel Journal*, Vol. 35, p. 307.

prestige are nicely ranked in terms of the degree to which each individual has internalized its values.[8] Here too, the ambivalent reaction proves disqualifying. A chronic "outsider," he has learned anxiety defenses that often stress skepticism, rejection, and distrust.[9] His rewards include a feeling of uniqueness and the flaunting of the conventional values that saturate organizations. Their precious distinctions of rank, status, seniority, and their manipulative interpersonal ethos leave him between anger and despair.

In explaining this reaction, psychological theory seems more useful than sociological theory. The latter tends to focus upon group and collective determinants to the extent that individual behavior may be viewed purely as a social function. Although society clearly plays the major role in shaping personality, this conception neglects personality's role in organizational behavior. If the individual is seen essentially as a group product, we may ask: But which of his several membership groups receives his primary allegiance? Is his work group more critical than his family or his church? Mannheim has said: "The motives and desires of a single man may vary with the groups in which they are expressed." [1] The

[8] G. Homans: *The Human Group* (New York: Harcourt, Brace & Co.; 1950), p. 141; O.J. Harvey and C. Consalvi: "Status and Conformity to Pressures in Informal Groups," *Journal of Abnormal and Social Psychology*, Vol. 60, pp. 182-7; P. Blau: "A Theory of Social Integration," *American Journal of Sociology*, Vol. 45, pp. 545-56; R.F. Bales and P.E. Slater: "Role Differentiation in Small Decision Making Groups," in T. Parsons and R.F. Bales, *et al.*: *Family Socialization and Interaction Process* (Glencoe, Illinois: The Free Press; 1955).

[9] T. Leary: *Interpersonal Diagnosis of Personality* (New York: The Ronald Press Company; 1956), pp. 269-76; for clinical data on group reactions to nonconformists, see D. Stock, *et al.*: "The Deviant Member in Therapy Groups," *Human Relations*, Vol. 11, pp. 341-72; D. Cartwright and A. Zander: *Group Dynamics* (Evanston: Row, Peterson & Co.; 1953); for literary and philosophical portraits of the "outsider," see also Albert Camus: *The Stranger* (New York: Alfred A. Knopf, Inc.; 1946); Colin Wilson: *The Outsider* (Boston: Houghton Mifflin Co.; 1956).

[1] Karl Mannheim: *Man and Society in an Age of Reconstruction* (New York: Harcourt, Brace & Co.; 1951), p. 335.

ubiquity of role conflict also suggests the weight of personality in individual behavior. The ambivalent's rejection of work group values may be explicable in such terms.

This temperamental inability to identify with group values frustrates the hopes for mobility and autonomy that his idealism has led him to expect. The majoritarian ethic of organizations repels him. He will not understand that if they are to compete, they must deal in averages. Their standards and their product must suit the majority. They must seek control through hierarchy. Both their ends and their instruments must be collectivized. However, the ambivalent confuses the ideal of individual autonomy with the reality of such barriers to self-realization. Each time these untenable hopes are dashed, he is disenchanted. A less rigid perception might include hope in its calculus, but the ambivalent often sees his own position and that of the organization as going from bad to worse. Insofar as his own mobility is concerned, he is correct, since his inability to accept the organization's terms excludes him from its rewards. The closer an individual comes to realizing in his behavior the norms of the group as a whole, the higher will be his rank, and in turn the greater his influence.[2]

This generalization holds in many contexts. In the U.S. Senate, for example, as Matthews has shown, members may be divided into an elite "inner club" and those who remain outside.[3] The critical standard for membership in the club is the acceptance of the traditional values and behavioral norms of the Senate. Significantly, the men who conform most closely to its folkways are the most influential members of the Senate, as measured by their ability to get their bills passed. This Senate type who "cares more for the

[2] G. Homans: op. cit., pp. 141, 145, 169, 257.

[3] D.R. Matthews: *U.S. Senators and Their World* (Chapel Hill: University of North Carolina Press; 1960); Matthews: *The Social Background of Political Decision-Makers* (Garden City, New York: Doubleday and Co., Inc.; 1954), Ch. 3; W.S. White: *Citadel: The Story of the U.S. Senate* (New York: Harper & Brothers; 1956).

esteem of like-minded colleagues than any other type of approval,"[4] shares many of the values of our upward-mobile. He is above all "a prudent man, who serves a long apprenticeship before trying to assert himself, and even then talks infrequently. . . . More than anything else, he is a Senate man, proud of the institution and ready to defend its traditions and perquisites against all outsiders. He is a legislative workhorse who specializes in one or two policy areas. . . . he is a conservative, institutional man, slow to change what he has mastered at the expense of so much time and patience."[5] Here again, note the acceptance of typical organizational values of seniority, authority, group norms, and continuity.

On the other hand, the ambivalent role seems nicely comparable to that historically played by "outsiders" in the Senate. Such men may consciously elect *not* to become members of the inner club. Their disengagement is not necessarily a matter of personal or social disability, but is often the result of deliberate choice. However, temperament again underlies this accommodation: "the outsider feels impelled to stand for principal absolutely, preferring defeat on those terms to half-a-loaf. He likes to tell people what they should and frequently do not want to hear. He is never so confident of his opinions as when he holds them alone. He is as comfortable alone against the crowd as the Senate type is in the bosom of the club."[6] Unlike the latter who is a "local," the ambivalent-outsider plays a "cosmopolitan" role: he

[4] R.K. Huitt: "The Outsider in the Senate: An Alternative Role," *American Political Science Review*, Vol. 50, p. 571. It is significant that Huitt does not regard the "outsider" as a deviant type, but rather as an "alternative" type, for whom the Senate has historically had considerable tolerance. To some extent, however, this conclusion violates one well-documented aspect of group behavior, namely, the fact that both acceptance and influence are normally a function of the individual's internalization of majority group values.

[5] Ibid., pp. 566-7.

[6] Ibid., p. 571.

"typically looks elsewhere—to his constituents and to his ideological allies across the nation." [7] The cost of this independence may be high, however, for he rarely exerts great and continuing influence within the Senate group.

Here again the interpersonal phenomenon of becoming "locked into" relationships may be seen. The ambivalent's rejection of group values may result in a progressive worsening of his relations with its members. Robert Merton says: "What the individual experiences as estrangement from a group of which he is a member tends to be experienced by his associates as repudiation of the group, and this ordinarily evokes a hostile response. As social relations between the individual and the rest of the group deteriorate, the norms of the group become less binding for him. For since he is progressively seceding from the group and being penalized by it, he is the less likely to experience rewards for adherence to the group's norms. Once initiated, this process seems to move toward a cumulative detachment from the group, in terms of attitudes and values as well as in terms of social relations." [8]

The ambivalent's accommodation proves disqualifying in another way: it prevents him from developing a rational perception of bureaucratic interpersonal relations. He fails to understand that size, rationality, and anonymity inspire "universalistic," tough-minded choices. When Mailer's General Cummings says: "The army works best when you're frightened of the man above you and contemptuous of your subordinates," the ambivalent loses contact.[9] Not only is he temperamentally incapable of admitting that action is often immoral, he cannot avoid seeing people as individuals. Partly

[7] Ibid.

[8] R.K. Merton and A.S. Kitt: "Reference Group Theory and Social Mobility," in R.K. Merton and P.F. Lazarsfeld, eds.: *Continuities in Social Research* (Glencoe, Illinois: The Free Press; 1950), p. 94.

[9] Norman Mailer: *The Naked and the Dead* (New York: Signet edition; 1950), p. 152.

as an anxiety reaction, but also because he believes individualism cuts both ways, he cannot make decisions that affect others adversely without undue personal strain. Always on the lookout for evidence that will document his "tender-minded" orientation, he idealizes human relationships. He has never learned that many individuals *want* structured relationships and find in their dependency a cue that reinforces their own preference for hierarchy and their need to believe that its gradations are the result of merit.

In an organized society where individuals are often viewed instrumentally, personal influence is often achieved by combination and compromise. One must join some organization if his will is to be felt. He must accept its values. But here again, the ambivalent's values often prove disqualifying. He resists organized "causes" because they are imperfect and require what he regards as a "sacrifice of principle." Disdaining half a loaf, he usually ends up with nothing. As a result, his preconceptions about his personal impotence are reinforced. Withdrawal serves a self-confirming function. It also reinforces his neurotic tendencies. Significantly, withdrawal and alienation are often associated with neurotic disturbances. J.A.C. Brown says: "If this need [for group acceptance] remains unsatisfied, nothing else can compensate for its lack. Loss of status leads to social isolation, and is one of the commonest causes of neuroses." [1]

The difficulties experienced in interpersonal relationships are often aggravated by frustration. Since a classical generalization of social psychology is that aggression mediates frustration, we may assume that the ambivalent's behavior

[1] J.A.C. Brown: *The Social Psychology of Industry* (Baltimore: Penguin Books, Inc.; 1954), p. 281; cited by E.L. Brown, *et al.*: "The Applications of the Science of Social Behavior in Ward Settings," in Greenblatt, *et al.:* op. cit., p. 482; a similar relation between isolation and neuroses was found by R. Fraser: op. cit.; authorities believe that neuroses of one kind or another provide the largest single cause of problem workers, amounting to 20-40 per cent of all patients referred to industrial physicians. Moreover, from 30-60 per cent of all individuals who consult doctors are estimated to be suffering from psychoneuroses.

will often be unpredictable and aggressive.[2] As we have seen, ritualistic behavior and the concentration of culturally valued rewards at the top inevitably evoke frustration and hostility among many members of the organization. Unsatisfied claims for success and power skew the ambivalent's behavior from an effusive bonhomie to a failure to honor ordinary social amenities. Lacking a sense of proportion, he often takes a stand on the basis of principle over relatively insignificant issues. This tendency to do the right thing at the wrong time may be aggravated by an insistence upon a degree of frankness that paralyzes human relations. He may also retain quaint and passionate beliefs about the relevance of objectivity in human affairs and the importance of hard work and merit in career success. Here he often fails to distinguish between what is and what he thinks ought to be. Indeed, he usually operates in an "ought" framework, providing himself with an idealistic and irrelevant standard that proves once again that everything is usually for the worst.

Such a self-system makes the ambivalent a tragic figure in big organizations. On the one hand, he wants success yet resists paying the price in collectively validated behavior. On the other, he disdains success, as popularly defined, yet feels that his individuality must be validated by others. Unable to reject or to rise above majority values, he is also unable or unwilling to play the roles required to achieve them. While the upward-mobile is sustained by status rewards and great expectations, and the indifferent accommodates by limiting his aspirations, the ambivalent is chronically disturbed. While upward-mobile anxiety seems to reflect mainly a *fear of failure*, the latter's fear mirrors *ethical conflict*, arising, for example, from bureaucratic claims for exploitative roles. Although incapable of playing the roles required for success, he badly needs success to validate his

[2] J. Dollard, *et al.*: *Frustration and Aggression* (New Haven: Yale University Press; 1939).

intense need for recognition. Although majority values must be honored, he is temperamentally incapable of accepting them. He demands self-realization; he wants to count, to put his ideas into practice. Yet in big organizations such demands are usually honored only through the subordination of individual claims.

The ambivalent evaluates himself by the same unattainable standards he sets for others, and builds up more anxiety by his inevitable failure to measure up. Since (unlike the upward-mobile) he demands immaculate causes, he is immobilized a good deal of the time. His inability to identity with the organization not only disqualifies him for success on its terms, but aggravates his anxiety as its leaders exchange loyalty to the organization for its rewards. If he were self-sufficient enough to reject such claims, the conflict might be resolved. If he could adopt unconventional behaviors without disqualifying strain, he would probably not be neurotic. If he had the upward-mobile's facility for "positive thinking," the organization might provide him security through recognition. Finally, if he were exceptionally productive he would personify Rank's "creative artist," who can rise above majority values. But the ambivalent's conflict is always the conflict between such values and the idiosyncratic alternatives he enlists to dramatize his individuality.

Such efforts to escape his cramping environment take several forms. He may develop a compulsive interest in his work, not so much for its intrinsic value, but as a means of obtaining sufficient recognition to set him off from the rank and file. Creative work is difficult for him, however, since he is often hypercritical of his own efforts. Moreover, his anxiety makes him afraid to project his ideas upon a world perceived as hostile. He may seek easier ways of differentiating himself and securing the independence that will permit escape from the bureaucratic mold. Unusual mannerisms or the aping of those who are successful may follow as he attempts to borrow status and clip a security dividend.

But he is always inhibited by a fundamental anxiety which may provoke extreme variations of behavior, from rebellion in an effort to validate his autonomy to submission which reduces anxiety. Toward the pathological end of the continuum, he may hope that something cataclysmic will break the monotony of his unsatisfying role. He may entertain fantasies such as the well-known "magic helper" delusion which insures that he receives preferential treatment. In all this he is attempting to escape the stereotyping of big organization.

His ambivalence is intensified not only by the organization's acquisitive demands but also by its structure and procedure, which seek control by limiting individual discretion. Collective goals and values always have priority. By ascribing specific roles with limited jurisdiction, bureaucratic structure aims at predictability, which necessarily assumes control. This creates a situation unalterably opposed to the ambivalent's demands for autonomy. We can now restate an earlier hypothesis: the ambivalent finds bureaucratic structure uncongenial because his value preferences deny its functional requirements. The latter include an uncritical acceptance of the legitimacy and rationality of the organization; the supremacy of its manifest goals; the honoring of tradition and precedent; structured, authoritative interpersonal relations; and collective decision making, hence collective irresponsibility.

Unlike the indifferent, however, who rejects and displaces such claims, he can neither reject them nor find work situations in which they would seem less compelling. One might assume that he would seek an unstructured environment in small business or the "independent" professions of law, medicine, and university teaching. But the possibilities are limited because in these callings too, big organizations often provide the main avenue for cashing in personal claims. Skill is no longer enough. Large, prestigious law firms, for example, now "want men who also have pleasing personalities, are from the 'right' schools with the 'right' social backgrounds, have a 'cleancut' appearance, and are endowed with tremendous stamina."[3] The dysfunctions of size are suggested by the recruitment themes of those firms which play down the common anxiety of law graduates that they will be forced to specialize too soon, will fail to receive "proper training," or will "get lost" in the large organization. A related indication of bureaucratization is the gentlemen's agreement among such firms that they will not lure men away from another office, nor will they exceed the "going rate" of beginning salary. The highly specialized "law factory"; the big state university with its utilitarian ethic and programs; medicine's demand for cohesion, as evidenced, for example, by the compulsory subscription policy of the American Medical Association in its campaign against "socialized medicine"—all underscore the changing conditions of professional work.

Fundamentally destructive reactions may follow. Disenchanted by unrealized claims for status, frustrated by an alien environment, the ambivalent may become embittered and his perceptions increasingly distorted. The organization's elite may appear to be unrestrained Machiavellians. The normal disappointments of life may be perceived as evidence of conspiracy, particularly since chance no longer fits into his calculations. Here again his error is in generalizing from an individualized perception of a partial truth. The obvious rationality of the elite, its preoccupation with the "political" consequences of its actions, and its fairly patent manipulations suggest clearly enough that probability has been harnessed; but the ambivalent concludes that it has been eliminated. As Freud observed, such distortions meet his needs in two ways: he escapes a painful reality, which might show that his failure is really his own fault; and he

[3] E.O. Smigel: "The Impact of Recruitment on the Organization of the Large Law Firm," *American Sociological Review*, Vol. 25, pp. 56-66.

can exploit the neurotic claim, often by using it to rationalize his inability to work productively.[4]

Contrary to the Indian proverb, "It isn't how much one can do, but how much he cares," the ambivalent's tragedy is that he cares too much, but can do too little. Alienated by bureaucratic conditions and by his own distortions of them, he finds little satisfaction in work. The security which identification with the organization would provide is denied him. Since he has little faith in either its rationality or legitimacy, both are foreclosed. In some cases, and at great cost, a compulsive effort to escape anonymity and futility may result in achievement that brings the recognition he needs. But such solutions are unlikely in a milieu whose ground rules stress seniority, co-optation, and conformity. Both the situation and his personality inhibit self-realization.

In this chapter we have traced the dysfunctional results of the ambivalent's adjustment to the bureaucratic situation. The most critical item is his fear of authority which often distorts his interpersonal relations. His inability to accept the organization's collective goals, which violate his need for personal autonomy, is also at work. His "tender-minded" view of human relations disqualifies him for the "universalistic" decision making required for success on organizational terms. Since his preferences include a desire for creativity and for a work environment that permits spontaneity and experiment, the structured personal relations, stereotyped procedures, and group decision making of big organization prove stifling. He rejects its systems of authority and status which often seem to rest upon subjective bases rather than upon the objective, professional claims that motivate him. Nor can he easily identify with the small group in which he works, for here too the conditions of participation are similar to those of the larger system. If his values did not include prestige and influence, a happier

[4] Sigmund Freud: *Introductory Lectures on Psychoanalysis* (New York: W.W. Norton & Co.; 1935).

accommodation might be possible; but these again emphasize his ambiguity and his inability to assume the roles required to achieve them. In sum, with the exception of his critical function as the agent of change, the ambivalent type is uniquely unsuited to the bureaucratic situation.

CHAPTER 9

THE SOCIAL DYSFUNCTIONS OF ORGANIZATION

THE LAST few chapters have stressed the internal aspects of big organizations, particularly their impact upon the individuals who work in them. We now turn to some of their larger *social* consequences. Are their vaunted contributions to our economic power and our affluence the only grounds upon which they should be assayed?[1] Or do they have other, less positive, consequences that must be included in any assessment of their critical role in American society? Big organizations do indeed have vital social dysfunctions over and beyond their failure to provide a democratic-humanistic work environment. Significantly at this historical stage, such dysfunctions give rise to grave questions about our competitive ability in the international arena.

The dominant theme in the antiorganizational refrain has usually been that bureaucracy stifles individual demands for self-realization and autonomy. While this is all to the good,

[1] These achievements, of course, rest upon factors such as natural-resource wealth, technology, capital, and a highly skilled labor force. The organization's unique contribution is to combine such factors into a productive synthesis, mainly by centralizing authority and control.

the larger implications of big organization are perhaps even more significant today, since they touch upon our very capacity for survival. Certainly we have never faced a challenge comparable to that now posed by Russia and China. Our democratic values and political system are also threatened by the rise of authoritarian governments in many new states where for some time poverty, illiteracy, and insecurity will make democracy untenable. Meanwhile, there is at this critical juncture evidence of our declining superiority in atomic weapons and missiles, and also some question whether our rate of economic growth is rapid enough to provide jobs for an expanding work force faced with increasing automation.

In this larger context, then, what are the dysfunctions of the organizational logic that pervades our society? This question requires some prefatory consideration of the *utility of conflict,* a concept that has come into wide disrepute during this era of conventional wisdom and good cheer. Both conflict and change have been stoutly resisted. But even the slightest historical perspective reveals that the survival chances of a society are largely a function of its ability to meet change. As Arnold Toynbee has shown, civilizations have always been confronted with successive challenges, such as the alternating cycles of drought and humidity that occur in the Eurasian and African steppes, forcing nomadic tribes to seek food by invasion of surrounding agricultural countries.[2] When unable to harness their values and institutions to the demands of social, economic, and climatic change, civilizations have rapidly declined. Challenges emerge within the existing order, while others are the result of external pressures. One might assume the former to be easier to accommodate since their elements are embedded in the existing culture, in contrast to alien influences that are not only novel but less amenable to control by the threatened society.

This distinction between internal and external challenge

[2] Arnold J. Toynbee: *A Study of History* (New York: Oxford University Press; 1934), Vol. 3, pp. 7-22, especially p. 17.

underlines the gravity of our present situation. For not only is the challenge essentially alien and novel, but as the uncertain course of our diplomacy suggests, we seem to have lost the initiative. With the grand exception of the Marshall Plan, for the past decade our diplomacy has been mainly one of parry rather than of thrust. The present conditions are unique in that, while threats to American security have traditionally occurred along a single dimension, the challenge now proceeds simultaneously along social, political, economic, technological, and military lines. The main challenge, moreover, seems to exist in the very areas where we have enjoyed supremacy, namely in technology and economic growth.

These unprecedented developments pose the most urgent demands for critical inquiry into time-honored patterns of organization, thought, and behavior. We can probably agree that the present challenge is not only unique, but that its successful resolution will require a major advance in creative areas. Not only in weaponry, but also in the design (or at least in the acceptance) of the new social and economic models that change is forcing upon us. Here again our very success is a potential handicap to us. This irony can be seen, for example, in the insistence of many political and business leaders that economic growth in the underdeveloped countries must follow the impressive American pattern of free enterprise. But such societies cannot afford free enterprise as we have known it, mainly because of their lack of venture capital (per capita income in these societies is less than $200 per year) and because of the complex technical and managerial skills that our system requires. If such unrealistic and nostalgic attitudes persist, what hope is there for the acceptance of new ideas here, such as the thought that our own national state may have become an anachronistic form of political organization?

In both weapons development and social organization, then, creativity is required to meet global shifts in power and to accommodate the demands of poorer countries for political and economic equality. Yet both our social values and our organizational forms inhibit the conflict and criticism which are the very beginning of creativity. Because it is so vital today, let us consider for a moment the sociology of conflict. What is its utility value; and why do organizations inhibit it?

The aversion to conflict in big organizations rests in part upon the perspective of its leaders who see the organization as a disciplined, cohesive system for achieving a common goal. They regard it as a rational instrument which binds together the interests of its members in a kind of all-for-one, one-for-all ethic. The other face of organization with its informal power centers and its function of satisfying individual needs for status and self-realization is neglected. Organizations are not defined this way by those who direct them. As Coser says: "The decision makers are engaged in maintaining and, if possible, in strengthening the organizational structures through and in which they exercise power and influence. Whatever conflicts occur within these structures will appear to them to be dysfunctional."[3] Moreover, many social scientists with a conservative bias regard conflict as anathema because they define society as an organic system in which by definition all values and groups operate smoothly as vital parts of the whole system. Conflict or disagreement about basic values or the roles assigned to each group thus tends to be regarded as destructive.

Similarly, in American political life, the liberal ideal of a co-operative society in which everyone works together for the public interest has gone virtually unchallenged. This romantic pluralism holds that there are really no basic (or at least no irreconcilable) conflicts between classes, between labor and management, between big business and small business, etc. Adjustment, not conflict, is the theme. To hold otherwise is to fall victim to an unlovely economic determinism. Thus both political and sociological analysis often

[3] L.A. Coser: *The Functions of Social Conflict* (Glencoe, Illinois: The Free Press; 1956), p. 27.

has a built-in conservative bias which abhors conflict. In the everyday world, organizational leaders share this bias; and much of their time is consequently spent showing that we must all hang together or we will surely hang separately.

Organizational logic is essentially conservative, for it honors consistency, tradition, the minimizing of individual ends in favor of collective ends, and the wisdom of history rather than the wisdom of men. A resulting major quality and dysfunction of big organizations is, therefore, their inflexibility in the face of social and technological pressures for change. They resist conflict and creativity because they tend to assume that what is, is good. Perhaps the revival of conservative ideals among some American writers is a by-product of the organizational society in the sense that the organizational ethic has needed, certainly, a more compelling rationalization than mere efficiency or profit. It seems less ingenious, moreover, to praise organizations and modern technology than to attribute our national achievements to tradition, to history, and even to heredity, as conservative theory does.

In a larger social context, conflict is further inhibited by the pervasive American need to be liked, to pursue conformity for the sake of popularity. As we saw earlier, socialization inculcates conventional values to the extent that the individual feels guilty when he expresses unorthodox views. Moreover, as organizations become more systematic in their demands for predictability and conformity, the penalties for heterodoxy become more severe. When career chances are threatened by independence, independence becomes a luxury. Bureaucratization plays its part relentlessly as the trend toward spending one's work life in a single organization ties the individual more and more closely to the demands of a given organization. The piling up of fringe benefits and seniority rights encourages the tendency to rationalize one's work place as the best of all possible worlds. Professional training and commitments similarly increase one's personal mortgages and his tendency to play it safe.

Despite the traditional aversion to conflict, a few sociologists have stressed its positive, desirable side. Robert E. Park, for example, insists that conflict is a normal and necessary part of social life. "Only where there is conflict is behavior conscious and self-conscious; only here are the conditions for rational conduct [found]."[4] Among its useful aspects is its tendency to further and intensify group cohesiveness, particularly in the face of external threats. Our present conflict with Russia, as earlier with Germany and Japan, suggests how external threats can bring unity and resilience to a society. A similar phenomenon is apparent in minority groups where hostility may produce an exceptional capacity for survival and competition. One may assume that Jewish child-raising patterns, which seem to inculcate great security in the children, originate in this structural condition of minority existence.

The utility of conflict is seen again in its role as a reality-testing device, as sharpening the quality of decisions through debate. Unopposed policies often appear infallible, especially in organizations where they are often imposed full-blown by elites. But when put to the test of critical inquiry, policies can lose their luster. The common reliance upon authority to sustain policy is not surprising, inasmuch as the validity of most decisions depends upon many unforeseeable factors and is therefore tentative. Nevertheless, men operate at many levels of rationality, and we can safely assume that a decision which has been sharply debated will be more rational than one which rests merely upon traditional or hierarchical authority.

In real life, however, as distinguished from logic, the utility of conflict is undercut by the irrelevance of facts when decisions involve normative issues; or when decisions involve factual alternatives that can be supported by equally impressive evidence. In such cases, conflict may actually be a waste of time, a kind of ritual, duly observed, and having

[4] R.E. Park and E.W. Burgess: *Introduction to the Science of Society* (Chicago: University of Chicago Press; 1921), cited in Coser: op. cit., p. 20.

little impact upon either the participants or the outcome. Despite this qualification, history shows quite clearly that criticism is often the beginning of innovation. Moreover, a premium is placed on the rigorous advocacy of new ideas by the resistance that often greets them. We are told that Galileo was unable to persuade the professor of astronomy in Padua University to look through his telescope. General Custer refused to take the Gatling gun, the forerunner of the machine gun, into the Battle of the Little Big Horn. His men were thus obliged to face Winchester repeating rifles with single-shot Springfields. Szilard and Fermi had to enlist the political art to gain support for atomic research, and Admiral Leahy, one of the wartime Chiefs of Staff, was sure that the atom bomb would not work.

But the monumental resistance that meets social and economic change makes scientific innovation seem relatively easy; technical change can occur swiftly, but man's social values remain inveterate. The rise of unions, which in retrospect seems to have been an inevitable correlate of the national organization of industry, was greeted by violent conflict. The pluralist rationalization which now accepts unions as an essential part of highly organized society came after the fact. The widespread demand for governmental social-security programs required a tragic depression to validate its claims. The recognition of Russia took twenty-five years and a "radical" in the White House before necessity overcame virtue. A similar myopia prevails at the present time with regard to Communist China, although here it seems virtue will prove less durable. In such cases conflict helped bring about changes that might not otherwise have occurred.

In the political arena, the benefits of conflict are apparent in the British system. His Majesty's Loyal Opposition is explicitly charged with presenting alternatives to the policies of the party in power. Here institutionalized conflict pays off in responsible criticism. A related mechanism is the Parliamentary Question, whereby a certain period must be set aside each week during which legislators may direct questions to cabinet members concerning their departments. In this way conflict is built into the British political system, in sharp contrast to the logic of most organizations which regard conflict with horror.

Essentially, conflict and criticism shake us out of the complacency that is uniquely the danger of a rich, hedonistic society. While our complacency is surely reinforced by an inclination to regard as significant only those things which happen during our lifetime, it also reflects the blind nationalism that inheres in every society. It has been said that Greeks today retain the Platonic opinion that the rest of the world is, unfortunately, but nevertheless clearly, composed mainly of barbarians. To the French syphilis was always the "Italian" disease, while to the Italians it remained the "French" disease. Such complacency is all the more seductive when one is living, as we are today, near the zenith of our country's historical influence. In this condition it is difficult indeed to accept Cromwell's admonition: "Conceive it possible, in the bowels of Christ, that you may be mistaken."

However well founded our complacency may have been in the past, the evidence now suggests that it has become a luxury. However difficult it may be to develop a higher toleration for ambiguity on a national scale, criticism and conflict must again become fashionable. This brings us back to organizational logic which is the root of the matter, since its premises discourage experiment and iconoclasm. What evidence exists that such dysfunctions affect basic research and weapons development, our most immediate challenge?

In what follows, let the scientists speak for themselves. In terms of our organizational types, it will soon become evident that these individuals tend to fall in the ambivalent category, particularly in their resistance to bureaucratic norms of order, of consistency, of hierarchy, and of uncritical acceptance of organizational goals. It is equally clear that if change is to occur, it must come from these innovative types to whom change is the norm. We begin by reviewing the essentials of scientific creativity, and then set them against the organizational claims traced earlier. What are the conditions of pure science? Percy Bridgman, Nobel Laureate in physical science, answers as follows:

> Pure science, in the first place, gets done by individuals, and these individuals have rather specialized characteristics which must be recognized if their turning out of pure science is to be properly encouraged. One of the most important of these characteristics is disinterestedness—the pure scientist is not primarily interested in the practical consequences or in the applications that may be made of what he finds. . . . Feeling as he does, the man who does pure science cannot help being a little bewildered by the clamor of the public that he should get busy and turn out pure science in order that the United States may stay ahead of Russia; nor can he help feeling that if he should yield to the clamor he would lose something in personal integrity. . . . It is stylish at present to think of science as essentially a public activity and even to incorporate its publicness into the definition of science. It seems to me on the contrary the most fundamental things about scientific activity are private and individual.[5]

One sees here several values that defy organizational logic, not only in Bridgman's tribute to individualism, but in his concern with work for its own sake and not, as organizations often insist, for its practical consequences or for its status dividends. But most significant, in view of the problem of loyalty and security, is the rejection of nationalistic motivation implicit in his "being bewildered" by the popular demand that the scientist should "turn out pure science in order that the United States may stay ahead of Russia." In the scientist's view, research and knowledge are not the

[5] Cited in T.C. Schelling: "Surprise Attack and Disarmament," *Bulletin of the Atomic Scientists,* Vol. 15, p. 413. Reprinted by permission of the author.

possessions of any single nation to be used to enhance its competitive power position. Instead the scientist feels an obligation to spread knowledge across the earth. This disparity in values between the scientist on the one hand and the government and its officials (and most of the American public) on the other, helps explain the intensity of the loyalty-security issue mentioned below.

The effects on science of hierarchical distribution of rewards are suggested by another scientist, E. Orowan:

> In the nineteenth century a scientist was generally fruitfully active beyond what is retiring age today; the French chemist Chevreul, discoverer of the nature of fatty substances, worked in his laboratory past his 100th birthday. Today an unusually able scientist, figuratively speaking, is on the scrapheap sometimes at the age of thirty or forty; he becomes director of research of a large unit, or head of a large department, a dean, or an important committeeman oscillating between his home town and Washington, D.C. In other words, he is snatched by the social assembly line at an early stage of his career. Not that he ceases to be useful; but he is doing work that many others could do equally well or better; and he has to abandon work, usually more important in the long run, in which there is no substitute for him. The cause of this shocking waste, of course, is the system of values originating in business life. The last step of selling or manufacturing is usually simple and does not require exceptional intelligence; the important work is done by the executive, and his importance is measured by the number of people under him. . . . The hero of our age is the executive who does not work personally; he merely tells others to do the work. Unfortunately, it is rarely realized that science, literature, and the arts differ radically from business and industry in this respect: most of the important work has to be done personally,

> not by supervision. If an outstanding scientist succumbs to the higher salary and prestige of an "executive" position, his opportunities for high-level work do not increase with the number of those under him; they probably diminish very sharply. Roentgen discovered X rays because he found a box of photographic plates fogged on a shelf close to a cathode-ray tube; had he been director of a large research institute, the man in charge of the tube would probably have thrown the plates away without telling his boss about it.[6]

Here again it is made clear that contemporary social and organizational values may inhibit creative work. The dysfunctions inherent in the uncritical extension of big organization to all kinds of work are also indicated. There is a striking implication here regarding scientific method: once again we find that a vital discovery was the result of chance, luck, and the ability to see the meaning of an unusual event. This frequent result is sharply at odds with the current infatuation with method in social science, suggesting again that we may be going overboard for techniques and large-scale research, both of which reflect to some extent organizational claims.

The director of the French Atomic Energy Commission, L. Kowarski, concludes that:

> Patterns of hierarchy, "family trees," and rigid forms of subordination which have worked well in other fields of cooperation—industrial, military, etc.—may suddenly fail when applied to a situation in which, as so often happens in scientific practice, it can be said literally that nobody knows exactly what he is actually doing or going to do. Quick twists of direction or quick changes of emphasis may suddenly call on somebody's hitherto-

[6] E. Orowan: "Our Universities and Scientific Creativity," *Bulletin of the Atomic Scientists,* Vol. 15, pp. 237-8. This and the following extract reprinted by permission of the author.

unused skill and put him in a position where he will have to give orders to those who were giving him orders a week before. . . . The imposition of an organizational framework, no matter how flexible or syncopated, may cause a not unjustifiable regret to professional scientists, most of whom have lived the lives of independent small holders.

On the dangers of specialization, he repeats the following ironic anecdote: one young radar worker says to another, "What is this physics of which we hear so much?" to which the answer: "I believe it is part of radar." [7]

The changed conditions of research are again noted by A.M. Brues, scientist-director, Argonne National Laboratory:

Basic research is no longer the avocation of the professor whose job allows him time for contemplation and experimental work. It is now a well-financed industry, with the contemplation somehow getting lost from it, and with the output somehow not quite measurable in either quantitative or qualitative terms. It has even come to pervade universities as we see clearly from the attempts that are made to quantitate the output of those faculty members who have not gained tenure. . . .

[The] recipe for success [under this system] is to publish lots of papers, [whose quality is measurable] on the basis of prizes such as employment offers from other institutions. . . .

We acquired the organizing habit with a vengeance and have not since had time to reflect that there may be things in the world that it would be a profanation to organize—courtship, for example—or not worth organization—a vacuum, for example—or things that

[7] L. Kowarski: "Psychology and Structure of Large-Scale Physical Research," *Bulletin of the Atomic Scientists,* Vol. 5, p. 187. Reprinted by permission of the author.

cannot be organized, or if organizable, better left as they are—scientific research, perhaps.[8]

But the most dramatic and unhappy of the dysfunctional aspects of organizational claims has been the loyalty-security program. At the outset "loyalty" and "security" must be defined. Loyalty tests, as Ralph S. Brown, Jr., points out, really refer to "disloyalty," to those who would "reject our form of government and society and would supplant it, by violence if need be, with communism." [9] In time, however, the program was broadened to include people who *might* be Communists, just as in the public mind the concept was expanded to include anyone who disagrees with conventional values. Since disloyalty is tantamount to treason, it is unfortunate that it cannot be defined precisely and that people may be adjudged disloyal without committing disloyal acts and without the protection of procedural due process. Disloyalty, that is, does not require an overt act but may presumably be determined by associations, by hearsay evidence, by writings, etc. Loyalty is a state of mind, and the criteria for judging it are many and diverse.

Security, on the other hand, is somewhat more precise, since it concerns *sensitive positions* in which the individual could do serious harm to the national security. Does a particular person in a particular job constitute a risk to the security and to the preservation of our military, economic, and political systems? But here again definitions of precisely what is a threat to security will vary widely. As Brown says:

[8] A.M. Brues: "The New Emotionalism in Research," *Bulletin of the Atomic Scientists,* Vol. 11, pp. 344-5. Reprinted by permission of the author.

[9] For these definitions and observations about loyalty and security, I rely upon R.S. Brown, Jr.: *Loyalty and Security: Employment Tests in the United States* (New Haven: Yale University Press; 1958), pp. 4-9. Brown concludes "that loyalty and security tests have been used with too much vigor and too little humanity, and . . . that these tests needlessly impair the great freedoms of belief, of speech, and of association enshrined in the First Amendment"; p. 485.

"It is universally accepted that successful espionage or sabotage injures the national security. But, as we move away from the simple facts of selling secrets or blowing up bridges, consensus eventually turns into controversy. There are people who sincerely believe that open debate about touchy issues of foreign policy injures national security. Criticism of Chiang Kai-shek, for example, destroys national unity and invites a Communist attack on Formosa. On the other hand, others fear for the security of the country unless there is the fullest possible debate on such matters." [1]

In sum, the program's effects are difficult to assess, and its proper limits are matters of debate, reflecting the values, personality, education, and experience of those concerned. The following comments of scientists and public officials indicate the extent of such conflicting views. The official point of view is expressed clearly by Thomas E. Murray, former member of the Atomic Energy Commission: "The American citizen in private life, the man who is not engaged in governmental service, is not bound by the requirements of the security system. However, those American citizens who have the privilege of participating in the operations of government, especially in the sensitive agencies, are necessarily subject to this special system of law. Consequently, their faithfulness to the lawful government of the United States, that is to say their loyalty, must be judged by the standard of their obedience to security regulations. . . . Where responsibility is highest, fidelity should be most perfect." [2]

The former chairman of AEC, Mr. John H. McCone, shares this official point of view. In July, 1958, he appeared before the Joint Committee on Atomic Energy to testify about his financial interests, his views on the classification of AEC materials, and his beliefs about the scientists' proper

[1] Ibid., p. 9.

[2] Thomas E. Murray: "In the Matter of J. Robert Oppenheimer," U.S. Atomic Energy Commission (Washington, D.C.: Government Printing Office; 1954), p. 62.

role in political affairs. Senator Clinton Anderson asked McCone, a trustee of the California Institute of Technology, about a letter he had written to Thomas Lauritsen, one of ten California Technology scientists who signed a statement supporting Adlai Stevenson's proposal that the United States suspend nuclear testing. Mr. McCone wrote that he thought it "an improper statement for a group of scientists at Cal. Tech. to make because the statement in [his] opinion was misleading to the American public and [he] thought there was some purpose behind the statement other than that of getting a professional viewpoint into the hands of the American public." [3]

This exchange then followed:

SENATOR ANDERSON: "The scientists felt that it might be all right to have a halt in nuclear testing?"

MR. MCCONE: "Unilaterally; that is right."

SENATOR ANDERSON: "Are we not now discussing with Russia a halt in nuclear testing?"

MR. MCCONE: "Yes sir."

SENATOR ANDERSON: "They were just a little ahead of us."

MR. MCCONE: "No, they were advocating a unilateral stopping."

SENATOR ANDERSON: "Do you have their statement?"

MR. MCCONE: "Yes sir, here are the first two paragraphs. 'For some time Governor Adlai Stevenson has urged that the U.S. take the lead and renounce further H-bomb tests for as long a time as other nations likewise refrain from testing their devices.' This suggestion has been attacked as advocating a dangerous unilateral action and as advocating a step which would permit the Russians to get ahead of the U.S. in nuclear technology."

[3] Cited in H.C. Allison: "John McCone, New AEC Chairman," *Bulletin of the Atomic Scientists,* Vol. 14, p. 334. Reprinted by permission of the author.

SENATOR ANDERSON: "You say that that was unilateral? They did not recommend unilateral action." [4]

The views of AEC officials are endorsed by Senator Kenneth Keating (N.Y.), who believes definitely that the scientist should be on tap, but not on top. In a recent debate on the scientists' role in politics, Keating conceded that they had "marvelously educated the general public of free citizens to the major implications of man's achievement in tapping atomic energy both for war and peace." But, he added, when they campaign for banning or controlling atomic weapons or when they rush into a crusade to compel the U.S. Administration to reach some sort of peaceful understanding with Russia without realizing the difficulties involved in such steps, they often contribute "to the confusion of free men everywhere." [5]

This official rationale, which is probably shared by the great majority of Americans, is an uncomplicated, organizational point of view. It holds that the official definition of "national security" is always the overriding claim and that individual interests and judgments must always submit to it. It is a utilitarian standard easy to understand and to justify, especially when evidence exists of espionage and a critical challenge to our security. The opposing argument that true security and progress require conflicting points of view; that the really vital elements in atomic theory have never been secret in any case; that the whole program is actually endangering democracy and security by adopting arbitrary methods and by driving scientists away from government work—this argument is often too theoretical, too philosophical, to gain much headway in a pragmatic society.

Our national forte has never been nice, philosophical distinctions or theoretical brilliance, but rather the

[4] Ibid.

[5] Cited in M.M. Simpson: "The Scientist in Politics: On Tap or on Top?", *Bulletin of the Atomic Scientists,* Vol. 16, p. 28.

painstaking and brilliant organized development, often on a breathtakingly grandiose scale, of basic ideas usually conceived in Europe. Occasionally it was the provision of the raw material from which a great synthesis was to be built overseas, as in the case of Michelson's experiments which laid the foundation of the theory of relativity. This is true in technology as much as in pure science; to mention only recent instances, modern radar, television, nuclear fission and chain reactions, and antibiotics were discovered or invented in Europe and then developed on a large scale mainly in America. Even the technological emblem of American life, the automobile, is of almost purely European origin.[6]

Our genius has been the process, the machine, the organization, rather than creativity and speculation. We have been more Roman than Greek. The loyalty-security program rests upon this ethos, and our social heritage explains the acceptance of its premises and methods. A recent historical survey indicates that we have always had loyalty tests, from the earliest days of the Republic.[7] We have long felt that loyalty is a matter of allegiance, something owed to the state as a result of contractual obligation in which government preserves order and security and the citizen in turn obeys the laws. The common-sense view that only those who have something to hide could object to loyalty oaths follows as naturally as the "don't-take-a-chance" rationale of federal security officers. The security system, in effect, is part and parcel of the organizational logic which unquestioningly subordinates individual claims to collective security. This condition is less a matter of right or wrong, of official attempts to push scientists around, than a reflection of deep-seated historical and intellectual definitions of reality and

[6] Orowan: loc. cit., p. 236.

[7] H. Hyman: *To Try Men's Souls: Loyalty Oaths in American History* (Berkeley: University of California Press; 1958).

of man's relation to the state. The impact and rigidity of these definitions have been aggravated by our great social and technical achievements and by international tension and fear. Such values accommodate the vested interests that develop in organizations of all kinds and that make the acceptance of change terribly difficult.

But returning to the security system, let us again look at the record. First, what is the extent of this program? Is it a system covering only a few scientists whose access to the press and the journals has enabled them to exaggerate its scope and impact? Actually, as the following table suggests, the system now affects about one out of every five Americans in the labor force.

EXTENT OF SECURITY PROGRAM[8]

CLASSIFICATION	TOTAL
Professions, including teachers	1,600,000
Managers	300,000
Government and Military	7,200,000
Manufacturing, construction, and transportation industries	4,500,000
	13,600,000

As Brown shows in his definitive study, thousands of investigators, officials, and clerks are involved in this program, which at the federal level has (1955) cost about $350,000,000 and resulted in the discovery and firing of "between one twentieth and one thirtieth of one per cent" of those covered by the programs.[9]

Confining ourselves only to its impact upon research scientists, what are some of the results? Here again we shall rely on the comments of distinguished men who have personally felt or observed the system. A well-known example is Edward U. Condon, former Director of the National Bureau

[8] Brown: op. cit., p. 181.
[9] Ibid., p. 182.

of Standards. Speaking of his own experiences, Condon said:

> During the past two months there has come about a general public awareness that America is not automatically and effortlessly and unquestionably the leader of the world in science and technology. This comes as no surprise to those of us who have watched and tried to warn against the steady deterioration in the teaching of science and mathematics in the schools for the past quarter century. It comes as no surprise to those of us who have known dozens of cases of scientists who have been hounded out of jobs by silly disloyalty charges, and kept out of all professional employment by blacklisting. . . .
>
> I [have] . . . been under steady political attack for seven years, and [have] won at every hearing. But now (in 1954) I was told that I would have to go over all the same material again . . . In those seven years so much of my nervous energy had gone into the struggle that I decided to withdraw from it, and my resignation from an industrial position for which security clearance was needed was announced in early December. You might think that now I would be allowed to go back to work. I came East in January, 1955 after giving my retiring presidential address to the American Association for the Advancement of Science and was offered the post of chairman of the department of physics in a leading university. In March the chancellor of that university told me that he could not follow through on the appointment because a high government official threatened one of the university trustees that if my appointment went through, that university would lose all of its federal funds.[1]

[1] E.U. Condon: "Time to Stop Baiting Scientists," *Bulletin of the Atomic Scientists,* Vol. 14, pp. 80-1. Reprinted by permission of the author.

The reason for these actions against Condon was, in his words, his "having been interested in the American-Soviet Science Society, an organization which received a grant from the Rockefeller Foundation ten years ago to foster translation and wider distribution in this country of Russian scientific literature."

Brown estimates that 300,000 scientists, engineers, and public administrators have been subject to loyalty-security tests, and that about one twentieth of one per cent of them were security problems. But this figure is only a rough estimate. It does not, of course, include those who have elected not to work for the government or who, working for it, have been dissatisfied with the program's character and effect and left. The personal hardships of those dismissed can only be imagined: their inability to secure other jobs, the high costs of defending oneself against accusations of disloyalty, etc. Such questions cannot be considered here; our major interest is in the program's effect on our ability to carry out scientific research and development.

Authoritative evidence on this issue has been presented in legislative hearings by many scientists, some of whom will be cited below. The Chairman of the "House Committee on Government Operations," Representative R.W. Riehlman, outlined the objectives of the hearings as follows:

> Each day's news reminds the people of the United States that our military power in the world political scene is inseparably related to our ability to maintain superiority in scientific research and development. Our human resources in the field of science are a precious commodity which must be husbanded . . . this subcommittee's inquiry into military research and development programs stems from several questions concerning the organization and administration of the program in the Department of Defense.[2]

[2] U.S. 83rd Congress, 2nd Session, Subcommittee, House Committee on Government Operations: *Hearings, Organization and Administration*

The major questions were as follows:[3]

> 1. *Are there any characteristics inherent in military organization which are incompatible with the administration of an effective program of scientific research and development?*
>
> 2. *Does the military organization of a research and development program tend to create conditions which retard the work of scientists or make it difficult to obtain and retain the services of highly qualified civilian scientific and technical personnel?*

Answering these questions, James R. Killian, Jr., President of Massachusetts Institute of Technology, commented:

> I feel that the inherent characteristics of a military organization make it very difficult to operate a creative research organization, but it can be done and has been done. It requires a breaking away from conventional military organization and usually the development of an effective combination of military and civilian management. The difficulties of military organization are obvious. The rapid turnover in personnel and in general the absence of any officers who are creative scientists make it very difficult to manage research directly. . . .
>
> Research is a kind of creative activity that generates new developments and ideas. Neither of these is effective simply by the rule of spending money. The real effectiveness comes from brilliance and from the capacity of the men who are conducting the research and development. A hundred mediocre or even average scientists, or even a thousand, cannot be equivalent to one first-rate man working in an environment where he has freedom to exercise his imagination.[4]

---

of the Military Research and Development Programs (Washington, D.C.: U.S. Government Printing Office; 1954), pp. 1-2.

[3] Ibid., p. 2.

[4] Ibid., pp. 429, 436.

On the matter of security, Killian testified as follows:

> There has been [1955], unhappily, a deterioration in recent months in the relationships between Government and science. The reasons for this deterioration are much more fundamental than the simple problem of relationships between members of the military services and scientists. . . . The problem has now come to be one of various trends, movements, and policies in this country which have created a condition where members of the scientific community are clearly discouraged and apprehensive about the lack of understanding of scientific methods, and about an undue regard to what sometimes seems to be a preoccupation with security procedures and policies at the expense of scientific progress.
>
> I believe that the whole problem of security procedures and policies at the present time may be one of the things that is most hazardous to our future research and development activity in this country. The feeling that the present security procedures can be handled and administered in a manner to damage creative activity, and if they are, the feeling that the giving of an unbiased and objective judgment can be, under certain conditions, dangerous to the giver because this unbiased judgment does not accord with somebody's policy—all of these things add up to a great discouragement on the part of people in the field of science.[5]

Killian's testimony was reinforced by Vannevar Bush, President of the Carnegie Institute of Washington, and wartime head of the Office of Scientific Research and Development.

> I think there are two serious weaknesses today that impede our program of research and development.

[5] Ibid., p. 444.

First, the security system as now practiced is, in my opinion, doing great damage to the relation between science and government, and particularly to the relations between scientists and weapons development. Second, it seems to me we have lost our effectiveness in getting new weapons tested, tried out, produced on an experimental basis, and finally introduced in use.[6]

Regarding the effects of the security system Bush said:

During the war there was developed a partnership between military men and scientific men. It was not brought about automatically; it is not a thing that occurs readily. These men came from different backgrounds, and it is hard for each group to understand the other; but nevertheless, by the end of the war an excellent situation had developed. . . . That partnership, which was a healthy one . . . is, in my opinion, now almost destroyed, and one of the primary reasons is the security system.[7]

Scientists today are discouraged and downhearted and feel that they are being pushed out, and they are. . . . The morale is very low indeed, and it is quite natural that it should be. Let me give you an example. I could give you dozens of examples. I met a week ago a man who was a member of the scientific community that is advisory to the Security Council, and he said to me, 'Well, we have practically stopped working. It is quite impossible to accomplish anything in this atmosphere.' Now that is the sort of reaction I would get out of three out of four scientists today. They go on working but they feel that they are not welcome, that they are regarded with suspicion, that some of the men who led them during the war are now being questioned and their loyalty and security are in doubt.[8]

[6] Ibid., p. 452.
[7] Ibid., p. 454.
[8] Ibid., pp. 261-2.

Speaking of the common practice of placing line military officers at the head of research organizations, Wallace R. Brode, Associate Director of the National Bureau of Standards, commented:

> Actual research in the last war was done primarily by civilian scientific organizations with military officer liaison where needed to provide the logical contact between research and the armed services. . . . It was a matter of considerable disappointment to many that in the recent assumption of operation by different branches of the armed services, of civilian-operated laboratories . . . , these were not established as civilian-operated research laboratories under the Assistant Secretary of Defense for Research, with a continuation of the same highly efficient and productive program. . . . Yet on transfer a complement of officers was assigned as a superdirection echelon over the existing civilian direction.[9] The military characteristics of acceptance of leadership decision and discouragement of independent thinking and action are an impediment to creative thinking and effective production of research and development in the military framework. Delegation of authority is possible, but is seldom passed from military to civilians.[1]

Another scientist adds that "military officers usually have demonstrated little or no understanding of the scientific method, nor of the scientific aspects of the effort over which they have been assigned authority." [2]

The conflict between organizational logic and research needs is well stated by a major scientist who insists that in scientific efforts "all real achievement is measured by the creativity and originality of individuals"; while in the military, "by force of necessity the system must be largely impersonal." An army "is designed to absorb the human

[9] Ibid., p. 641.
[1] Ibid., p. 640.
[2] Ibid., p. 674.

material that flows into its ranks and to weld that material into an effective unit to accomplish certain simple and well-defined objectives."[3]

Again, on the problem of security, Brode observes:

> There is an apparent feeling of distrust and suspicion which pervades some military establishments regarding civilians and especially civilian scientists. Rather than trying to understand and aid in the scientific method of problem solution, there seems to be a direct effort to alter and suppress the scientific approach. There are many known cases where the administrative decision that the scientist does not have the "need to know" certain information has resulted in the loss of time and needless duplication of research.[4]

The "command" logic of big organizations is probably suitable when one is mass-producing a standardized product, but the common subordination of scientists to military men, lay administrators, and industrial managers has probably been dysfunctional. As Walter Lippmann concluded: "I am afraid the reason why the Soviets are ahead of us is that their military weapons and their space rockets are under the control, not of the soldiers and not of the factory managers, but of the scientists. Men of genius cannot do what they are capable of doing if, as is the case today, they are herded into separate compartments and told to devote themselves to limited aims."[5]

[3] Ibid., p. 696.

[4] Ibid., p. 644.

[5] *The New York Times* (January 30, 1960). C.P. Snow has pointed out an essential difference between the administrative and scientific type of mind: "I spent twenty years of my life in close contact with the English professional administrators. I have the greatest respect for them. . . . They are extremely intelligent, honourable, tough, tolerant, and generous. Within the human limits, they are free from some of the less pleasing group characteristics. But they have a deficiency. . . . Their tendency, which is strengthened by the nature of their job, is to live in the short term, to become masters of the short-term solution.

The tension between organizational logic and scientific creativity is patent in the words of Admiral Rickover, a central figure in the development of the atomic submarine:

> All organizations tend to perpetuate themselves and to keep things in a status quo. You cannot do new things, you cannot do exceptional or unusual things by usual methods, but the tendency of the organization is to keep everything at a beautiful even level where no problems rise above the surface. So when a man comes up with a new idea, and if it is a difficult new idea which necessarily requires the use of new methods, he is *ipso facto* opposed by the existing organization.[6]

In regard to the present military command organization of weapons research, the following exchange occurred:

> REPRESENTATIVE HOLIFIELD: Do you mean to tell us that you absolutely break down the line of authority in your managerial organization?
>
> ADMIRAL RICKOVER: Certainly, sir.
>
> REPRESENTATIVE HOLIFIELD: And you do not insist upon civilians being subordinate to military people?
>
> ADMIRAL RICKOVER: You are darn right, I do not. If the officer is better than the civilian, the civilian is subordinate; but if the civilian is better, the officer is subordinate.
>
> REPRESENTATIVE HOLIFIELD: I don't think this obtains

Often, as I have seen them conducting their business with an absence of fuss, a concealed force, a refreshing dash of intellectual sophistication, a phrase from one of the old Icelandic sagas kept nagging at my mind. It was: 'Snorri was the wisest man in Iceland who had not the gift of foresight.'" *Science and Government* (Cambridge: Harvard University Press; 1960), p. 83; see also, Snow: *The Two Cultures and the Scientific Revolution* (Cambridge, England: Cambridge University Press; 1959).

[6] U.S. 86th Congress, 1st Session, Subcommittee, House Committee on Government Operations: *Hearings on Organization and Management of Missile Programs* (Washington, D.C.: U.S. Government Printing Office; 1959), p. 603.

over in the Pentagon. . . . Regardless of the fact that the officer does not have this expert background, he is nevertheless superior to the expert civilian over there.

ADMIRAL RICKOVER: That is correct, sir. Of course, I don't see how a system like that can operate efficiently. . . . How can a man possibly take charge of complex technical matters, say a man who has been captain of a ship and has not had the requisite scientific and engineering experience . . . ? The present system encourages the good civilians to leave.[7]

The weight of organizational logic is perhaps suggested by Representative Holifield's reaction to this information. But the problem is more deep-seated, involving conflicting views about the nature of scientific research and its appropriate organizational framework. As Caryl P. Haskins, President of the Carnegie Institution, says: "It is somewhat startling to realize that there may indeed be a wide gulf between men whose training, concerns, and values have lain in the general areas of scientific pursuits, and men of nontechnical background. . . . More serious than the gulf of intellectual content . . . is the accompanying danger that the divergence of experience may set and harden a real and fundamental dichotomy of attitudes and values between the two worlds, and encourage an unbridgeable hostility between them." [8]

This same scientist also points out the tension between organization and individual, noting both normative and operational consequences. "The very threat of bigness in a vast technological society like our own must menace the sanctity and maintained sense of worth of the individual.

[7] Ibid., pp. 606-7. According to *The New York Times* (February 25, 1960), p. 1, W.H. Pickering, Director of the Jet Propulsion Lab, Connecticut Institute of Technology, told Congress that the space program was being hampered by confusion, indecision, and increasing military domination.

[8] Caryl P. Haskins: "Society and Scientific Research," *Bulletin of the Atomic Scientists*, Vol. 16, p. 147.

. . . It is far too easy to identify the organized group with the members who compose it. It is far too easy to forget that the very essence of creativeness must be with the individual as contrasted with the group. . . . This, above all, is what the research environment must stand for." [9]

The difficulty of maintaining such conditions is suggested by the severing of research arrangements between the Army and Johns Hopkins University, a "decision made against a background of mutual recriminations over freedom of research, breaches of security, and withholding of funds." [1] Dr. E.A. Johnson, for twelve years head of the University's Operations Research Office, indicated that ethical differences had developed between the Army and the university. He said that "conservative" army leaders had sought to maintain "strict control in detail" over the research efforts of the Operations Research Office, whereas he believed that once given an assignment the researchers must do "a complete and honest job." [2]

The bases of such tensions are apparent in the following summary of the logic underlying current industrial research management:

> The basic assumption is that having been in research, the research manager "knows" research people and will know how to manage them. The second assumption is that human behavior is anarchic and chaotic and impervious to systematic understanding, the behavior of scientists being especially chaotic and peculiar. Third, research management assumes that the organizational environment consists only of facilities, salary scales, and merit and achievement rewards. Fourth, research management assumes that tempering its authority with friendly informality of a "happy family" variety contributes to a colleague [permissive] authority system. Fifth,

[9] Ibid., p. 150.
[1] *The New York Times* (May 28, 1961), pp. 1, 31.
[2] Ibid., p. 31.

research management assumes that scientists have come to accept the definition of themselves as employees. Sixth, research management assumes that defining its method of supervisory selection as "natural leadership" will avoid organizational rigidity and contribute to flexibility. The fact that all of these assumptions are fallacious is not without its impact on strain in the laboratory organization.[3]

In sum, big organizations typically seek control, discipline, and standardization. They apply pragmatic, often quantitative standards to measure their activities. For such reasons, basic research and the unstructured conditions which nourish it are fundamentally contrary to organizational logic. Such research is hard to control. Those engaged in it do not know what they will find, if anything, how long it will take, nor how much it will cost. As a former Secretary of Defense said: "Basic research is when you don't know what you're doing." Unfortunately, not all critical problems nor the motivations of individuals can be handled according to such logic. The very success of our mass-production system and its applied-research orientation seems to aggravate the resulting dilemma.

The consequences of conflicting values of scientists and military-organization men can usefully be presented in the context of interpersonal theory. We saw earlier that organizational conflict is often the result of distorted perceptions among its members, both of themselves and of each other. Such misperceptions, moreover, became self-inforcing, locking individuals into relationships that aggravate tension and hinder the organization's attempts to achieve its goals. In the case of the executive group reported in Chapter 6, the self-deceptions of the men (the disparity between their self-perceptions and the way their associates saw them)

[3] S. Marcson: *The Scientist in American Industry: Some Organizational Detriments in Manpower Utilization* (New York: Harper & Brothers; 1960), p. 146.

made effective working relations impossible. A similar mechanism seems to be at work in the government's weapons-research program.

One way of portraying this perceptual disparity is by constructing a rough "index of alienation" based upon the common images that research scientists and military-organization men have of themselves and of each other. Such an index is necessarily crude; indeed, in a technical sense it is not precisely an index since it includes no quantitative difference among the items comprising it. The index, moreover, reflects both the selectivity of those who made the statements and the writer's selectivity in choosing the specific items which are included. However, the index is representative in the sense that the items were collected randomly from a wide variety of sources. The validity of each statement is less significant than the indication it offers of opposing definitions of reality by individuals working toward similar goals in a similar organizational context.

INDEX OF ALIENATION

Military-Organization Men	*Research Scientists*
The overriding significance and priority of the ICBM and IRBM programs dictate that special administration procedures and controls be established (Chief of Staff suggested draft memo).	The real ruler of government-sponsored research [is] the Bureau of the Budget (university scientist).
An ounce of loyalty is worth a pound of brains (government security officer).	Unfortunately, secrecy and progress are mutually incompatible. This is always true of science (research physicist).
This [claim that military	The key positions at the

Military-Organization Men	*Research Scientists*
	ternal controls imposed by industrial methods of organization—in fact they are held to be inconsistent with the basic tenets of professionalism.[7]
The trouble with these research people is that they go ahead and do research without any appreciation of the cost) (manager, industrial laboratory).[8]	Many of these people, used to command, are impervious to new ideas. . . . The same type of people, the same type of treatment as they apply to ship operation, they apply to . . . research and development. You simply can't do that (Navy research director).
Most of the troublesome people have left—you really can't have research people who think they're God Almighty (development engineer, industrial corporation).[9]	The great point in the scientist's code is full and honest reporting to all his colleagues (university scientist).
Our job is to recruit individuals and to try to broaden them to the interests and the point of view of the company (research administrator, industry).[1]	My technical people would quit rather than work on anything they didn't believe in (director, research organization).

[7] H.A. Shepard: "Nine Dilemmas in Industrial Research," *Administrative Science Quarterly*, Vol. 1, p. 300.

[8] Marcson: op. cit., p. 19.

[9] Tom Burns: "Micropolitics: Mechanisms of Institutional Change," *Administrative Science Quarterly*, Vol. 6, pp. 257-81.

[1] Marcson: op. cit., p. 41.

Allied with the consequences of such disparate self-images and judgments is the problem of goal displacement. We have seen that the results of organizational logic often include a reduction in the intrinsic satisfaction in work. This results from the breakdown of work and decision making into such minute compartments that any given individual finds it difficult to derive the psychic satisfaction of producing a finished product. But psychologists find that variety and complexity in most kinds of work are required for high morale and identification.[2] Organizations tend to inhibit these satisfactions by dividing and standardizing work in order to gain control and efficiency.

The breaking down of university disciplines into departments, and then into special fields within a given department, may alienate the scholar because his work is seen as only a fragment of a larger whole. This not only prevents him from defining his field in large compass, but it interferes with his role as citizen by providing a handy rationalization that every problem has its experts who must define the issues and work out the solutions. In Veblen's phrase, he becomes a victim of "trained incapacity." By dramatizing the irrelevance of his special knowledge to vital public questions, such results tend to undercut pride in work and to divert one toward alternative rewards such as income, prestige, and leisure.

Organizations further encourage such displacement of values by the tendency to replace creative work and independence as the basis for rewards with subjective criteria of loyalty, seniority, dependence, adaptability, "personality," and community service. Traditional values tend to be displaced by a marketing ethic characterized by self-promotion, status borrowing, and mock conviviality. In creative kinds of work, where (after initial training and certification) standards of achievement are much less precise, and where, indeed, one may in effect set his own pace, the results are far-reaching.

[2] S. Wyatt and J.A. Frazer: *The Effects of Monotony on Work* (London: H.M.S.O.; 1929).

We have seen that physical scientists do not have to work for the government, and that many prefer not to. Organizational logic, which has been essentially authoritarian, has often failed to recognize this permissive aspect of highly skilled work. Like all of us, its advocates find it hard to change their ways in the face of new conditions. As the Defense Department's Special Assistant for Research and Development insisted:

> When the vital urgency of the military development and research mission is considered . . . it is clear that an optimum climate for research work by civilian scientists cannot be the only consideration. Certain disciplines are essential to insure that development schedules are met and that research remains in areas of direct relevance to the problems at hand. The investment of public funds in the production of weapons . . . represents such a large part of the national economy that certain checks and balances which may be regarded as restrictive are absolutely essential for the protection of the public interest. Some or all of these factors may occasionally lead to the frustration of an individual scientist, but this, it is feared, is inevitable under any system of management sensitive to its responsibilities to the public.[3]

This dictum expresses well the military-organization man rationale. It points up a common premise of such thinking, namely, the assumption that organization and controls by themselves can create something. It points up also the assumption that basic research can be controlled when by its very nature it cannot. Organization's role must indeed be

[3] *Hearings, Organization and Administration of the Military Research and Development Programs,* p. 197. For an analysis of the "public interest," its various meanings and its strategic use by organizational elites, see G.A. Schubert, Jr.: *The Public Interest* (Glencoe, Illinois: The Free Press; 1960). The significance of the "public interest" as a guide and motivation for government officials is traced in J.M. Pfiffner and R.V. Presthus: *Public Administration,* 4th ed. (New York: The Ronald Press Company; 1960), pp. 556-62.

an auxiliary one of providing the conditions that will encourage individual creativity.

NAME INDEX

SUBJECT INDEX

Cornell political scientist ROBERT PRESTHUS is editor of the *Administrative Science Quarterly.* He has been awarded research grants by the Ford Foundation (1959-60) and the Social Science Research Council (1950-51 and 1963-64). In 1964 he gave the Southern Regional Training lectures in administration at the University of Alabama. His writings include *Public Administration,* 1960 (fourth edition), and *Men at the Top: A Study in Community Power,* 1964.

V-284 Lewis, Oscar *Village Life in Northern India*
V-384 Lindesmith, Alfred *The Addict and The Law*
V-76 Linton, Ralph *The Tree of Culture*
V-407 Mack, Raymond *Our Children's Burden: Studies of Desegregation in Ten American Communities*
V-209 Marcuse, Herbert *Eros and Civilization*
V-437 Nietzsche, Friedrich *The Will to Power*
V-462 Piaget, Jean *Six Psychological Studies*
V-258 Piel, Gerard *Science in the Cause of Man*
V-70 Rank, Otto *The Myth of the Birth of the Hero* and Other Essays
V-99 Redlich, Fritz, M.D. and Bingham, June *The Inside Story:* Psychiatry and Everyday Life
V-395 Rokeach, Milton *The Three Christs of Ypsilanti*
V-301 Ross, Nancy Wilson (ed.) *The World of Zen*
V-464 Sartre, Jean-Paul *Search for a Method*
V-289 Thomas, Elizabeth Marshall *The Harmless People*
V-310 Thorp, Edward O. *Beat the Dealer,* Revised
V-109 Thruelsen & Kobler (eds.) *Adventures of the Mind, I*
V-68 *Adventures of the Mind, II*
V-239 *Adventures of the Mind, III*
V-299 Watts, Alan W. *The Joyous Cosmology:* Adventures in the Chemistry of Consciousness
V-466 Watts, Alan W. *The Wisdom of Insecurity*